BACKCOUNTRY SKIING

Authors Martin Volken, Scott Schell, and Margaret Wheeler have undergone internationally recognized training and certification exams in the highest levels of professional guiding. Although the content of this book does not officially represent American Mountain Guides Association (AMGA) guiding techniques, the AMGA does endorse the authors, who are certified guides, and the content of this book which provides the most current techniques used in the craft of technical mountaineering.

Backcountry Skiing is a brain-dump of some of the most dialed ski mountaineers in the U.S. Intermediate to the most advanced ski mountaineers will find answers to their burning questions [inside].

—*Backcountry* magazine

[A] backcountry bible.

—*Skiing* magazine

Backcountry Skiing is the skier's equivalent of *Mountaineering: Freedom of the Hills*, and should prove a valuable resource for any skier looking to be well-informed and make good decisions in the mountains.

—*Off-Piste* magazine

D1361479

MOUNTAINEERS
OUTDOOR EXPERT
series

BACKCOUNTRY SKIING
Skills for Ski Touring
and Ski Mountaineering

**Martin Volken, Scott Schell,
and Margaret Wheeler**

Photography by Scott Schell

THE MOUNTAINEERS BOOKS

THE MOUNTAINEERS BOOKS
is the nonprofit publishing arm of The Mountaineers Club,
an organization founded in 1906 and dedicated to the exploration,
preservation, and enjoyment of outdoor and wilderness areas.

1001 SW Klickitat Way, Suite 201, Seattle, WA 98134

First edition: first printing 2007, second printing 2008, third printing 2009

Manufactured in the United States of America

Editor: Julie Van Pelt
Cover and Book Design: The Mountaineers Books
Layout and Illustration: Jennifer Shontz, Red Shoe Design
Illustration (figure 6.10) on page 209 by Simon Mentz
Illustrations on pages 264 and 265 reproduced from *Mountain Weather* by Jeff Renner.
Illustrations on page 268 reproduced from *Mountaineering: The Freedom of the Hills,* The Mountaineers.
All photographs by Scott Schell unless otherwise noted. Photographs on pages 13, 16, 224, 228, 310
    (figures 10.25 and 10.26) by Martin Volken.
Cover photograph: *AMGA ski mountaineering course heading out for a full day of ski mountaineering,*
    Thompson Pass, Alaska
Back cover photograph: *Martin Volken enjoying powder near the Ice Fall Lodge in the Canadian Rockies*
Frontispiece: *Mason Stafford capturing the essence in the Slot Couloir, Snoqualmie Pass, Washington*

Library of Congress Cataloging-in-Publication Data

Volken, Martin, 1965–
    Backcountry skiing : skills for ski touring and ski mountaineering / by Martin Volken, Scott Schell, and Margaret Wheeler.
        p.   cm.
    Includes bibliographical references and index.
    ISBN 978-1-59485-038-7
    1. Cross-country skiing. 2. Ski mountaineering. I. Schell, Scott, 1972– II. Wheeler, Margaret, 1974–
III. Title.
GV855.3.V64 2007
796.93'2—dc22

                                                                                2007022273

Contents

CHAPTER 3
Navigation

CHAPTER 4
Uphill Movement

CHAPTER 5
Transitions

CHAPTER 6
Ski Mountaineering Techniques

Acknowledgments

Creating a book like this is truly an enormous effort, and we owe a gigantic thanks to all those who have contributed their time and energy towards this final creation!

Our special thanks for technical and professional advice, assistance, and information go to: Mike Hattrup, Tom Murphy, Colin Zacharias, Bruce Edgerly and Steve Christi (Backcountry Access), Dale Atkins, Howie Schwarz, all the authors of the AIARE curriculum, John Hereford, Ken Schiele (K2 Skis), Lowell Skoog, Freddy Grossniklaus, Marc Chauvin, Kaj Bune (Outdoor Research), Martin Poletti (Montana Sport), Chris Solomon, Mason Stafford, Carolyn Parker, Erik Moen, Chris Miske and Welling Savo Justin.

We are lucky enough to have friends and colleagues of great skill and patience who allowed us to take their pictures for this project. We look forward to going skiing with you all in the future for *fun*, not just to take technical photos of excruciating detail: Mason Stafford, Ben Haskell, Chris Miske, Adam Justin (Pro Ski Service – Seattle), Dave Jordan, Chris Solomon, Ben Wheeler, Howie Schwarz, Kasha Rigby, John and Erin Spiess, and Sarah Bruce. Thank you also to all the participants in the AMGA ski programs during which Scott was shooting photos, and to all our clients who have been subjected to the lens! Thanks to Pro Ski Service (Seattle and North Bend, WA) and Marmot Mountain Works of Bellevue WA for helping us get photos of cutting edge gear.

In addition to the main body of photos, professional photographers Dan Patitucci (www.patitucciphoto.com) and John Scurlock were generous enough to provide us with a few excellent images, and we are very grateful for them.

We would also like to thank K2 Backcountry, Outdoor Research, Black Diamond Equipment, Backcountry Access (BCA), and Garmont boots, for their support in all our guiding and professional endeavors.

Extra thanks go to Gina Volken, for putting up with us and our furrowed brows around her kitchen table, again and again over the past few years.

In embarking on this project, we had only the slightest inkling of what we were getting into. Without the help of Julie Van Pelt (JVP Editing), Jennifer Shontz (Red Shoe Design), Christine Hosler, Mary Metz, and Kate Rogers (The Mountaineers Books), this book would never have made it. Thank you!

Finally, thanks to our parents and families for their love and support.

On the upper portion of the Nisqually Glacier, Mount Rainier, Washington
(Photograph by Mike Hattrup)

Introduction

If your friend called to see if you wanted to go ski touring, what image would come to mind? Do you see a snowy slope bathed in sunlight along a California highway, with cars pulled over and tracks being laid in the corn by a sporty group of sunglass-clad thirtysomethings? Or do you picture bearded young men wearing telemark gear moving together up a broad bowl in Colorado? Perhaps you see the gate at your local ski area, beyond which access is for those who carry avalanche gear and who want to hike up a ridge to reach untracked snow.

Now imagine the same friend calling to ask if you're interested in ski mountaineering. You might picture the clean lines of a Bradford Washburn black-and-white photo of mountains in Alaska. Or you might see the outline of a mountain hut in the Alps, perched precariously on rocks over the gaping maw of an icefield. If you've read a ski magazine lately, you probably see a figure with skis strapped on his or her back, wearing a harness, and using a rope to rappel into a couloir of steep, untracked snow.

This mental slideshow is a testimony to the diversity of ski touring and ski mountaineering. The two sports are inherently connected; in order to achieve complicated ski mountaineering objectives you must first master the basics of ski touring. Wouldn't it seem dangerous to attempt the Haute Route in the Alps or the Forbidden Tour in the North Cascades if you had never been ski touring before? Ski mountaineering is a blend of multiple disciplines involving everything from snow safety to alpine rope skills to winter camping. It requires a depth of knowledge, skill, and experience that goes beyond what you must know in order to ski laps in the woods or the back bowls of your favorite ski area. Ski touring is the foundation upon which ski mountaineering is built.

Summiting an unnamed peak in the Chugach Range, Alaska

Ski touring and ski mountaineering have experienced amazing growth and development in recent years. More and more people are beginning to understand that the mountain experience—human beings spending time outside of their cities and suburbs and moving through the mountains alone or with companions—is something that can occur during the winter season. Folks in Europe and Canada have known this for years, but it seems that Americans are just beginning to catch up: when the climbing or backpacking season comes to a close, swap your rock shoes or hiking boots for skis and skins and continue to enjoy the mountains.

Another factor in increased winter backcountry use is the growing cost (and crowds) of in-area skiing. There is also the natural progression of people experienced in mountain travel looking to expand their horizons: for example, the skier who has been quietly farming her backyard stash for the last twenty-five years and is setting her sights on technical summits, or the alpinist who has been climbing for ten years and is considering where he could get to on skis. Climbers in particular are adopting skis as a better tool for accessing rock, ice, and mixed-climbing objectives. The net effect of all these factors is that more and more people are looking outside the ski-area boundaries for their skiing experiences.

Leaps and bounds have also occurred in the gear available for ski touring and ski mountaineering, and in the techniques for using that gear. Boots for telemark and alpine touring (AT, also called randonnée)

have evolved in multiple directions—some ski better downhill, some walk better uphill, some are designed to be light and fast, and some have morphed into objects that look strangely like the in-area alpine boots designed for ski racing. Manufacturers have been battling each other to develop a telemark binding that is releasable, or an AT binding that is lighter and stronger, which has meant new designs as well as updates to products that have been the same for years. Skis, which have undergone a complete makeover in alpine skiing, have also evolved for the backcountry, performing more like an in-area ski but with the added criteria of being lightweight enough for sustained walking uphill. Avalanche transceivers, soft-shell outerwear, and ski-specific packs...the list goes on. And we would add one more piece of vital "gear" required in the backcountry: knowledge. Compared to the alpine skier in a ski area, the backcountry skier must have a much larger skill set to safely negotiate the hazards of backcountry terrain.

WHAT IS AND IS NOT IN THIS BOOK

This book arose out of a desire to keep pace with the recent evolution of the skiing population, the improvement and proliferation of gear, and the development of new techniques. Our aim is to provide an in-depth explanation of all of the various skills, knowledge, and techniques that are so crucial to safety and success in the diverse activities of ski touring and ski

Mike Hattrup testing skis in the Cosmique Couloir, Chamonix, France

mountaineering—all in one place. Our goal is to reach people who are coming into the sports of ski touring and ski mountaineering from all directions, giving you the necessary skills to begin traveling in the backcountry and the tools to build upon those skills as you gain experience in the mountains. Many of these topics have been covered in great depth in other places, and we hope that you will seek out those resources for use in conjunction with this book.

What is not included in this book? You won't find skiing lessons or snowboard-specific skills. We assume that readers are intermediate to advanced in-area skiers. Insofar as we do discuss skiing skills, they pertain to those techniques unique to back-country skiing. For instance, how do you navigate breakable crust with an overnight pack on? Learning basic skills like weight transfer, turn initiation, and so on, is best

done with a real person who can observe and instruct you as you go...preferably a cute one. For the snowboarder, you can still use this book to improve your general backcountry travel skills in areas like snow safety, tour planning, and the like.

This book is generally organized according to the progression of a ski tour. We begin with an extensive look at gear. We then discuss decision making and big-picture preparation such as snow safety and avalanche awareness, navigation, and tour planning. Launching into the tour itself, we deal with uphill travel, with transitions that take place while moving uphill and between skinning up and skiing down, with the technical systems involved in ski mountaineering, and finally with descent. There's also a chapter on the mountain environment. We close with rescue and emergency situations, and appendixes offer additional resources.

TOOLS OR PLAYTHINGS?

Arnold Lunn wrote in the early 1900s, "Ski mountaineering is the result of the marriage of two great sports, mountaineering and skiing." But is it mostly mountaineering, or mostly skiing? Are skis tools to achieve some end, or is skiing itself the end? The ski mountaineer crossing a glacier on a high-level traverse and the extreme skier linking turns on a must-not-fall descent have answered these questions very differently.

Marcel Kurz, who pioneered the Chamonix-to-Zermatt Haute Route in 1911, wrote, "In the high mountains the ski ceases to be a plaything. Circumstances make it a tool—the most useful aid to the winter mountaineer—but a simple tool intended to make traveling easier—something which we put on or take off like crampons and which is only a means to an end." Kurz's viewpoint was typical of the early 1900s. The pioneers of ski mountaineering used skis for winter ascents and high-level traverses. They wanted to go places in the mountains, and skis were tools for the job.

The pioneering era of ski mountaineering ended around the time of World War II, when mechanical lifts became common in Europe and North America. Skis, for the vast majority of skiers who rode lifts, were simply playthings. Just a tiny minority of skiers continued to do mountaineering. For three decades, they were largely content to repeat the accomplishments of the prewar pioneers.

Arnold Lunn, the Englishman who did so much to promote ski mountaineering before the war, invented modern slalom racing in the 1920s. He did it, he later wrote, "inspired by the naive concern that downhill racing would help to develop the kind of technique suitable for ski mountaineering." (Slalom was supposed to simulate "tree-running" during the descent from a peak.) By the 1960s, Lunn lamented that ski racers had become "a bunch of ballet dancers on skis" and that the sport was infected by "downhill-only disease." He recalled, "In the remote past, skis were the passport to untracked snow and unexplored slopes." That was no longer true, it seemed.

Ironically, slalom racing and other developments from lift skiing began to profoundly influence ski mountaineering soon after Lunn's death in 1974. In North America, former lift skiers fleeing the crowds and constraints of ski resorts rediscovered Nordic touring and the telemark turn. Although it was not as suitable for downhill skiing as the alpine gear of the day, lightweight Nordic gear was much more mobile and it became the preferred tool for North American skiers to leave the beaten path. Telemark skiers sparked a renaissance in backcountry skiing in the 1970s and 1980s, pioneering high-level ski routes in North America's wilderness mountains similar to those done earlier in the more civilized Alps. They had rediscovered the ski as a tool for mountaineering.

In Europe, a small number of ski instructors and mountain guides began using alpine skis to descend steep climbing routes where a fall would likely spell death. Such feats would not have been possible without the advances in equipment and technique driven by ski racing.

By the late 1970s, competition for first ski descents in the French Alps grew so intense that ethical disputes arose over the use of helicopters for the ascent and rappels for the descent. Skis, for these mountaineers, were a far cry from Marcel Kurz's "tools to make traveling easier." They were playthings, employed in an elaborate and deadly serious game.

Since the 1990s, Nordic and alpine touring have converged. Nordic equipment has become more downhill-capable and alpine equipment has become more touring-friendly. The new balance is illustrated by randonnée racing, a European invention that has recently taken hold in North America. Racing up, down, and across the mountains, this sport is something that Arnold Lunn would certainly have recognized. Randonnée racing is likely to spawn new developments that will make it easier for tomorrow's ski mountaineers to return to the roots of the sport—exploring the mountains.

Lowell Skoog has been a ski mountaineering pioneer in the Pacific Northwest for decades and has done much work in compiling its history of ski mountaineering.

TELEMARK VS. ALPINE TOURING

Free the heel and the mind will follow.
Fix the heel and fix the problem.

Which do you think is true? We believe the answer is not so much a matter of good or evil, but of which is the appropriate tool for the conditions and your intent.

Once upon a very long time ago, people used wooden boards that were strapped to their feet in order to simplify their winter travel needs. Probably no one knows who first used skins to climb uphill, but it's safe to say that this also happened a very long time ago.

Historically, the region of Telemark in Norway might be the single-most important area for the sport of skiing. In this region, skiing was taken seriously enough that people started doing it for fun. Of course,

once a fun sport reaches a certain standard, some people start getting all serious about it, and this is where the telemark prophet Sondre Norheim comes into the picture.

By the 1880s the sport of skiing had matured far beyond a simple mode of winter locomotion. Championships were held and a true master had to test his or her skills in three categories: the ski jump, a cross-country race, and the infamous downhill slalom. All this had to be done on the same gear. The overall winner of these three disciplines was the true ski champion.

Norheim appeared on the scene as a bit of a renegade. He insisted that the current skis were way too long and straight—they were about 10 feet long and had next to no side cut. His idea of a good time was a 7-foot ski and a ski geometry that was actually no different from the side cut used in some alpine skis up to the late 1980s.

Norheim, originator of the telemark turn, then invented the alpine turn (Norwegians are quite adamant about this), and he introduced it during a competition in the small town of Christiania. According to Norheim, he would strap a strong birch twig across the top of his foot to keep his heel down. He would then bring the skis around with a more open parallel stance, the basis of the alpine turn. Norheim demolished his competitors with his new turn, and the debate raged over whether he had cheated or not. He had modified his gear, after all, and had departed from the pure telemark turn.

Here is where a new faith was born. The Norwegians believed strongly in the idea of the all-around champion who could jump, race cross-country, and slalom ski. Since all these disciplines had to be accomplished using the same gear, the modified gear idea that came along with the "new school Christiania Schwung" (the stem christy) did not take hold in Norway. But it did catch on in the Alps. Once this turn was introduced in Austria and Switzerland, it was embraced right away. Within a few years, all the downhill races were won with the newly developed alpine turn.

Development of the pure downhill sport has been steady over the decades and has turned into the backbone for both AT and telemark ski development. The power of a pure downhill setup outperforms both AT and telemark systems, but is just about useless for uphill travel.

During the 1960s, uphill travel with the alpine bindings seemed clunky and inhibiting compared to the telemark system, and telemark boots had a relatively soft-flexing boot that allowed for a much more ergonomic gait progression. Sometime in the late 1960s, it was found that most of the negative effects of the stiffer alpine sole could be compensated for by placing a hinge under the toepiece of the binding. Of course, the toe- and heelpiece needed to be connected so that the whole thing would move as one unit, and thus was born the AT binding.

The advent of the AT binding allowed the backcountry skier to move uphill with relative ease, and the locking mechanism assured the superior power of the alpine

Backcountry gate in Niseko, Japan

turn. Since then, enormous strides have been made in both the AT and telemark setups. A key difference between them is the flex or pivot (or lack thereof) between the boots and the bindings, not just how much each setup weighs (a traditional complaint against AT that has become moot—modern AT and tele boot-binding combinations weigh about the same). Because of the relatively stiff toe flex of telemark bindings, AT bindings have surpassed them in walking efficiency. The newly released hinged tele bindings, however, will improve walking performance dramatically.

A significant disadvantage of the AT system on the uphill occurs when the skier needs to transition between uphill to downhill and back to uphill again in a short distance. The AT skier must determine whether to be in the uphill mode or to stop and put the binding in ski mode. Ski mode allows for better control of the ski, but the skier will need to switch back to uphill mode in short order, which all takes time. Meanwhile, the tele skier skins by and skis down those smaller slopes with ease and control.

In truly rugged terrain, it's hard to argue with the power and relative efficiency of a modern AT setup, just as it's hard to argue with the elegance of the telemark turn. Arguing about the tele vs. the AT turn is like debating your favorite color and can only be debated so far. It's hard to deny the exquisite feeling of dropping your knee in a tele turn in light Utah powder, and it's hard to disagree with the control provided by the fixed-heel alpine turn in Cascade breakable crust or Sierra cement. We come back to where we started: the best answer remains to choose the right tool for the job, or quite possibly to go with whatever style you prefer. Happy reading, and be safe out there.

A NOTE ABOUT SAFETY

Safety is an important concern in all outdoor activities. No book can alert you to every hazard or anticipate the limitations of every reader. The descriptions of techniques and procedures in this book are intended to provide general information. This is not a complete text on backcountry ski mountaineering. Nothing substitutes for formal instruction, routine practice, and plenty of experience. When you follow any of the procedures described here, you assume responsibility for your own safety. Use this book as a general guide to further information. Under normal conditions, excursions into the backcountry require attention to traffic, road and trail conditions, weather, terrain, the capabilities of your party, and other factors. Keeping informed on current conditions and exercising common sense are the keys to a safe, enjoyable outing.

The Mountaineers Books

CHAPTER 1

Mason Stafford starting a good day in the Snoqualmie Pass backcountry

Gear and Equipment

Backcountry skiing comes with its own gear and equipment needs, but before launching into gear specifics, we'd like to address the weight dilemma. Innumerable conversations in ski shops, in mountain huts, on lift rides, in tents, and in bars debate the virtues of light and even lighter gear, namely the ski-boot-binding setup. The lighter the load, the greater the efficiency, or so assumes many a backcountry skier. But overall efficiency, going both up- and downhill, comes from an overall caloric economy—that is, expending as little energy throughout the tour as possible—and, regrettably, this does not run parallel to weight savings.

By way of analogy, it would be nice if a hammer weighed just about nothing on the upswing and then had the necessary heft to drive a nail home. A good framing hammer weighs a significant amount and still appears to be the most efficient tool for the job. If the hammer were too light,

the framer would expend too much energy driving the nail into the wood, and overall energy output would be increased.

So it is with ski touring. Most of a ski tour is spent going uphill, and so getting a light ski can become a focus in choosing gear. But what happens with a superlight ski on the way down? At some point the ski will lose its driving power—it won't hold an edge very well because of its inability to absorb vibration, and it will be very difficult to steer the ski properly through its designed radius. Once snow conditions become difficult, any energy saved on the way up can easily be wasted on the way down if the ski is too light.

So what is the right ski weight? People want different things out of a ski tour, but principally there are two ways to look at the question of weight: by looking at the qualitative aspects of the tour and by looking at the overall caloric efficiency of the tour.

The qualitative assessment. You may

be perfectly happy to carry heavier gear because you are accessing an amazing and challenging ski line that requires top-notch ski performance. A superlight setup would be a poor qualitative choice. Furthermore, it could turn into a safety issue.

On the other hand, you may be setting out on a multiday traverse that offers moderate skiing and you want to carry as little gear as possible in order to make the traverse as enjoyable as possible.

What if you want to ski an amazing line, but it is way in the backcountry? Some people would choose a lighter setup, assuming that their superior skiing skill will compensate for their gear's lack of performance. Other people decide they are fit enough that a few extra pounds will not detract from enjoying the tour.

There are about as many right choices in these scenarios as there are attitudes. When thinking qualitatively, most experienced backcountry skiers end up with a very carefully chosen setup that tends toward the lighter side of things. And thanks to new technology, skis, boots, and bindings have become lighter while still retaining a good amount of performance.

Caloric efficiency. Now let's consider the overall caloric efficiency of a tour. This means that you choose equipment around the principle of expending as few calories as possible. This is a popular way of thinking among guides and mountain professionals, since they have to retain energy levels for weeks on end and optimize recuperation time.

The resulting setups are not necessarily

the lightest, though they trend light. The type of terrain, length of tour, rhythm of touring, and general conditions are all factors. And some considerations will change from skier to skier depending on skiing ability, even if the skiers share the same goals for a tour. But, in general, if caloric efficiency is your goal, you will most likely end up with more than one ski touring setup.

Some examples: a 65-millimeter waisted superlight randonnée rally racing ski that weighs only 800 grams is certainly light and is hard to argue against (fig. 1.1)—until you have to plow uphill through 4 feet of

Fig. 1.1 A randonnée rally racer's gear is superlight and superfast.

deep powder and the ski submarines below the surface. If your ski weighs about 1400 grams but boasts a 90-millimeter waist, you'll have a more efficient tool for the powder job, on the uphill and the downhill, and certainly in terms of overall caloric efficiency.

As for boots, if you anticipate very difficult snow, committing ski descents, or will carry a heavy pack, you might be better off with a slightly heavier and more supportive boot for minimal caloric consumption— you'll be carrying more boot weight uphill, but you'll expend less energy going down.

To make matters more complicated, boots of equal weight do not necessarily offer the same amount of efficiency, depending on how freely the boot cuff hinges in walk mode. The less resistance you feel against your shin and calf during your stride, the more efficient you can be on the uphill.

Bindings are also part of the caloric efficiency equation. Different bindings have different amounts of resistance in their hingepoints due to the position of the hinge relative to the boot tip. Greater resistance means lower efficiency walking uphill. Often you must choose between a binding's downhill performance and weight. A glorious exception to this situational gear conundrum is the Dynafit AT binding, which should be a consideration for any skier interested in ultimate caloric efficiency. It offers exceptional reliability, low weight, and good power transfer (see "Boot and Binding Compatibility" below).

For the most part your touring setup will be on the lighter side if caloric efficiency is your ultimate goal. Just keep in mind that the lightest setup is not necessarily the most energy efficient.

SKIS

Choosing skis used to be a rather simple affair. There was not a great selection, and innovation for backcountry skis was slow because of the economics of ski building. For a long time telemark skis looked like fat versions of cross-country skis (which are called backcountry skis these days... very confusing). Let us explain: backcountry skiers use telemark or alpine touring (AT) skis, both called touring skis. Cross-country skiers use track (classic) skis, cross-country skis, skating skis, and backcountry skis.

From the early 1970s to the late '80s, AT skis had a generic side-cut geometry (90 millimeters at the tip, 70 at the waist, 80 at the tail), a tip that was turned up farther than an alpine (downhill) ski, and a very bright top-sheet color for some added avalanche safety.

Things seemed a little stuck until shaped skis came along. Manufacturers started experimenting with side cuts, and by the late-'90s any traditional idea of what a telemark or AT ski should look like was thrown out.

Telemark and AT skis started to look a lot alike, then they started sharing molds, and these days the only difference lies in the construction of the ski and how the ski is designed to flex (fig. 1.2 shows modern AT and tele skis). A telemark turn applies

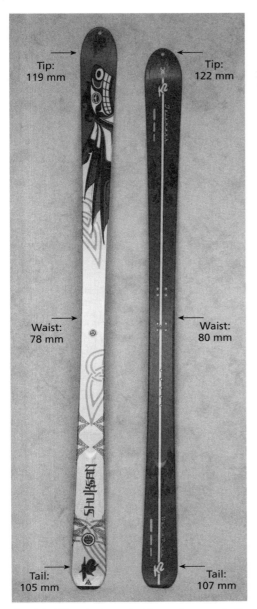

Tip: 119 mm

Tip: 122 mm

Waist: 78 mm

Waist: 80 mm

Tail: 105 mm

Tail: 107 mm

Fig. 1.2 AT and telemark skis can be very similar.

less force to a ski than the equivalent alpine turn. As a result, some telemark skis are designed with a flex to accommodate the forces of a tele turn. Several manufacturers are blurring the lines by producing telemark skis that have stiffer longitudinal flexes (the flex of the ski lengthwise, tip to tail) than their AT counterparts.

Manufacturers are struggling with differing attitudes and the complicated economics of niche ski manufacturing. However, a few things seem to remain consistent. Telemark and AT skis tend to be lighter in overall weight than alpine skis. They are also a bit softer in flex. Many AT and some tele skis have a hole drilled in the tip, and if the ski is supposed to be any kind of multifunction tool, it should not have a twin tip. Twin tips make it difficult to plant the ski tail-first in the snow in order to build ski anchors, or to prevent a runaway ski in steep or exposed terrain.

Let's turn to the several criteria for choosing a ski: platform and side cut, weight, size, intended application, and boot/binding compatibility.

PLATFORM AND SIDE CUT

A ski's platform is how much surface area it has. Side cut refers to the relationship between tip, waist, and tail dimensions, and this relationship dictates the turning radius of the ski.

Platform. Historically, ski platforms were dictated by the conditions associated with their expected use. For a long time the European standard of around a 70-millimeter waisted ski seemed common for ski touring platforms. In the Alps, ski touring often occurs in high alpine terrain and, because of that, the touring season actually starts a bit later. This means the snowpack is often more consolidated and sometimes very hard-packed, thus the skinnier platform. Ski touring in the United States and Canada often happens in deeper snow and the season starts earlier than in Europe, which means platforms tend to be fatter.

From our perspective, a fatter platform makes the majority of snow conditions easier to ski. But all things being equal, a fatter platform means the ski will be heavier, and hard-snow performance will decrease.

Conversely, a skinnier platform will have quicker edge-to-edge transfer on hard snow and will translate the applied power better (it will also skin better in hard conditions). But a skinnier platform will not float as well in varied and generally unconsolidated snow conditions.

Side cut. Side cut determines the radius that the ski will carve.

Turn initiation is almost always easier on a ski with substantial side cut. The bigger the side cut, the shorter the turning radius and more immediate the initiation. That remains correct until you need to bring your skis around in a radius that is shorter than the intended radius of the ski (pivoting the ski).

If pivoting your ski around is an issue, consider that less side cut translates into a more neutral behavior in a ski. Aggressive skinning on hard terrain can be improved with less side cut. Side slipping and snow plowing and general skiing in difficult snow is definitely easier with larger radius skis

(i.e., skis with less side cut). A ski's radius changes with the ski's size, but generally a turning radius between 18 and 22 meters is ideal for ski touring.

While we're on the subject of how skis behave in a turn, a note about ski tips: ski manufacturers have experimented a lot with various tip profiles (the actual shape of the tip). Most often a relatively neutral profile is chosen for an AT or telemark ski. If the profile is too aggressive (i.e., is designed to initiate a turn very quickly), turn initiation can be twitchy in difficult snow conditions.

Here are a few guidelines for choosing a ski for the backcountry:

- Choose the waist size of your ski along with the radius you would like it to ski. Skis with 75- to 85-millimeter waists are considered all-around platforms. Once the intended radius is chosen, the tip and tail dimensions fall into place.
- If you choose a ski that is skinnier than 70 millimeters underfoot, you are most likely in a more specific category than general backcountry touring (an in-bounds tele ski or a randonnée rally racing ski).
- If you choose a ski waist that trends toward 90 millimeters and up, your intended application should be mostly soft-snow ski touring. There are fat skis out there that have amazing hard-pack performance, but they are probably too heavy for big days of ski touring.
- Choose a ski that has enough side cut to make turn initiation easy, but make sure the side cut is small enough that

the general ski behavior remains fairly neutral. This means you won't run into trouble in crusty snow and skinning on steep slopes, and the deep waist of the ski won't keep you from performing optimally on hard skinning conditions.

WEIGHT

Since most backcountry skiers earn their turns, we spend an amazing amount of time talking about the weight of skis, and light skis remain popular. With good engineering and a lot of care a ski can be built quite light and still perform very well.

But at some point in the weight-loss program, the downhill performance of a ski decreases dramatically. According to K2's ski builder guru, Ken Shiele, engineering properties alone can't make up for certain benefits that mass brings to a ski.

To ensure decent ski performance in terms of edge hold, steering power, and general performance at speed, be suspicious of a ski that weighs less than about 1500 grams per ski. A lighter ski can perform well, but it needs to be very carefully built; the construction materials will most likely be quite exotic and the resulting price will reflect that.

In a ski, a certain amount of mass results in inertia, better edge hold, better steering, and generally more stable behavior. On the other side of the scale, if a ski gets too heavy it becomes unresponsive; a World Cup downhill ski will not be a snappy ski.

Telemark and AT skis currently range from a featherlight 800 grams per ski to nearly 2000 grams (fig. 1.3). At around 1800 grams, you might as well wander over to the alpine rack and marvel at the incredible selection available there.

Do not choose by weight alone. Shop at a store where the salespeople can answer technical questions and can point you in the right direction for your intended application.

SKI LENGTH

It used to be popular to choose a shorter ski for ski touring than for downhill skiing. This was a simple way to lighten your setup and make it more maneuverable.

But this came at the expense of general ski performance and fore and aft stability. If you're skiing in difficult snow, with a backpack and softer boots, a lighter ski (that's harder to control) can make your first downhill experience with your new AT or telemark outfit quite an awakening.

For some of the considerations mentioned above, in-area and backcountry ski length selection have melted together. Some people even prefer a slightly longer AT or telemark ski in order to increase fore and aft stability.

INTENDED APPLICATION

Because of the diversity of intended applications, there is not one best ski for ski touring. To make the right choice, it helps to be as clear as possible about what kind of touring you are going to do.

- Are you strictly weight conscious and willing to forego a certain amount of ski performance?
- Are you accessing "the goods" or that difficult descent and willing to carry the

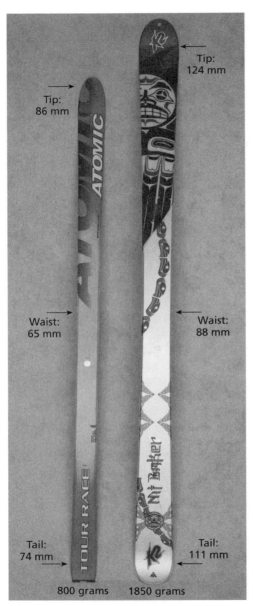

Tip:
86 mm

Tip:
124 mm

Waist:
65 mm

Waist:
88 mm

Tail:
74 mm

Tail:
111 mm

800 grams   1850 grams

Fig. 1.3 The far ends of the spectrum of top-notch backcountry skis

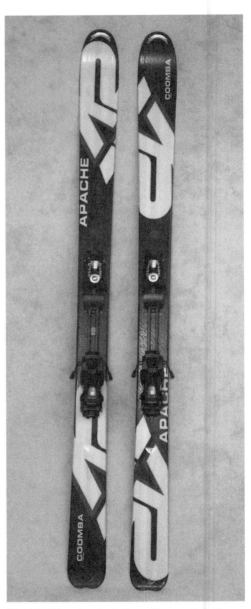

Fig. 1.4 This setup is designed to excel on the downhill—concerns about weight don't apply.

load for optimal performance on the way down (fig. 1.4)?

- Do you want it all and are you willing to pay for it?
- Will you be skiing mostly in unconsolidated conditions, or do you anticipate a hard spring snowpack?
- Do you need a crud buster or does your ski need to handle all of the above?

BOOT AND BINDING COMPATIBILITY

Make sure that your boot and binding system is appropriately matched with your ski (see the "Boots" and "Binding" sections below). It would be silly to use a powerful binding and boot combination on a rando rally racing ski. It would be just as silly to buy a powerful ski to counteract the inadequate ski performance of a superlight AT or telemark boot; these lighter boots simply don't have enough power to steer heavier skis properly.

That said, a heavier binding doesn't necessarily produce the best power transfer. The Dynafit binding in particular has shattered the traditional image of what a lightweight binding can do.

SKIS AS MULTIFUNCTIONAL TOOLS

Regardless of whether you choose a narrow or wide ski, a heavy or light ski, two things demand careful consideration when selecting a touring ski: first, snow conditions are vastly different in the backcountry than they are in a resort and, second, your skis aren't merely for skiing—they're also tools.

Even if you remove all the grooming and snow-making equipment that can turn even the most difficult conditions dreamy, the sheer volume of resort skiers prevents truly difficult conditions from developing or lasting very long. When is the last time you saw powder hang around a resort long enough to develop a sun crust? And in the rare case that superchallenging conditions do persist, you simply don't ski them. When the temperature plummets and turns yesterday's slush bumps into corrugated cement, dont tell me you don't traverse over to the groomed slope. I do.

You don't have this luxury in the backcountry. Safety aside, if you have to get to the bottom of a particular slope, you're going to ski it, even if that means zigzagging down the whole pitch.

Since backcountry conditions are less forgiving and predictable, your skis must possess those attributes instead. The same design features that make skis dynamic and exhilarating in resorts make them more unpredictable and less forgiving in difficult backcountry snow. For example, deep side cuts are super-precise, have great edge hold, and are a blast to ski on groomed terrain, but they behave erratically in wind or sun crust. Or, a reactive tip will draw you into the turn quicker and put more edge on the snow, which is awesome on consistent snow, but that same tip will be hooky and inconsistent in tricky conditions.

Better to give up a bit of precision and hard-snow stability and gain predictability and forgiveness in your touring ski. That's not to say the ski shouldn't be high performance; you still need solid edge hold and stability. But shallow to moderate side cut, moderate to stiff torsion, medium-round flex, and a less reactive tip profile can provide that forgiveness and predictability.

Not only are you more likely to encounter tough conditions when touring, but the consequences are more severe. At best, multiple crashes sap valuable energy reserves. At worst, if you crash in the wrong place—like the top of a steep slope or above rocks, cliffs, or crevasses—the consequences can be fatal. If you twist a knee because your ski was erratic and hooky, backcountry evacuation is much more daunting than simply waiting for the patrol to bring you to the first-aid shack in a big, solid toboggan.

Which brings us to the next function of a touring ski: utility. If you want to cut down on weight in the backcountry, the multifunctionality of all your equipment is crucial. If you can construct a sled with your skis, you don't need to carry a rescue sled. If you can use your skis as a belay anchor or to stake out your tent, pickets and tent stakes can be left at home.

With that in mind, look for skis that have holes drilled in the tips and tails to facilitate rescue sled construction, tail notches to secure skin hooks, bright colors for visibility, and, one of the most overlooked designs, straight tails. Twin-tipped tails are great for going backward or throwing up a smokescreen of powder, but they prevent you from jamming your tails in even the softest snow—not a big deal until you try to build an anchor by jamming your tails in the snow. Even trivial tasks like securing your skis on a steep, firm slope while taking off your pack or putting on your crampons become challenging, if not impossible, with twin tips.

So when picking out a touring ski, realize that most alpine skis don't have the utility features you need for an efficient backcountry tool; they are designed for different conditions than you're likely to find in the backcountry. Choose your touring ski wisely—not only does your skiing enjoyment depend on it, your safety does as well.

Mike Hattrup is the director of development for the K2 telemark and AT divisions, is an AMGA-certified ski mountaineering guide, and has appeared in several ski movies.

BOOTS

The most dreaded ski gear purchase is often the ski boot. Many skiers endured their first turns in toenail-crushing torture chambers foisted upon them by race-fit-obsessed ski shops. The alternative boot experience, feet swimming in an enormous hand-me-down boot, is no better. We'll say it once: this kind of suffering does not need to be associated with backcountry skiing.

The boot, whether telemark or AT,

plays a crucial role in the overall performance of your backcountry setup. Boots for the backcountry must fulfill a dual purpose: uphill function and downhill performance. We all want to carve turns in breakable crust with the power of an alpine boot, even as we demand efficiency while skinning uphill.

To that end, all telemark and AT boots have a walk/ski switch in the back. When in the walk position, this switch allows the rear of the boot to flex backward, increasing comfort and stride length on the uphill. Ski mode locks the upper cuff of the boot in position, giving the skier better control for the ski down.

MOLDABLE LINERS

Both telemark and AT boots are available with heat-moldable liners (fig. 1.5). These liners, made of moldable ethylene vinyl acetate (EVA) foam, contour nicely to your foot and provide an excellent fit. For best results, have your liners molded in a qualified shop with a special oven and a skilled fitter. These moldable liners have several advantages over

Fig. 1.5 Several types of moldable boot liners

conventional liners: custom fit, light weight, added warmth, and low water absorption (a great feature for a multiday tour).

BOOT FIT:
SHELL AND LINER SIZE

We all know the saying: if the shoe fits, wear it. The overall fit of a boot will most likely be the biggest determining factor in your final boot choice.

First, accurately determine the size of your foot by having the salesperson measure it. Then, to fit the plastic shell, remove the liner and place your foot in the empty shell. Slide your foot forward and let your toes touch firmly against the front of the boot. With your fingers, see how much space you have between your heel and the back of the boot: you want around 0.75 inch. For backcountry racing performance, round down in size; if you're heading to the Arctic and need a little more warmth, err on the bigger side. Once you have figured out your shell size, reinsert the liner into the shell and try it on.

First make sure that the length of the shell is still good with the liner inserted. When you stand straight up and lean back a little, the tips of your toes should lightly touch the end of the boot. Touching the liner with your toes when the boot is new is not a bad thing. When new, the boot is the *smallest* it will ever be, and if your toes touch lightly this gives you the right amount of thickness to keep the boot snug after the liner packs out. If you're in a boot with a moldable liner, expect to feel pressure around your toes. Once correctly molded to your foot, the liner will allow for enough room in the toe box.

Once you determine the shell size for the model of boot you're buying, stay with it. Don't try to adjust the length of the boot to take care of other fit issues. This will only lead you down the road of severe fit problems.

The final aspect of fitting is the overall volume. In a nutshell, you want a firm and hugging pressure around your entire foot. A critical fit area is the heel of the boot. You want your heel to be secure in both ski and walk mode; too much heel lift invites devastating blisters. If the liner is a moldable one, discuss any hotspots you've experienced in other boots with the boot fitter prior to molding.

Prior to molding, consider an aftermarket footbed, or insole, that suits your foot. These not only improve comfort, but also can help with better energy transfer from your foot to your boot and ultimately to your ski.

WOMEN'S BOOTS

For many years, women had to use the only boots available to them: men's boots. But women's versions of most models are now in shops and generally have the following differences: smaller sizes available, wider and lower upper cuff, narrower heel, and narrower forefoot.

TELEMARK BOOTS

Modern telemark boots have come a long way, and most backcountry telemark skiers now use plastic boots (fig. 1.6). These modern plastic boots consist of shells that have multiple plastics injected into them, which allows the manufacturer to control and vary the flex of the boot. Depending on the intended purpose of the boot, the flex may be stiffer in one area and softer in another. As a general rule, boots having a higher cuff and more buckles often lend themselves to better downhill performance. Be sure to consider your backcountry objectives when perusing the boot wall.

Fig. 1.6 Modern plastic telemark boots offer a range of performance capabilities.

When trying on different models, the fitting discussion above applies, with one additional consideration: the fit and flex of the bellows. The ideal fit will allow you to flex forward onto the ball of your foot without any pinching.

Tip: Ask the salesperson to provide you with a tele ski and binding to place on the floor to better determine to flex and position of the bellows. Another thing to consider when fitting a tele boot is the addition of an insole. Unlike in an AT boot, the insole in a telemark boot must remain flexible so as not to crack when the boot flexes.

In 2007 the telemark industry saw one of the biggest evolutions since the plastic boot: the new telemark norm (NTN). The NTN is the first telemark system designed as a cooperative effort between the boot and binding manufacturers. The most noticeable difference between the NTN and the 75-millimeter Nordic norm is the removal of the "duckbill" from the toe of the boot. This new boot standard closely resembles the sole of an AT boot, while still retaining the bellows of a classic telemark boot. This new sole will give the skier better mountaineering performance—something many tele skiers have been yearning for. The NTN also features improved lateral control over the ski while at the same time greatly improving uphill efficiency with the use of a free rotating pivot point. Will the NTN become the new standard for the telemark skier, rendering cable bindings a thing of the past? Only time will tell!

ALPINE TOURING BOOTS VS. ALPINE SKIING BOOTS

If you're a downhill skier looking to get out into the backcountry, chances are you already own a set of alpine skiing boots. Many people make their first turns in the backcountry on a set of these boots. For the downhill experience, this works fine; carving turns is the primary function of the alpine boot.

The trouble with an alpine setup in the backcountry comes when it's time to go uphill. In order to skin up the mountain, you need to slide one ski in front of the other. In order to do this in an efficient manner, the boot needs to allow for range of motion both frontward and backward. This added range of motion, especially toward the back, is not considered in the design of the alpine boot (see fig. 1.7).

An additional problem with the alpine boot in the backcountry is the weight. In

Fig. 1.7 The shape and function of alpine boots significantly impede your range of ankle motion, shortening your stride.

Fig. 1.8 A collection of modern AT boots

order to create a strong skiing boot, manufacturers increase the overall stiffness (in all directions) in an alpine boot, which often means a thicker plastic shell made of different material and thus more weight.

The bottom line for alpine boots? They work great going down, but going up the mountain they'll be inefficient and uncomfortable.

SKI TOURING BOOTS: WALKING UP VS. SKIING DOWN

Even the type or model of an AT boot affects uphill performance. A key element in the selection of a touring boot (AT or telemark) is the cuff height and the overall range of motion of the upper cuff. Imagine a boot with a very stiff forward flex and considerable forward lean. This boot may ski well, but your stride on the uphill will be limited to short choppy steps (see chapter 4, Uphill Movement). In the ski shop, you can compare similar models for the range of motion in uphill mode: for each boot, check how far you can flex forward and how far your lower leg can angle backward.

Once you have selected the boot for the uphill, take a look at the skiing performance. Comparing boot models for skiing performance in the shop is severely limited, but you can get a general idea by looking at a boot's three directions of flex, in order of importance for skiing performance: backward (or aft) flex, lateral flex, and forward flex. The stiffer the aft and lateral flex, the better the boot will ski. Forward flex is complex: the stiffest boot may not ski the best, but the softest boot won't ski well either. Figure 1.8 shows a selection of AT boots.

BINDINGS

Bindings are often the last and least deliberated piece of gear in the ski-boot-binding package. By the time most people waddle (in their new boots) from the ski wall over to the binding side of the store, they are worn out from the complicated decisions about boot flex and ski design. But telemark and AT bindings play a large role in the comfort and skiability during both downhill *and* uphill performance.

Simply put, the binding holds the boot to the ski. This is true in either the telemark or AT system. We want this attachment to provide a connection to the ski that gives us good control. For AT and some modern telemark bindings, we want to release from the ski when we crash.

In addition to the specifics discussed below, consider the following things when purchasing bindings: weight, ease of use, uphill efficiency, lateral response, release mechanism, heel lifters, durability/reliability, and field repair options.

TELEMARK BINDINGS

Most telemark bindings adhere to the 75-millimeter Nordic norm. This requires the classic duckbill toe that we've all come to recognize. This norm has been standard for decades, although it is undergoing change with the advent of the new telemark norm (NTN; see "Telemark Boots," above). Over the years, bindings have been developed using various designs: the classic 3-pin style, cable bindings, and—most recently—bindings designed with a low-resistance pivot point.

Before you head to the ski shop to purchase bindings, ask yourself these questions:

- How much time will you spend in the backcountry vs. in-area skiing?
- How much weight are you willing to carry?
- What is more important: downhill performance or weight?
- Are you interested in a release mechanism?

Classic 3-Pin

These bindings were once the standard for the telemark skier, but they have fallen by the wayside with the advent of the modern cable binding (see below). This is most likely because the classic three-pin lacks torsional stability and control over the ski, especially when paired with a high-performance plastic tele boot. Another issue with these bindings is the pinhole wear in the boot sole associated with the pins.

The classic three-pin binding works well for the skier looking to do very light-duty touring; beyond that, cables should be part of your binding.

Cables

Cable bindings have become the standard telemark bindings for both in-area and backcountry skiing (see fig. 1.9). The cables affect both uphill and downhill performance: depending on your skinning-to-skiing ratio, they can be beneficial for control...or they can hinder your ability to tour efficiently.

On the downhill, cables serve several functions. They provide a significant increase in torsional stability, which allows better control of the ski in aggressive terrain or difficult skiing conditions. Second, cables are the primary attachment mechanism between the boot and the binding, a great improvement over the three-pin attachment on its own. Cables solve the problem of pinhole wear in the boot sole and also take care of lining up the boot sole and the binding.

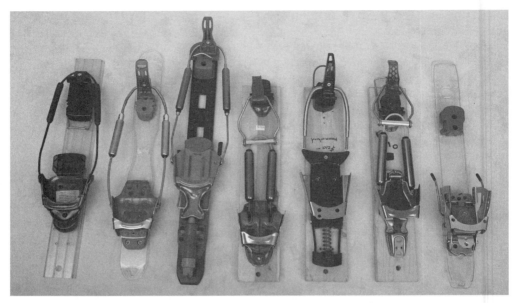

Fig. 1.9 Telemark bindings available on the market offer a wide range of designs.

On the uphill, cables cause a loss of efficiency (and can make kick turns difficult) because they add resistance in the pivot of each step. As a result, some still prefer the older-style binding with three pins and a removable cable, which allows you to remove the cable for uphill touring and replace it on the downhill.

Most modern bindings come with cables that have adjustable tension, allowing you to adjust the tension of the cable to better suit your weight or preference. To adjust the tension, place the boot in the binding and adjust so that there is positive snap when you close the heel lever. Some bindings are a little more complicated and may require assistance from your local shop.

Tip: Loosen the cable tension on the uphill for efficient skinning and easier kick turns, and retighten on the downhill for torsional stability and control.

Depending on the model, you may be able to purchase cables with stiffer or softer springs. For the average skier, we recommend soft to medium springs for the backcountry. This allows for a more efficient stride and helps to minimize pressure on the ski tip while breaking trail.

Dual Mode Pivot Telemark Bindings

Recently, several binding manufacturers have addressed the uphill efficiency problems of high-performance telemark bindings. As discussed above in "Telemark Boots," the resistance provided by the sole and bellows of a stiff telemark boot help the skier to control the ski on the downhill, yet dramatically reduce the uphill efficiency of the system.

To solve this problem, some companies are producing tele bindings featuring a dual mode (fig. 1.10). The bindings have a switch that allows the skier to differentiate between tour mode and ski mode. In tour mode, the entire binding and boot pivot around a single point, allowing very low resistance similar to many AT bindings. Place

the binding in ski mode and it delivers performance equivalent to high-end cable bindings.

An added advantage of the pivot tele binding is that it allows more efficient execution of a kick turn (see "The Kick Turn" in chapter 4). The advent of these modern telemark bindings is quickly narrowing the gap between tele and AT touring systems.

Heel Lifters

For the backcountry, you should consider the addition of heel lifters (fig. 1.11). Many

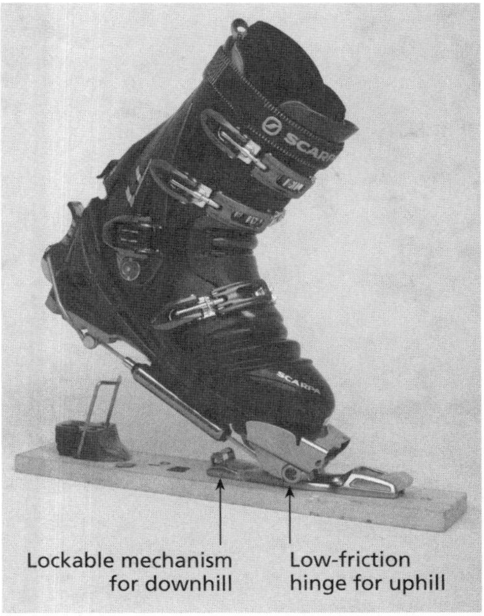

Lockable mechanism
for downhill

Low-friction
hinge for uphill

Fig. 1.10 The Black Diamond O1 is one of the new telemark bindings with dual mode pivot.

Fig. 1.11 Integrated heel lifter in a telemark binding

modern telemark bindings have them built into their design. These allow for a variety of boot positions while skinning uphill (more on this in chapter 4, Uphill Movement). If your bindings don't have lifters, there are several aftermarket kits available and we highly recommend getting them.

Release Mechanisms

Several release mechanisms are now available for telemark setups, partly because of the correlation between higher boots, shaped skis, and the increase in knee injuries. The mechanisms vary from simple release plates mounted under your existing bindings to complete binding release kits.

Release mechanisms are a great safety advantage when traveling in avalanche terrain. They do add considerable weight and complexity to an otherwise simple ski setup, and considerable cost. But if you travel in avalanche country, they may be worth it.

ALPINE TOURING BINDINGS

The AT bindings available today are solid, reliable, and easy to use (fig. 1.12). Most of the bindings on the market are reasonably well built, so your choice should be

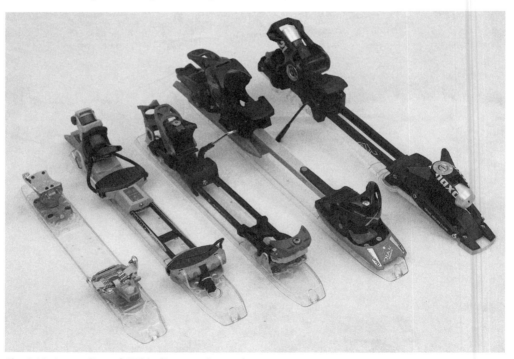

Fig. 1.12 A sampling of AT bindings on the market

determined by your criterion of use. We tend to think about these three main criteria: boot compatibility, uphill performance, and skiing performance.

Boot Compatibility

At the point of making the binding purchase, most people have already decided on, or already own, a boot. This can make the binding choice easy or not. There are three main binding types.

Standard AT. The standard AT binding fits both alpine boots and AT boots. AT boots have a rubber sole and a rocker to improve walking and climbing, giving them thicker toe height than a regular alpine boot.

Dynafit. The binding is superbly designed for many applications and is an excellent solution to the weight dilemma, but there are some limitations. The binding requires special fittings on the toe and heel of your boots. Boots without Dynafit compatibility can't be retrofitted. These bindings require a bit more skill and practice to operate. The Dynafit binding also lacks mass and therefore does not dampen the ski as well as a heavier binding. In spite of these limitations, the Dynafit is one of the strongest and lightest bindings available—and it has full release capabilities.

Mountaineering. Mountaineering bindings are compatible with ice-climbing or mountaineering boots as well as with AT and alpine boots.

Uphill Performance

Several factors affect the uphill touring performance of an AT binding. The location of the hinge, or pivot point, plays a huge role in uphill efficiency. The farther back on the binding the pivot point lies, the more efficient and ergonomic your stride will be. Weight of the binding is another thing to consider. All other things being equal, the lighter the binding, the more efficient uphill travel will be. Keep these factors in mind based on the amount of time you plan to spend walking uphill.

Downhill Performance

The heavier the binding, the better it will ski through crud and hardpack. The more the binding weighs, the less it and the ski will get pushed around.

Take a look at the bindings the World Cup racers use. These very stout and heavy bindings allow them to steer through a turn with very little deflection. As a backcountry skier you shouldn't necessarily do as the racers do, but it's something to consider in your binding purchase. The cost, of course, is weight.

Several newer bindings are designed more toward skiing down than touring up. These bindings have a higher DIN setting (or binding release value) and are built with durability in mind.

Other Considerations

All AT bindings have a heel lifter built into them. This is usually a multiheight lifter that is often easy to operate with your ski pole.

Mounting and adjustment of an AT binding is slightly more complicated than a telemark binding. This work is best done by your local backcountry ski shop.

SKI CRAMPONS

Ski crampons, also called *harscheisen* (the German term), are a very important tool for the backcountry skier. These metal devices attach to ski bindings and augment traction provided by climbing skins. In softer snow, skins themselves provide plenty of traction. But when the conditions become too firm, as in the early mornings of a spring tour, attaching ski crampons can save you a tremendous amount of energy and can increase your margin of safety.

Ski crampons are available for all AT bindings (fig. 1.13), and they recently became available for telemark bindings. For many years, the lack of a useable ski crampon in the tele market was a big drawback if you wanted to tele ski a high-alpine spring tour. The fact that ski crampons are now tele compatible is another factor narrowing the gap between AT and tele setups.

SKI STRAPS VS. BRAKES

Another binding-related gear decision is what kind of stopping mechanism to use: ski straps or ski brakes. Tele skiers skiing at a resort must have straps or a releasable system with a brake to board the chairlift. What about in the backcountry? This topic is hotly debated, and instead of weighing in definitively we'll give you a couple of things to think about in making your decision.

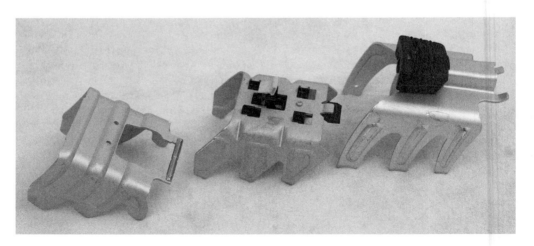

Fig. 1.13 Ski crampons for Dynafit, Naxo, and Fritschi bindings

First off, brakes are convenient and easy to use. It's much quicker to step into a binding and start skiing than to fiddle around with fixing a strap around your leg or to your boot.

Then there are the safety concerns associated with straps. If you crash and release from your bindings, each ski becomes a rotating, metal-edged projectile that can give you a beating. And in an avalanche, being permanently connected to your skis is not ideal: the skis act as anchors pulling you under the moving snow.

When should you use straps? They are still applicable for certain situations. Losing a ski in a ski area is an unfortunate event; losing a ski in the backcountry can quickly turn serious. On spring tours when the snow is firm and on deep powder days, you may want to consider straps to augment your brakes. Glacier travel in heavily crevassed terrain is also an appropriate time to use straps.

Tip: Unbuckle or remove straps when crossing avalanche terrain.

SKINS

By most accounts, skis and skins have been used together for several thousand years. In fact, for the longest time skiing was called *skilaufen* (ski walking) in German-speaking countries. The term *skifahren* (ski riding) was not born until the 1920s and '30s. Technological advances during the First World War and the postwar revitalization programs in Austria and Germany led to the first gondolas which, along with ski lifts, changed the face of skiing forever.

But before lift-assisted skiing, the masses earned their turns by attaching skins to their skis for traction. As the name implies, mammal skins were most often used. Some skiers even used fir twigs strapped under their skis, certainly a cheaper option than animal skins.

The plush, as the climbing skin surface is called, has to fulfill two contradictory purposes. Ideally it should provide next to no gliding resistance when you're striding forward, and then it needs to provide as much traction as possible when you step down on your ski.

Seal skin was a popular material because it fulfilled this dual function. The hair grows at a very narrow angle out of the actual skin of a seal, which makes both the gliding and catching actions possible. Mohair, the material used after seal skins fell out of favor, has similar qualities.

Contemporary climbing skins consist of three parts: the plush, the backing, and the attachment system.

THE PLUSH
The plush is the surface you're gliding on. Mohair (or goat hair) continues to be popular in Europe, perhaps because of tradition, while synthetic materials have come into wide use elsewhere. Synthetic skins provide superior longevity to natural fiber skins. A recent study conducted by the Swiss Federal Institute for Snow and

Avalanche Research concluded that mohair skins show better gliding properties in colder snow (less than 3° C/37° F), and nylon skins have better gliding properties in warmer snow (greater than 3° C/37° F).

If the plush of the skin is too short, you will not get as much initial traction, but you will enjoy better glide. If the plush is longer, over time the skin will not lay as flat against the backing anymore. This will hinder both the gliding and climbing performance. In spring conditions you might also experience more glopping up of snow under the skin (glide wax can help skinning performance in gloppy conditions).

Over time the plush will get somewhat contaminated, scratched, and worn down. Of course this depends on the type of snow and terrain you use and abuse your skins on, but after about half a million feet of climbing—the estimated life cycle for skins—the plush will simply not be the same. It may still look quite good, but the gliding and climbing performance will not be optimal.

You can prolong the life of the plush and improve performance on a day-to-day basis by actually combing the skins (tip to tail) and by regularly applying skin wax. You can apply wax as needed on a tour, to deal with gloppage (snow stuck to skins), or you can apply wax every time you go out to improve glide.

THE BACKING

The backing is what the plush adheres to on one side and the adhesive adheres to on the other.

Most backing is made of nylon. The quality of the weave and the actual thickness of the nylon determines to a great extent the overall weight, suppleness, and durability of the skins.

There seems to be a general difference between European manufacturers and their North American counterpart. Generally, the backing on European skins seems a little thinner, and so the skins are lighter and take up less space in your pack. This also means they can be more easily cut by a rock or a sharp piece of wood, and they can also be more difficult to deal with in windy conditions when it comes time to stow them away.

THE ATTACHMENT SYSTEM

For a long time skins were simply attached by strapping a leather strap around the ski. This caused a lot of problems in traverses where lateral stability is important. The Swiss Army solved the problem in classic army-style by drilling a few holes through the skis and bolting the skin to the base of the ski. More elaborate attachment systems came later, with tip and tail attachments and neatly integrated strap systems that went around the middle of the forebody and between the heel piece and the tail attachment.

Montana Sport of Switzerland invented the adhesive skin in 1968 and changed the industry forever. Today, skins come with a variety of attachment systems at the tail (fig. 1.14).

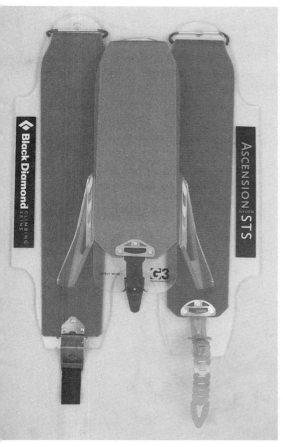

Fig. 1.14 Different tail attachment systems for climbing skins

Tip: In choosing an attachment system, bring your ski to the shop to make sure that both tip and tail attachments fit your ski. Twin tips and wide tip profiles can make it tricky for skins to stay attached.

Skin glue is like no other glue. It is designed to stick to a cold, smooth surface but not leave any residue. It should not permanently bond to itself. And, most of all, it should not lose adhesive power over time and after multiple uses. That's a tall order.

In the matter of skins sticking to themselves, a recent addition has been the "cheat sheet." It is actually for helping get your skins apart when they're new, but it can also prolong the life of the adhesive. If you use the cheat sheet, make sure to store skins in a cool, dark place. In warm conditions, when the adhesive softens, the cheat sheet can become imbedded in the adhesive, and you'll never get it off your skins without leaving parts of it behind.

SOME SKIN RECOMMENDATIONS

- Choose skins with a reliable adhesive. If the adhesive is not excellent, it will fail in cold and wet conditions and will most likely end your tour prematurely. In remote situations this can even become a safety issue.
- Make sure that the attachment system of the skins matches the tip and tail profile of your skis. Any qualified retailer should be able to help you out.
- Make sure that the skins are fat enough to provide optimal coverage, base edge to base edge, in the central 80 percent of your skis. See the sidebar, "How to Cut Skins." If you're nervous about getting it right, buy skins from a good shop and they'll cut them for you. You only get one chance to do it right!

HOW TO CUT SKINS

Most skins come with a tail clip-type attachment, so let's assume this is the type of skin you are cutting for your ski. Make sure that your working area and the base of the ski are clean.

Fig. 1.15

Fig. 1.16

1. Peel the wax paper off the tail area of the skin. Adhere the tail section of the skin to the tail section of the ski base, making sure that the tail clip is somewhere in the middle of its adjustment area (fig. 1.15).

2. Peel most of the remaining wax paper off the skin, but leave a short section of the paper attached to the skin that extends beyond the length of the ski tip (fig. 1.16).

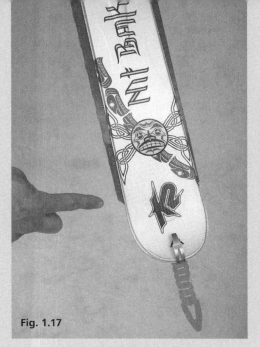

Fig. 1.17

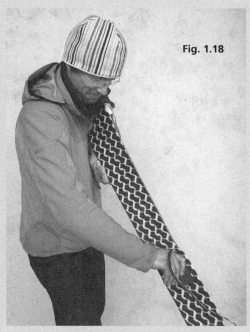

Fig. 1.18

3. Stick the rest of the skin to the ski from tip to tail. In doing so, make sure the full length of the skin is offset to one side by about 3–4 millimeters (fig. 1.17). Check to ensure that the skin is well adhered to the ski base.

4. Using the cutting tool (this comes with the skins when you buy them), cut from tip to tail on the thicker side of the skin (this is the side offset by 3–4 millimeters from step 3). Focus on making the cut in one smooth, constant motion; this will give you a clean, straight edge on the skin (fig. 1.18).

5. Pull the skin off the ski base, allowing only the tail attachment to stay hooked to the ski. Now stick the skin back on the ski, this time with it aligned so that the newly cut side (of the skin) allows some ski base to show. The amount of base showing should be equal to the width of the metal ski edge (fig. 1.19).

Fig. 1.19

Tip: Check that you have the alignment right: you want to see the metal edge plus one edge's worth of base material.

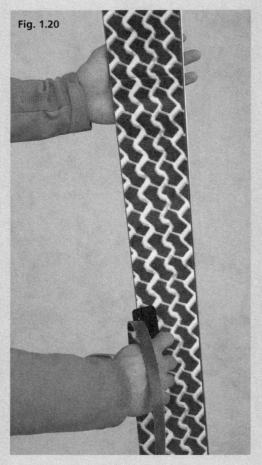

Fig. 1.20

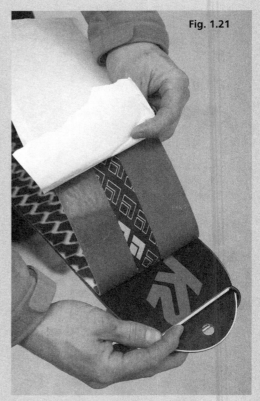

Fig. 1.21

8. Remove the remaining wax paper from the skin. Take the tip loop (included when you buy the skin) and place it over the ski tip. Take the skin and press it against the ski base and tip loop (fig. 1.21). This will leave you a reference mark in the adhesive for sizing the skin to the ski's length.

6. Using the cutting tool, cut the other side of the skin (the overhanging side after your alignment in step 5) from tip to tail (fig. 1.20).

7. Pull the skin off and reapply it to the ski. The skin should be centered on the ski, leaving only the edges exposed on both sides of the skin.

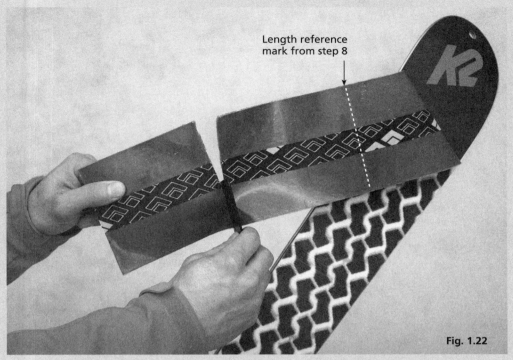

Fig. 1.22

9. Using your length reference mark from step 8, measure 15–20 centimeters longer on the skin and cut the excess skin material at that point (fig. 1.22).

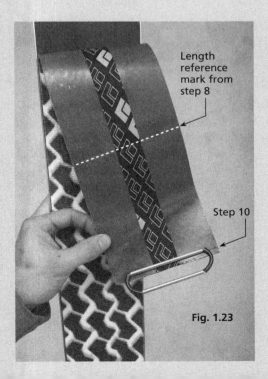

Length reference mark from step 8

Step 10

Fig. 1.23

10. Stick the tip loop to the skin at the very end of the skin. This gives you a width reference mark to which you will trim the skin in order to slide the tip loop down the skin (fig. 1.23).

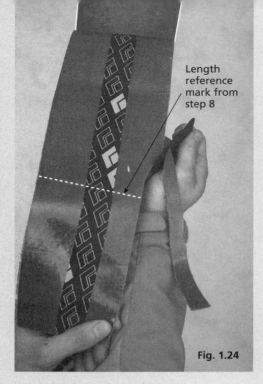

Length reference mark from step 8

Fig. 1.24

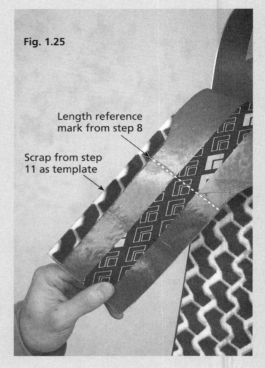

Fig. 1.25

Length reference mark from step 8

Scrap from step 11 as template

11. Using the cutting tool, trim one side of the skin 2 centimeters past your length reference point (from step 8). This cut should be straight (parallel with the skin edge) and should use your width reference mark from step 10. Finish the cut by curving smoothly to the outside skin edge (fig. 1.24).

12. Use the scrap piece from step 11 as a template to cut the opposite side of the skin. Stick the scrap piece to the skin, adhesive-to-adhesive and with the straight edges and corner lined up. Using the cutting tool, cut the mirror image in the skin (fig. 1.25).

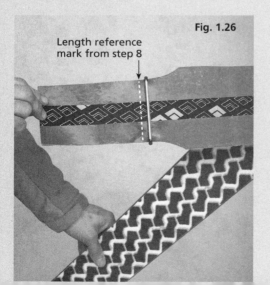

Fig. 1.26

Length reference mark from step 8

13. Slide the tip loop onto the skin, placing the loop beyond the length reference mark (from step 8) by several millimeters. Fold the skin onto itself around the tip loop (fig. 1.26).

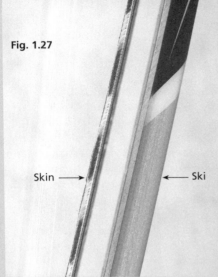

Fig. 1.27

Skin →   ← Ski

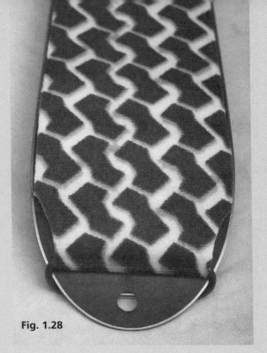

Fig. 1.28

14. Check the length of the skin relative to the ski. Remove the skin completely from the ski, hook the tip loop on first, then attach the tail clip without allowing the sticky skin surface to adhere to the ski. The skin is the correct length if it is stretched between the tip and tail with enough tension to keep the sticky surface off the ski base (fig. 1.27). To finish, run your hand over the skin from tip to tail, centering the skin on the ski and adhering it to the ski base.

When you have finished, the skin should cover the entire base of the ski, leaving only the metal edges exposed (fig. 1.28).

Repeat this whole process to cut the skin for your second ski.

POLES

Ski poles come in a variety of types. The set of downhill poles you use in the ski area will, for the most part, work fine for the backcountry.

If you plan on doing a lot of touring, it is worth investing in the telescopic or adjustable type. Adjustable poles allow you to dial in the length you prefer for the conditions. For example, your tour may culminate on a logging road requiring a long ski out. Longer poles will keep you more upright when skating out, which can significantly increase skating power and reduce lower-back strain.

Some poles convert into avalanche probes. This can come in handy in a rescue if you happen to break your probe, but should never replace a dedicated probe (see "Avalanche Probes" later in this chapter).

SIZING POLES

We tend to size poles for backcountry skiing the same as for downhill skiing. First, turn the pole upside down. Next, place your hand under the basket. Now align your upper arm with your torso and look for a 90-degree bend in your elbow. This is less of an issue with adjustable poles—you can change their length to fit your needs and most are one size fits all.

Tip: If you plan on using your downhill poles, consider purchasing a larger basket for the backcountry.

As for the material of the pole, get the one with the lightest swing weight you can afford. The number of times you swing your poles throughout the course of the day is a lot. The heavier your poles are, the more fatigued your arms will be.

POLE ATTACHMENTS

For sportier ski descents, consider an ice ax attachment, which puts an ice ax pick on the handle of your ski pole. We recommend the type that can easily be removed when the terrain is not so steep. This should help minimize the chance of impaling yourself when trying to enjoy powder.

BOOT CRAMPONS

Boot crampons are an important piece of gear for the ski mountaineer. They can provide added security when conditions are frozen or icy, and they greatly expand your ability to move through technical terrain.

Choosing boot crampons is like choosing any other piece of technical gear: your goal is to select the right tool for your intended application. You should consider weight, material, number and configuration of points, flexibility, and the attachment system. Of these, weight is often the most important in the ski arena, and it's related to many of the other factors.

Why not simply choose the lightest? Consider that crampons are an essential piece of safety gear. Climbing in steep, technical terrain using the wrong crampons is a recipe for an accident. Many ski mountaineers have a quiver of crampons similar to their quiver of skis. Objectives with technical summits involving rock may not be suitable for lightweight aluminum crampons. But on a ski tour with only short sections of steep snow you may wish to take advantage of the reduced weight that aluminum crampons provide.

The materials comparison below outlines the key features to consider when choosing crampons for ski mountaineering:

STEEL	
Pros	Best purchase in ice and rock
	Most durable
	Can be resharpened
Cons	Increased weight

ALUMINUM	
Pros	Lightweight
Cons	Doesn't penetrate ice well
	Can break or bend easily
	Wears down easily

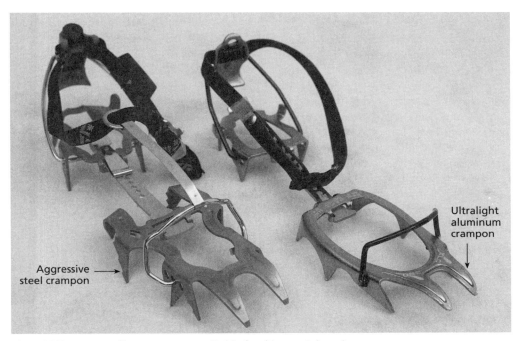

Fig. 1.29 Two types of boot crampons suitable for ski mountaineering

NUMBER AND CONFIGURATION OF POINTS

Classic 12-point. Crampons with 12 points have long been standard for technical climbing. The more points the better the purchase power. In fact, there are ice-climbing crampons with more than 12 points. The downsides of more points are increased weight and more difficult walking in mellow terrain.

10 points or less. Crampons with 10 points are popular for ski touring because they are lighter and are easier to walk in.

Configuration. The overall length of the points and their angle create different levels of performance. The longer the front points and secondary points, the more prone the crampon is to hanging up or tripping; if you don't plan on doing steep technical routes, look for a less aggressive crampon (with shorter and fewer points).

RIDGED OR HINGED

Ridged crampons are simply those that don't bend in the instep. These are more suited to steep ice then to general ski mountaineering and are not very common these days.

Most crampons are hinged. The toe- and the heelpieces are separate and joined by a bar or rail. Hinged crampons will fit a variety of boots and boot-sole stiffnesses.

ATTACHMENT SYSTEM

Having a crampon come off in walking terrain is a big inconvenience; having it come off while climbing is downright dangerous. The attachment system needs to provide a secure fit between the boot and the crampon. Some attachment systems work better than others depending on the model of boot, and how crampons attach also affects how easy they are to put on, which correlates to transition time (figs. 1.30 and 1.31).

Fig. 1.31 *A correctly adjusted boot crampon on an AT boot*

Tip: If you're using a classic tele boot, make sure the crampon toe bail fits over the lip of the toe and allows for adequate front-point purchase. Also make sure the crampons will work on a flexible sole.

Tip: To assure a good crampon fit, take your ski touring boots with you to the store.

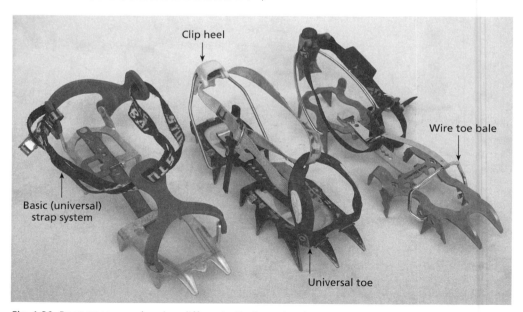

Clip heel

Wire toe bale

Basic (universal) strap system

Universal toe

Fig. 1.30 *Boot crampons showing different attachment systems*

Basic straps. This system uses front and rear parts to strap around the boot. It is the least expensive, least powerful connection and requires the most time to install. Many a climber has tripped on his own crampon straps, so pay attention to the length of the excess straps and keep them as short as possible. Put on correctly, straps work well with a large variety of boots.

Universal toe and clip heel. These crampons have a plastic toe bail that accepts the strap from the heel clip. These are the most popular for ski mountaineering. Make sure the heel lever clears the back of the boot and snaps up with a fair amount of tension.

Wire toe bails. This attachment is common on technical crampons. Wire toe bails are the easiest to put on and provide the most power. They require a solid toe lip (which all AT and tele boots have). As with the universal toe and clip heel, make sure the heel lever clears the back of the boot and snaps up with a fair amount of tension.

ACCESSORIES

Antiballing plates. These plates, made of rubber or plastic, snap on underneath crampons and help minimize snow buildup under crampons, a dangerous problem. The plates sometimes come with the crampons or otherwise must be added on. They are a worthwhile add-on purchase.

Crampon pouch. Whenever possible, it's best to keep all of your equipment in your pack. A good pouch keeps the sharp points of your crampons from coming in contact with your pack contents. Look for a simple pouch that is easy to open and close, allowing for quick and fluid transitions between skiing and cramponing.

ICE AXES

Ski mountaineering objectives warrant the use of an ice ax. An ice ax provides security on steep slopes, a means of climbing technical terrain, and a tool for self-arrest in the event of a slip. An ice ax can also be used to create ski platforms (discussed in chapter 5, Transitions) and anchors commonly used in ski mountaineering (see "Anchors on Snow" in chapter 6). Choosing an ice ax is similar to choosing crampons: try to balance function and weight (fig. 1.32).

LENGTH

For ski mountaineering, we recommend an ice ax length of between 50 and 65 centimeters, depending on your height. Longer axes are better suited for mellow terrain. A long ax (nearly touching the ground while standing on level ground) is not suited to steep terrain, which is where the ice ax is truly needed for ski objectives.

Furthermore, building ski platforms or ski anchors requires a fair amount of swing and chopping, something a long ax does not do well. Finally, longer axes extend above your pack, potentially snagging trees and other objects while skiing.

WEIGHT

Think lighter for ski mountaineering. That said, we don't recommend aluminum heads

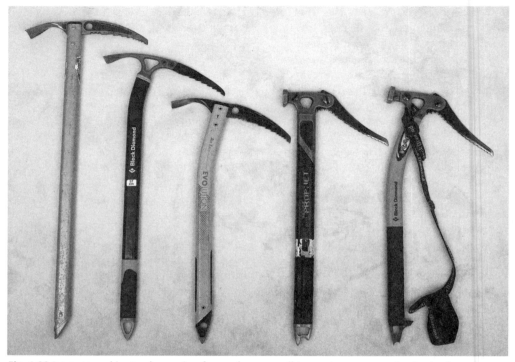

Fig. 1.32 Ice axes and ice tools ranging from a longer walking ax to an aggressive ice tool

for an ice ax; they are simply too light. If you need to swing aluminum into ice or hard snow, it bounces back. Remember, it's called an *ice* ax, not a snow walking staff.

SHAFT

A straight shaft is the most common because it plunges into the snow for added security while climbing steep snow. This contrasts with the fully curved shaft of an ice tool, designed for swinging overhead into the ice. Some ice axes have a straight shaft with a bit of a curve near the head, providing a little extra power and clearance when you swing the tool. This makes the ax more multifunctional: you can still plunge it, but it also swings better in steeper terrain and ice.

HARNESSES

A ski mountaineering harness differs from a climbing harness in several ways, and the harness you select should reflect those differences. The ideal ski harness is a minimal affair; consider the following in selecting your harness.

Weight and padding. Seek a light harness with minimal padding. Padding makes your harness more comfortable to hang in, but it adds bulk and can act like a sponge when it gets wet. The amount of time spent hanging in your harness will hopefully be minimal in ski mountaineering. You may wear a harness for glacier travel or for roped travel on rock or ice, but neither of these applications calls for hanging in your harness unless in the event of a fall—and the likelihood of a fall should be much smaller than in a vertical rock or ice climbing arena.

Easy on and off. A ski harness should be configured so you can take it on and off without having to take your skis (or crampons) off. There are several designs out there, but any harness with buckles in the right places will do the trick.

Gear loops. These are very handy for ski mountaineering, but seek gear loops that are light and pack down small—they don't need to be the rigid gear loops of a climbing harness.

Belay loop. Some lightweight harnesses have them, and some don't. Belay loops can help keep you moving quickly in transition-heavy and technical terrain.

Using the facilities. A harness with buckles on the bum straps will enable you to take care of business without taking off your harness. This is very handy for glacier travel, especially if you can't pee standing up!

CLOTHING

Proper clothing while ski touring and ski mountaineering can make an enormous difference in how much you enjoy yourself and even in how safe you are. Of course, we all want to look good, but your clothing has to be functional, and the selection of clothing available has never been better.

With the right clothing and movement rate, it's not that hard to stay comfortable. Most of the problems encountered by the backcountry skier originate with one of the following issues.

WATERPROOFNESS VS. BREATHABILITY

Let's get technical. In the late 1970s the Gore Company introduced a revolutionary principle: a PTFE (polytetrafluoroethylene) layer was manufactured such that pores were so small (9 million pores per square inch!) that only vapor molecules could pass through them—water molecules were too big. This resulted in a truly waterproof and breathable membrane.

Since then, the quest for the best waterproof and breathable materials has continued. Gore fabrics have been joined by competing moisture-management systems and the use of waterproof coatings on breathable materials. Each solution has its compromises and benefits.

Waterproofness. Waterproofness is measured in a "water column test," where a certain amount of pressure is applied to a fixed surface area of the membrane. For example, a Gore ProShell membrane is tested up to 40 pounds per square inch of water pressure (normal rain hardly ever exceeds a few pounds per square inch). This very high standard tries to take into account the pressure of backpack straps, kneeling on hard surfaces, and so on.

Making a waterproof-breathable garment using a membrane is effective, but quite expensive, and paying over $400 for a waterproof jacket has always been a tough sell. So manufacturers have discovered how to approximate membrane performance using waterproof coatings. (More on this below.)

Breathability. Breathability is based on the principle of equalization, meaning the relatively high humidity inside a jacket will get sucked through the membrane to the outside, where presumably humidity is less.

But during a storm, relative humidity (how much water vapor the air is holding at a given temperature vs. how much it *could* hold) is very often at or near saturation point, and the relative humidity inside the jacket also hovers around 100 percent. Breathability will still occur as long as the temperature outside the jacket is colder than inside, because cold air has a lower humidity saturation point than warm air.

Waterproofness and breathability both need to be taken into account when choosing an appropriate outer layer. All too often backcountry travelers complain that their outer layer is not working, when in reality the garments are not breathable enough or the wearer has not considered that his movement rate might have overwhelmed the garments' capabilities given the weather. Solid uphill movement on skis (or on

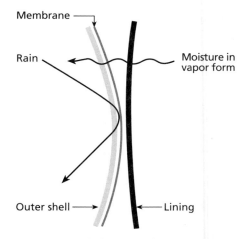

Fig. 1.33 Principle function of a PTFE membrane

foot) is a lot of work, and it's quite easy to overwhelm the vapor transport mechanism of just about any waterproof-breathable layer (fig. 1.33).

A properly manufactured garment with a membrane will outperform a coated one in terms of breathability and, most of all, longevity. In a coated fabric, the pores that ensure breathability are not as uniformly distributed as in a membrane fabric, making a coated garment less breathable. The actual waterproof layer in a coated garment is also exposed on the inside of the garment, which leads to the coating breaking down. Many of the newer coated garments perform amazingly given their cost, but their absolute performance is still not quite as good as garments with membranes.

Of course, all membranes are not the same. Some are geared toward breathability, which means that the garment will not be as waterproof. If your activity will be highly aerobic or if you sweat easily, this might be a good choice. Proper venting and carefully adjusting layers and your movement rate will also greatly enhance the breathability of a garment.

In addition to materials, design is important to consider. The world's best materials won't keep you dry if the hood design funnels water into the collar or the garment was not properly seam-taped.

INSULATION

No matter how waterproof or breathable your outer layer, if you stay out in wet conditions long enough you will get wet. It is therefore important that your under- and midlayers are made of fibers that retain their insulative qualities when wet. When choosing these layers, consider whether you anticipate getting cold because of the temperature alone or because of being cold and wet. Different fibers and materials work better than others for different applications.

Synthetic Fibers

Synthetic fibers such as polyester and all their derivatives are light, durable, and retain their insulative qualities quite well when wet. Primaloft, for example, mimics the insulative qualities of down—it's not quite as light, nor as compressible, but it does keep you warmer than down if it gets wet.

Synthetics also generally dry easily, an important consideration if you think you might have to dry a garment while outdoors. Your body heat may be the only drying force you have, and while drying

your underwear while wearing it in your sleeping bag is not fun, it may be the only option—in which case you'll appreciate a quick drying time.

Most new synthetic materials sport some kind of a bacteria inhibitor, which is supposed to reduce the unpleasant body odor that seems to become embedded, especially in long underwear. Even these, however, do not outperform wool in this respect.

SYNTHETIC FIBERS

Excellent vapor transport
Quick drying time
Retains insulating capacity when wet

NATURAL FIBERS

The ultimate renewable resource
Unsurpassed wearing comfort
Feature natural bacteria inhibitors (wool)
Modern manufacturing methods make wool fibers just about as easy to deal with as synthetic ones in terms of washing, drying time in the field, and durability

Natural Fibers

The most common natural fibers used in outdoor clothes are down and wool. One of the greatest insulators relative to its weight is down. But it loses just about all of its insulation properties when wet, so make sure that your down stays dry or wear it only in cold and dry conditions.

Down comes in different fill weights— 650 fill, 700 fill, or even 900 fill. This indicates how much loft (which is what keeps you warm) the down has relative to its weight. A 900-fill down jacket with the same loft as a 700-fill jacket weighs less. Higher-caliber down is also more compressible—and it costs more.

Wool is the other primary natural fiber, once supplanted by synthetics but now making a comeback. People used to worry about wool being itchy or smelling like a wet dog, but the use of merino wool has changed that. The merino wool fiber is finer and less barbed than traditional wool fibers, which makes for a softer and less itchy feel. The new wool fiber makes it more comfortable than synthetics, and textile engineers are finding that wool is hard to beat for overall performance.

Wool has excellent insulative qualities even when wet. The only drawback is its longer drying time and sometimes questionable durability. Blending wool and synthetics improves durability, for example, in socks.

THE RIGHT CLOTHES FOR THE JOB

- How durable do you need a garment to be? Will you be wearing it often, or is the intended use more of a specific application (e.g., emergency, ultra-lightweight)?
- Some clothing available is superlight, which can also mean it's fragile. Will this serve your needs?
- Are you trying to protect yourself primarily from wet conditions and are you willing to sacrifice a certain amount of breathability?
- Will your ski tour include high-intensity travel uphill? Does your garment need to ventilate well? Are you willing to sacrifice a certain amount of waterproofness?
- Will you be somewhere you can dry your wet clothes after your activity, or will you have to dry your clothes while in wet conditions? If the latter, consider a clothing system of multiple thin layers.
- You might be better served by erring on the more breathable side if you'll be in a high-humidity environment and your activity is high-intensity. Some of the new soft-shell fabrics are amazing in their comfort range.
- Can you bank on consistently cold weather? Then one warmer down layer would be a good choice. Or do you anticipate strong daily temperature swings? Then multiple thinner layers would serve well.
- Will being cold be due to actual cold temperatures (-26°C/-15°F)? Again, a warm down layer works well. Or will you be cold from losing body heat because of cool and wet weather (0°C/32°F, wet snow falling)? Then multiple thinner layers are a better choice.

BASE LAYERS

As if the whole concept of layering were not complicated enough, base layers come in several thicknesses. Let's try to simplify things.

If it's consistently cold and/or your activity level is moderate, you might choose a thicker, or so-called expedition-weight, base layer. Conversely, if the temperatures are relatively moderate and/or your activity level is high, choose a thinner layer.

If you'll be wearing the base layer for many days in a row and drying time is not an issue, you might try a merino wool product—you'll be impressed with its comfort and stink resistance. If your activity level is highly aerobic and quick drying time is crucial, synthetic base layers are still tough to beat.

Recommendation. Experiment. Everyone's metabolism is different and you'll have to find out for yourself what works for you. A good specialty retailer should be able to help you along.

MIDLAYERS

Midlayers are generally a bit heavier than base layers and provide insulation and a certain amount of weather protection. Midlayers can fulfill a couple of functions: they can fit neatly under your shell when it's nasty out or they can be the outermost layer in moderate conditions. Some midlayers are designed to work well either way, and some are designed to be just a midlayer.

Recommendation. Consider the end use. If you already have an outer layer, maybe take a midlayer along if you intend to wear it together with the outer shell. Ask yourself if the midlayer will be integrated into your layering system or if you'll be using it as a stand-alone piece. Some of the newer soft shells have good dual function capabilities.

OUTER LAYERS

The outer layer gets the most attention even though it spends a good amount of time in your backpack. Let's face it: when it's nasty out, a lot of people stay home. You might consider how much time your outer layer actually spends on your body vs. in your pack. Also consider whether your outer layer needs to be mostly waterproof or if breathability is a big issue. The array of offerings is staggering.

Design features are also important. For example, make sure that the hood adjusts the way you like it and that a helmet can fit under it.

Recommendation. Have a clear picture of your intended use. Ask what the claims of the various manufacturers are based on. The term *waterproof* is used quite liberally. Can a company back it up with technical data and guarantees? If you are leaning toward a more breathable garment, can a company back up its breathability claims?

GLOVES

Gloves are a big deal in ski touring. They need to keep you warm, they need to stay dry while you're grabbing stuff, they need to have sticky palms and allow for good dexterity, and of course they need to last forever. That's truly asking a lot, so we use one pair of gloves for uphill travel and a thicker pair for downhill travel.

For uphill, leather-palmed (or synthetic leather) gloves provide a good sticky feel when you're grabbing your poles (and they tend to last longer). The gloves should be just warm enough for uphill travel—any warmer and your hands will sweat. Drying out gloves (especially leather ones) can be a chore, so you want to avoid wet gloves the best you can. To do this, adjust your speed of ascent, wear a glove just barely warm enough for uphill travel, or just leave them in your pack if temperatures hover at or above freezing. (An old saying in the Pacific Northwest says that the driest glove is the one still in your pack.) Wrapping your ski poles with a bit of athletic or foam tape just below the grip will provide some extra warmth and grip.

For downhill, we prefer gloves with high gauntlets. They provide extra warmth and keep snow out. If you're buying Gore-Tex gloves, make sure they have taped seams. This process is labor intensive and raises the price.

Recommendation. If you want an all-in-one glove, consider a good-quality system glove (i.e., liner and shell that can be worn alone or together). These gloves cut down on bulk in your pack and they are easier to dry. Make sure you like the glove with the insert in the shell and that you can deal with wearing the shell alone. Surprisingly often, system gloves turn out very crammed with the insert in and loose and unrefined without the insert. Also make sure the insert alone can actually be used as a lighter, stand-alone glove.

SOCKS

Opinions differ here. Some people like liner socks coupled with a midweight sock, some like a heavyweight sock for more warmth.

Recommendation. Experiment to find what works for you. We've had excellent luck with wool-synthetic blends. They provide a lot of comfort, dry reasonably easily, and hold up very well.

HEADWEAR

The surface area of your head is surprisingly big compared to that of your whole body, which means your head plays a large role in temperature regulation. A hat can help keep you warm overall, or it can contribute to you overheating. Try to find a good middle ground.

One hat can probably not do it all. If you own a hooded insulated layer, you might be able to get away with a thinner hat. Also play with the position of the hat a bit. This may sound funny, but it actually makes a difference: maybe wearing no hat would be too cold, but having the hat on all the way would make you sweat. Just put it loosely on top of your head like an old-school Swiss farmer. You might be surprised.

Recommendation. Take a thin hat and a loose-fitting medium-size hat instead of one thick one. This is more versatile for the same amount of weight and bulk.

WARMTH IS PERSONAL

When you're wearing an insulated garment you're trying to trap heat produced by your body. Many people mistakenly think that when wearing insulation we're attempting to keep the cold out. While the layer of insulation (fleece, down, Primaloft) does serve to separate your warm body from the cold air, the most important job of insulation is to *retain heat*.

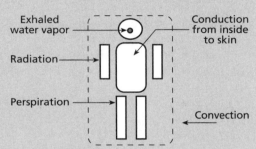

The shivers we experience at a rest stop are, very simply, due to a lack or loss of heat that occurs in five different ways (fig. 1.34). Knowing about them is a good start to arming yourself against the cold:

Fig. 1.34 Different kinds of heat loss

Conduction: The transfer of heat from a warm object to a cold one by direct physical contact. Conductivity varies—water conducts heat about 25 times faster than air.

Convection: The transfer of heat by the movement of a fluid (e.g., air). A good example is heat being carried away by the wind.

Evaporation: When enough heat is added to water on your skin, evaporation occurs. Water on the skin sucks heat by evaporation *and* conduction, so staying dry is doubly important for staying warm.

Respiration: Loss of heat by breathing is a combination of evaporation and convection. With every breath you lose considerable heat if the inhaled air is very cold.

Radiation: The transfer of energy primarily in the form of infrared radiation. Radiative heat loss is negligible relative to the other forms.

Of these five, conduction, convection, and evaporation are what well-designed clothing can do something meaningful about. Essentially, we need to protect ourselves from the heat-sucking tendencies of cold objects, from cold air movement, and from water (perspiration and otherwise).

Insulation creates a barrier against heat escaping by trapping air within its structure. Air is a very efficient insulator as long as it's not moving. When air moves it can carry heat with it (convection). To prevent moving air from disrupting the trapped air in the insulation and to keep the trapped air dry, a windproof and waterproof layer of fabric should cover it.

But here's where it gets really interesting. Two people wearing exactly the same apparel can, and often do, have radically different experiences in the cold. There are many reasons for this, but its implications are profound for the cold-weather enthusiast—there is no accurate way to rate a garment. To do this, a garment manufacturer would have to know how much heat is being kicked out by the wearer. So when deciding what to wear in the cold, each of us must rely on our understanding of our own bodies. Ask yourself:

- Am I a "warm" person or a "cold" person?
- How fit am I for ski touring?
- Am I well rested?
- Have I eaten enough?
- Am I well hydrated?
- Am I at high altitude?
- Am I healthy?

In short, understand your body before asking your apparel to keep you warm.

Kaj Bune is a lover of human-powered ski adventure and works as director of brand development for Outdoor Research in Seattle, Washington.

DAY PACKS

You should consider three categories when choosing a day pack: design and construction, fit and comfort, and features.

DESIGN AND CONSTRUCTION

Capacity. Day packs range from tiny water-holding packs to 40-liter ski mountaineering packs. For day trips you want a pack that is as small as possible given what you need to carry. Ideally, all of your gear will fit inside the pack—strapping things to the outside is a great way to lose them. Of course, if your pack has dedicated ice ax, crampon, or rope-carrying systems on the outside, this can be a great solution. Don't be afraid to bring all your stuff to the gear shop to test pack size, or to use gear in the shop.

Top-loading vs. panel. Top-loading packs consist of a main compartment with access through the top. These packs sometimes have zippers to access the compartment on the sides or the back of the pack,

TOP-LOADING	
Pros	Easy to pack
	Good carrying shape
	Top lid gives easy access to items like sunscreen, food, electronics, etc.
Cons	Must empty entire pack to get at things in the bottom
	No way to separate wet gear from dry

PANEL	
Pros	Packing in compartments means easier access, you don't have to empty entire pack to get your down jacket or water
	Good carrying shape
Cons	No top lid
	When very full, small pockets holding goggles, sunscreen, etc. can be difficult to access

and almost always have a top lid. Panel-designed packs are set up with multiple compartments, accessed with zippers into each compartment. These packs don't usually have a top lid.

Weight vs. durability. This is a balancing act. Lightweight packs tend to be less durable, and packs constructed with more durable materials are usually heavier. Skiing can be hard on packs, and the lightweight fabrics can be easily torn by a tree branch or cut by a sharp ski edge when you're carrying your skis.

It all comes down to application. If you're buying a pack for a ski mountaineering race, go light. If you need a pack for all-around ski touring, select one that strikes a balance between weight and durability. In doing so, be aware of your pack weight relative to the weights of your shovel, probe, and other equipment.

FIT AND COMFORT

Fitting a day pack is relatively simple. With the pack fully loaded, check that the pack fits your torso length: pull the shoulder straps tight and adjust any upper straps so the back of the pack rests against your back. At this level, the hip straps should rest right on your hips, taking some of the weight from your shoulders. Keep in mind what layers you'll be wearing when you're using the pack and how much weight you plan to carry.

Comfort is directly related to fit, but can also be affected by the amount of padding the pack has. Day packs are padded on the waist straps, shoulder straps, and back surface. The more weight you have in your pack, the more important padding becomes. Firmer padding can actually help you distribute weight more easily. But keep in mind that padding adds weight and can make the pack hotter if you are working hard.

FEATURES

It's all too easy to get a pack that is a picture of gadgetry, with straps and clips plastered all over it. To choose a pack that has the functionality that you need and no more, select between some combination of the following features.

Dedicated shovel and probe pockets. How fast can you get your shovel and probe out of your pack? Having it buried in a main compartment can make it difficult to access, with the added problem of getting your gear wet if you use your shovel and then repack it. Dedicated pockets for your shovel blade, shovel handle, and probe are an important feature to have in a ski pack.

One important note: these pockets should ideally be closed off completely with a zipper. Increasing evidence shows that a simple sheath or clip system for your shovel blade isn't enough to hold it if you're caught in an avalanche.

Carrying systems. Ski packs are configured to carry your skis either separately or apart (fig. 1.35). In choosing which system, consider ease of use and time it takes to put your skis on (and take them off) your pack.

Tip: Consider how well the carrying system will work if the pack is empty or stuffed overly full.

Fig. 1.35 One example of a ski carrying system

Carrying systems for ice axes range from simple ax loops to quick-clip buckles and sleeves for the ax shaft. Factors to consider include how many ax loops the pack has and ease of access to the ax: do you have to take the pack off to get to the ax?

Ropes can easily be carried inside or on the outside of a pack (see "Rope Handling" and "Roping Up" in chapter 6). Some packs have rope-carrying systems that attempt to refine this.

Hydration systems. Many packs include a pocket for a water bladder. These bladders are a great way to stay hydrated on a ski tour, but they do require a bit of management. Their hoses can freeze, and they can be prone to leaking or popping (especially if you sit on your pack!). Some packs include insulation for the hose or a pocket you can store it in on the shoulder strap. Keep in mind that a really full pack can exacerbate problems with the hydration system.

Integrated avalanche equipment. Packs are available with equipment designed to keep you alive if you're caught in an avalanche (see "Avalanche Survival Equipment" later this chapter).

OVERNIGHT PACKS

In selecting an overnight pack, you should consider the same basic categories of design and construction, fit and comfort, and features. The difference from selecting a day pack involves the importance of the various aspects of the pack.

DESIGN AND CONSTRUCTION
With an overnight pack it's especially important to get the smallest pack you can. Unless you're on a big-mountain expedition, it should be under 60 liters. Remember, you need to be able to ski with your pack on! This doesn't mean that you should get a pack so small it takes you three hours and 1000 calories to pack it. It simply means that you should take stock of what you'll be carrying, what you can do without...and then bring it all to the gear store. Stuff the pack full and try it on using the same fit guidelines as for day packs.

In balancing durability of construction and weight in an overnight pack, try to match the load you'll be carrying to the durability of the pack. For example, some ultralight packs may not be the best choice if you plan on carrying a bunch of heavy ski mountaineering gear, because they may have less structure and not carry well when loaded.

FIT AND COMFORT

In addition to avoiding the megapack, you want to get a pack that is comfortable for the loads and duration you plan on. Lots of padding makes for a heavy pack, so compare the weights of packs you try on and be aware of how much of your weight pie graph will be taken up by the pack. If you get the superlight pack, be prepared to suffer a bit... and if you get the superpadded pack, be aware that you've added weight to your load.

Features

Overnight packs also have options for dedicated shovel and probe pockets, carrying systems, hydration systems, and integrated avalanche equipment. Make sure to test the carrying systems when the pack is stuffed full, and be wary of overnight packs whose features add an unnecessary amount of weight.

ROPES

Backcountry skiers use rope in a variety of situations, depending on the terrain and skill level. Those uses include glacier travel, rappelling, roped climbing, short roping, and short pitching.

The primary factor dictating rope choice is your intended application, a theme we keep coming back to. Choosing a rope is a matter of understanding the different types and characteristics of ropes and then matching those with the application you have in mind. In ski touring and ski mountaineering, weight is especially important (if you can't ski because your pack is too heavy, aren't you missing the point?). Diameter and length dictate rope weight, so you will constantly be considering these when choosing a rope.

ROPE TYPES

Rope types are defined based on standards set forth by the International Mountaineering and Climbing Federation, or Union Internationale des Associations d'Alpinisme (UIAA). Ropes are rated as single, half, or twin and are defined by the tests they must pass and their intended uses.

Single Ropes

Single ropes are designed to be used individually and can be used in every application requiring a rope.

Pros. The single rope does it all. It can be used on glaciers and for crevasse rescue, and for technical climbing on rock and ice. The thicker diameters of these ropes make them abrasion-resistant and durable.

Cons. Weight. Single ropes are the heaviest way to carry a rope in the mountains. This is especially true if you need to carry two ropes for rappelling.

Half Ropes

Half ropes (also called double ropes) are intended to be used in pairs in lead climbing situations and are designed to be clipped separately to protection in order to reduce rope drag. It is becoming more common to see a half rope used as a single line in ski mountaineering contexts, especially on glaciers.

Pros. A set of half ropes weighs much less than two single ropes, so they can be a great option if you need to do a double-rope rappel. Two strands can be better protection against cutting or puncture by an ice ax or crampon. In moderate technical terrain where there is low fall and abrasion potential, a half rope can be used singly as a climbing rope.

Cons. Their smaller diameters make them much less abrasion-resistant when used singly. Using a half rope in this fashion has its best application in environments with low rockfall and abrasion, and with low fall potential. Note that this describes the environment on a glaciated ski tour.

Twin Ropes

Twin ropes are designed to be used together, as though they were one rope. Twin ropes provide the lightest scenario for a double-rope rappel. Some ropes that have come on the market as randonnée ropes are rated as twin ropes, although this seems to be more common in Europe than in North America.

Pros. Weight! Smaller diameters mean lighter ropes. They can be used singly for glacier travel and then paired for technical climbing objectives. Using twin ropes where there is high fall potential gives you the same performance (impact forces and number of falls) as a single rope, but longer rappel capability.

Cons. The smaller diameters of twin ropes can cause difficulties with friction hitches and devices in a crevasse-rescue scenario. The randonnée ropes often come precut to shorter lengths (30 meters), which can be problematic if you are carrying only one and need to rig a hauling system for crevasse rescue.

ROPE LENGTHS

Once you have determined the rope type and diameter you need, the next step is deciding length. Ropes come precut in lengths between 30 and 70 meters, with most of them being 60 meters. You want to bring the shortest rope possible for your intended use—remember, it's easy to just bring a long rope and cover all your bases, but for skiers weight is crucial. Ask yourself these questions:

1. What is the longest length you expect to need? Consider:
   - Climbing objectives with long pitches or lowers
   - Full-length rappels
   - Venturing into completely unknown terrain
   - Glacier travel with more than two people tied in to one rope
2. Are there any factors present that allow you to bring a shorter rope? Consider:
   - Known objectives with shorter than 50-meter rappels
   - Excellent prior knowledge of the terrain

- Glacier travel with small groups
- Strategy to carry multiple shorter ropes instead of one long one

Scenario 1: You want a rope for glacier travel in winter, and you expect to have a group of four people. You also want to use the rope for a 30-meter rappel into a rad couloir you've been scoping.

   Solution: The longest length you'll need will be 60 meters. You could bring one 60-meter rope, or you could bring two 30-meter ropes and split the weight between two skiers.

   Scenario 2: You want a rope for a five-day traverse with two other people on late-spring glaciers in the Cascades. Weight is paramount. You need the rope for glacier travel and don't expect to do any rappelling.

   Solution: You can bring a 50-meter rope, tie three people in 10 meters apart, and still have enough rope to create a hauling system if someone falls into a crevasse. Late-spring conditions mean some holes are beginning to open up, but bridges are still strong and you probably won't have the rope on unless the visibility is bad or you're traveling through broken sections.

   Scenario 3. You're planning a trip on early spring glaciers in the Swiss Alps with one other person. Neither of you has been there before, and you're planning to stay in huts for a week.

   Solution: This is a tough one. You might be able to get away with a 30-meter rope, but you're in unknown terrain. It might be best to give yourself more length and use a 40-meter rope.

Tip: Ropes can be cut! If a rope is not sold in the length you need, don't be afraid to cut it. You can usually have the shop do it with their rope/cord cutter.

Tip: Are you trying to find one rope to do it all? If so, understand that you'll find yourself using a rope that works in many situations, but that is ideally suited for only one or two. A rope for all applications may be master of none.

OTHER ROPE CONSIDERATIONS
Static Rappel Line

Another option for cost and weight savings is to carry a skinny static line. Static ropes have no stretch to them, so they are not safe to use in any scenario where dynamic or impact loading is possible, such as glacier travel and belayed climbing (see chapter 6, Ski Mountaineering Techniques). Static lines are appropriate for rappelling, and they come in any length and in 6- to 7-millimeter diameters. If you intend to use a rope solely to rappel, then a skinny static line can be a great option. Be aware that they provide less friction than a thicker rope.

   Pros. Lightweight and less expensive then a dynamic rope.

   Cons. Limited application. Static lines are for static loads only, and their skinny diameters mean they are less abrasion-resistant. Small-diameter ropes also tangle easily.

How is the Middle Marked?

Many manufacturers put a middle marker on their ropes. These are very helpful, but they wear out and become hard to find. Several ropes use the weave of the sheath to indicate the middle or the two halves of the rope. A rope with two weaves is extremely convenient, but more expensive. These patterns only work at the rope's original length, so they aren't a good option if you need to cut the rope.

Caution: If you try to mark the middle of your own ropes, make sure you use a marker approved for climbing ropes. Most permanent markers can greatly reduce rope strength.

Dry Treatment

Not all ropes are treated equally. For ski mountaineering, look for a rope with dry treatment. Dry treatment is essentially a waterproof coating on a rope. Dry-treated ropes still absorb some moisture, but the difference from a regular rope could save you several pounds of water weight for a 50-meter rope. Dry treatment usually adds to the cost of a rope, but it is crucial for use in any skiing application.

AVALANCHE SAFETY EQUIPMENT

If your tour takes you anywhere near avalanche terrain you need to have all the proper safety equipment to effect companion rescue. *Think of avalanche safety equipment as a system that consists of three essential parts: transceiver, probe, and shovel.* Without any one of these items your search time will increase considerably and survival chances will plummet.

AVALANCHE TRANSCEIVERS

Avalanche transceivers (also called beacons) have been around for almost forty years. The first was the Skadi that came out in 1968, and it's not all that different from the units we use today, though the technology has changed.

Transceivers are portable electronic devices that both transmit and receive a radio signal. When transmitting, beacons work by producing a current and pulsing it through a coil of wire wrapped around an antenna or antennae (the first transceivers used a 2.275 kHz frequency, modern ones use 457 kHz). This generates a magnetic field, which can be visualized using the concept of flux lines (fig. 1.36). The shape of a flux line is the path you take to the buried transceiver. The receiving unit uses its antenna(e) to pick up the magnetic field and then to generate a voltage, which is then delivered to the searcher's unit via lights, displays, and sounds.

Avalanche transceivers are designed to do one thing and one thing only: to decrease the burial time of the person caught and buried in the avalanche. Each person in a group must wear a transceiver so that he or she can either be found if buried, or can search in case another group member is buried. But nothing, including modern beacon

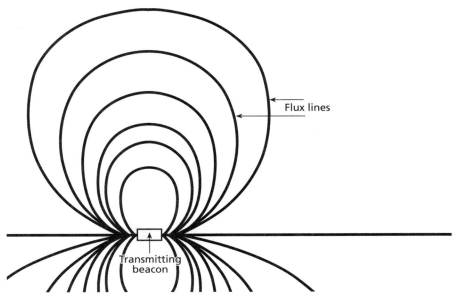

Flux lines

Transmitting
beacon

Fig. 1.36 Flux lines representing the shape of the signal of the transmitting beacon; all search beacons use this signal to find a buried beacon and will follow a path similar to one of those flux lines.

technology, can replace avalanche avoidance when it comes to keeping you alive in avalanche terrain.

Modern transceivers (fig. 1.37) all use the 457 kHz frequency and so are all compatible. The mid-1990s saw the rise of digital beacons, which differ from their analog counterparts by placing a microprocessor between the antenna(e) and the user interface. The microprocessor allows the beacon to interpret the data received, giving the searcher more accurate location and distance readings. The goal of digital beacons is to reduce the search time for single and multiple burials. Ortovox, Barryvox, Pieps, and Arva have joined the original Tracker

DTS in the race to solve the complex multiple-burial problem.

Multiple burials. Searching for more than one partner is every backcountry user's worst nightmare. When multiple people are caught and buried in an avalanche, all beacons buried are transmitting a signal. Multiple signals cause a very confusing array of flux lines, and determining the exact location of an individual takes extensive training in order to have any chance of a live recovery. The complexities involved in searching for multiple beacons grow exponentially from that of a single beacon search and therefore so do the search times and ultimately the burial times.

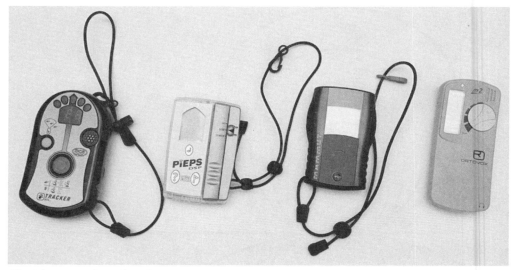

Fig. 1.37 A sampling of modern avalanche transceivers

In the early days of analog beacons, all beacons essentially worked the same; in the age of digital beacons, this is changing. The beacons have reduced the complexity of the search while at the same time increasing the complexity of the transceiver unit. Some of the newer beacons allow the searcher to mask buried beacons, essentially creating a series of single searches. Some transmit the victims' heart and respiratory rates to aid the searcher in deciding what person to search for first. Others use a screen to show the position of buried people relative to the searcher.

Regardless of which unit you choose, repeated practice in a variety of different scenarios is your only real chance of uncovering your partners alive. Even with the beacon in the hands of an experienced user, when searching for a single buried beacon the limiting factor is not the technology, but the speed of the searcher traveling over the avalanche debris and the time it takes to dig the victim out.

How to Wear a Transceiver

Being caught in an avalanche is an extremely violent event in which equipment and clothing can be ripped off. In order for your friends to locate you, your beacon must be attached to you when the snow comes to a stop. Properly wearing your beacon is the best way to assure that it stays on.

We recommend using the harness that comes with the transceiver and wearing it according to the manufacturer's specifications, which usually places the transceiver somewhere over your abdomen. Most importantly, the transceiver/harness must be worn under a layer of clothing. This helps keep the transceiver on you if you're caught and helps keep the batteries warm.

We've found that starting the day off by wearing the transceiver against your base layer and under all other layers works best. Then, as the tour progresses and you warm up, shedding layers, you won't take off the beacon and mistakenly forget to put it back on correctly.

Tip: For women, wear a tank bra and put the beacon over that and under your base layer.

Another option that works well, especially in the spring when you're not wearing a lot of layers, is to place the transceiver in one of the front pockets of your pants. The pocket should be zippered and located in the front near your groin. Avoid pockets on your hip and butt, where there is higher potential for trauma to the beacon. *The pocket you choose should be one you can remember to keep closed during the tour and should be dedicated to holding only the beacon.*

Transceiver Batteries

Transceivers are battery-powered devices. At present, all transceivers recommend using standard alkaline batteries. The European beacon manufacturing standard (there is no equivalent standard in the United States) says that a new set of batteries placed in a transceiver needs to be able to transmit at least two hundred hours and then provide enough power to perform a search for one hour. Rechargeable batteries tend to run on

a lower voltage and may not provide the adequate range for a search. Lithium batteries, although far better in the cold, were not factored in to manufacturers' parameters for measuring battery strength, so a transceiver using lithium batteries can't give you an accurate reading of remaining battery power.

Caution: The new "extra power" batteries designed for digital cameras have a higher output voltage, causing most digital beacons to function incorrectly in search mode.

Tip: Remove and recycle batteries after each season so they don't leak in your beacon during storage, and then start with a fresh set for the new season.

Transceiver Check

There are two main types of checks to perform: the function check and the range check. How do you know if your transceiver is working properly? In order to rely upon the rescue potential an avalanche transceiver provides, you must check the function of your beacon *every* time you ski in avalanche terrain.

Three-Part Function Check

The three-part function check should be performed at the beginning of every day at the trailhead parking lot or the hut you're staying in. If you discover someone's transceiver is not working correctly here, it's easier to replace the batteries or beacon before you leave than when you are standing on the side of a run, faced with deciding to ski or not ski without a fully functioning transceiver.

Have everyone gather around or near a leader. This can be best done in a circle with a large group or in a line with a small group.

1. Battery check: the leader asks if everyone has the appropriate battery percentage to safely complete the tour. Consult the beacon manufacturer's brochure for guidelines on battery percentage. Always carry a spare set of batteries.

2. Search check:
   - The leader asks everyone to turn their transceivers to search.
   - The leader has her beacon completely off.
   - Once all is completely silent, the leader turns her beacon on and to transmit (send).
   - The leader confirms that each person's beacon is correctly searching and finding a signal by holding her beacon next to each person's beacon and reading the number or signal on the searching beacon (fig. 1.38).

3. Transmit check:
   - The leader asks everyone to turn their beacons to transmit (send) and to stow them for the rest of the tour. This could take a moment. Make sure each person has his beacon properly stowed before this begins—you don't tour with the beacon in your hand, so you don't want to check its function while holding the beacon.

Fig. 1.38 Good technique for a beacon check: bring the searching beacon close to transmitting beacon and check the distance reading on the searching beacon.

   - The leader goes to each member of the group to confirm that everyone is correctly transmitting.
   - If the leader is using a digital beacon, slow down (three to five seconds per person) when approaching each person so the digital processor has time to pick up the signal. It's possible, when going too fast, for the searching beacon to still be locked onto the prior person.
   - The transmit check can also be done with the leader skinning up the trail 100 meters or so. Have the remaining group members ski by 10 meters apart directly in front of the leader.

After the three checks, the leader must make sure to stow her beacon correctly and to check that it is in send mode. The leader might communicate this action to the group: "I'm switching to send and stowing my beacon in my harness." Group members should not take their beacons out to check the leader; this defeats the purpose of the check, and the sending capabilities of the leader's beacon were tested in step 2.

Tip: "End in send." If you are the group leader, check everyone in search mode first, then in transmit (send) mode. That way, only one person (the leader) needs to do a visual check to make sure her beacon is in send mode.

Range Check

The range check ensures that your transceiver has a search and transmit range equivalent to the manufacturer's specs. Often this check is done at the trailhead with new ski partners, on the first day of a tour, or after your transceiver has suffered a blow (like a drop to the sidewalk). It's a great way to make sure your transceiver's fragile antenna has not been compromised. You can integrate this range check into the function check.

To start, someone will need to take the lead and have everyone get in a line.

- The leader turns her beacon completely off.
- The people in the line turn their beacons to search mode.
- The leader walks away approximately 100 meters.

- The leader turns her beacon to transmit.
- The leader begins to slowly walk toward the lineup.
- As the leader approaches, each member of the line notes the distance when he first receives a useable signal—this is the working range of the unit.

Compare your findings with the manufacturer's specs. If you find a large discrepancy (smaller than specified), change the batteries and repeat the test. If you still come up short, consider using another beacon and contact the manufacturer to have it professionally checked out.

It's also a good idea to do a range check for the transmit (send) range of your beacon. The steps are the same as above, but the functions are reversed.

AVALANCHE PROBES

Avalanche probes have, for many years, been the forgotten stepchild of the avalanche safety kit. Backcountry enthusiasts know they must carry a beacon if they want to be found and a shovel if they want to dig someone out. A dedicated avalanche probe is just as important. In a companion rescue, the three pieces of safety equipment (beacon, shovel, *and* probe) function together; without any one of these, recovery time goes up dramatically.

Dedicated Probe vs. Ski Poles

Why not simply carry ski poles that turn into a probe? The answer: time. It can take upward of a few minutes to turn ski poles into a probe, whereas a modern dedicated probe requires around ten seconds to construct. The mean rescue time for U.S. avalanches between 2000 and 2006 was eighteen minutes. If it takes three minutes to put your probe together, you've wasted 16 percent of your total rescue time fiddling with your probe.

Another reason is the potential for losing one of your ski poles. When caught in an avalanche, and unable to ski out of it, letting go of equipment is standard procedure. It's conceivable that both you and your partner could get caught in the slide and that you are not buried. Now you are your partner's only chance of survival, but you no longer have your probe poles.

That said, it's a good idea to carry both a dedicated probe and probe poles. You have to carry poles anyway, and probe poles provide backup in case of a broken probe during a rescue.

Probe Material

Probes come in three types of materials: steel, aluminum, and carbon. When you're frantically probing in avalanche debris the best probe is a steel probe. This is what most search and rescue probes are made of. Steel probes are extremely durable and penetrate the snow very well. The problem is weight. These probes can weigh upward of several pounds—not very practical for backcountry travel.

Aluminum probes have been the standard for the backcountry traveler. Both weight and cost are reasonable. An average 2.4-meter probe made of aluminum weighs in around 250 grams (8.8 ounces). Carbon,

on the other hand, weighs a little less, but will cost you more money.

A note on weight: Is light always right? *Not always.* Consider what you'll be using a probe for: saving your partner's life. This is a rescue tool, and if you ever need it you'll want the longest, strongest probe made. When standing in the ski shop, explore all the options. The weight difference between the lightest and heaviest backcountry probe is 170 grams (6 ounces). It's not uncommon for a backcountry ski pack to weigh in at 1800 grams (4 pounds). More modern, lightweight packs can weigh around 1100 grams (2.5 pounds). Before shaving grams from lifesaving equipment, consider saving the weight elsewhere; a lighter pack, lighter food, or less stuff overall are all better options than a broken probe.

Probe Length

The minimum length of an effective probe is 2 meters (6 feet). This provides enough length to probe to below the typical burial depth (fig. 1.39). That said, we recommend a longer probe of between 2.4 and 3 meters. The reason is twofold:

- Increased durability. As probe length increases, so does the gauge (thickness) of the probe. If you're frantically probing for your partner, this added durability helps reduce breakage.
- More efficient probing. Maybe you don't probe down the full length of your probe. But if you only have a 1.8-meter probe, you just might. A longer probe allows more space between your hands

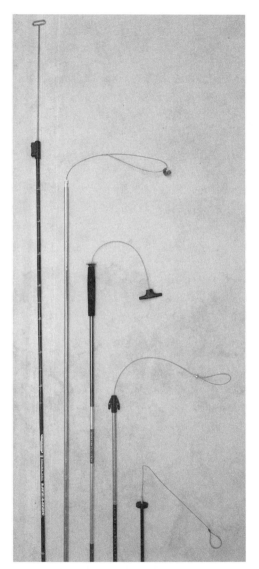

Fig. 1.39 Probes are available with a variety of locking mechanisms and in several lengths.

while gripping the probe. A wider space minimizes the chance of breaking the probe and it's easier on your back.

Other Probe Features

Markings. Some probes come with incremental markings on them (in centimeters, because the snow science standard is metric). This adds a few dollars in cost, but it's worth it. These markings are used for two purposes: to replace a standard ruler when creating a snow profile (see "Observing the Snowpack" in chapter 2) and to measure the depth of a buried skier, which is very important (see "Avalanche Companion Rescue" in chapter 10).

Locking mechanisms. One key difference you'll notice between the different probe brands and models are the locking mechanisms. All probes come in sections joined by some sort of cord or metal cable. When the probe gets tossed out to extend, the slack in the cord is taken up by the locking mechanism to produce a rigid probe.

In the store, try out different styles and see which one you prefer, although the main criterion is the time a probe takes to construct. Can the mechanism ice up or get stuck? You may also want to try the probes out while wearing gloves.

A probe with an adjustable locking mechanism can take up the slack in the cable as it stretches with use. Slack can develop over time if the probe is used frequently for snow profiles or to probe around on glaciers looking for a crevasse-free campsite (another great use for your probe).

AVALANCHE SHOVELS

Once you locate your partner with a beacon and pinpoint him with your probe, you still need to dig him out. The only effective way to uncover your partner is with a portable avalanche shovel (fig. 1.40). Studies show that the shoveling phase takes the majority of the time in a recovery (see "Shoveling Technique" in chapter 10).

The moment you need to use your portable shovel in a rescue situation you'll immediately yearn for a full-sized steel shovel not unlike the garden shovel in your garage. Keep this in mind when you waiver between models in the store, and consider the following.

Metal vs. plastic. *Shoveling* avalanche debris is a bit of a misnomer. When moving snow comes to a stop it sets up and can become rock hard. The correct technique for uncovering your partner is more of a *chop and then remove* sequence than it is shoveling. The best material for this job of chopping is metal. Metal blades are more durable and hold up much better than plastic ones under repeated chopping.

The characteristics of aluminum also allow for less deflection than a plastic blade. Deflection is when the chopping force of the blade bounces off a material because the blade bends. Less deflection allows for

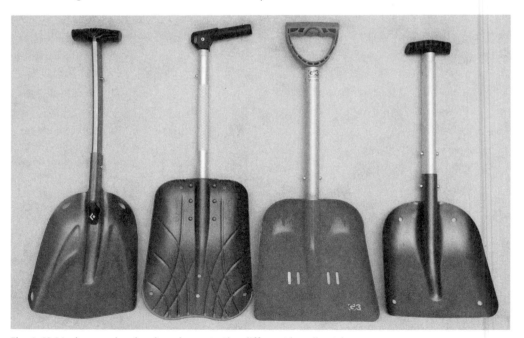

Fig. 1.40 Modern avalanche shovels – note the different handle styles.

better chopping, which is important for avalanche debris.

Handle. Does the handle telescope? This feature allows for better ergonomics while shoveling and also enables easy stowing inside your pack (remember that stowing everything inside your pack reduces lost items if you're caught in an avalanche and also minimizes the chance of snagging a tree limb).

Blade size. Not too big, not too small. Think efficiency. If the blade is too large, each time you throw snow out of the hole it will be too much weight, reducing the amount of repetitions you can do. This ultimately affects the overall amount of snow you can move in a given time. Too small, on the other hand, and you can't move snow quickly enough.

Blade shape. The shape of the blade can affect how the shovel works, though some of this is a matter of preference. Some people prefer a slight point in the shovel, others a flat end. If you plan on digging a lot of snow profiles or performing bonding tests (see "Observing the Snowpack" in chapter 2), a smooth (ribless) blade with a flat back works best.

Durability. Can you stand on the shovel? Any shovel worth its weight in the backcountry should be able to pass this test. Oval- or square-handle shafts are a bit more durable than round shafts. An oval shaft also helps align the pins into their holes when the handle gets extended—this saves time.

Weight. Once again, when you need a shovel, you really *need* a shovel. This type of critical safety equipment is not the place

to save weight. Look elsewhere in your backcountry kit if you want to shed grams.

Tip: When deciding on a shovel, bring your ski touring pack to the store. Try placing the blade into the shovel pocket of your pack—does it fit? Can the handle be stowed internally in the pack?

AVALANCHE SURVIVAL EQUIPMENT

The beacon-probe-shovel trinity is the cornerstone of companion rescue equipment, and research and development continually seek to improve each item's function and techniques for using them. In addition to these basics, new technologies are being developed to help people survive more avalanches: the Avalung, avalanche airbag systems, and the Recco system.

Avalung and Avalung Packs

In companion rescue, it takes roughly 20 minutes to find an avalanche victim with a beacon and dig her out. Survival rates for those victims not killed by trauma drop off after 15 minutes, with nearly all deaths from asphyxiation—carbon dioxide poisoning—coming between 15 and 35 minutes.

The basic goal of the Avalung is to extend the time a victim can be buried before asphyxiation occurs. It works by assisting your breathing. When you inhale, it functions as an artificial air pocket, with a breathing apparatus that pulls in air from the surrounding snowpack, which is porous. When you exhale, valves in the

Avalung redirect your breath—containing carbon dioxide—to a different part of the snowpack behind you.

There have been less than ten documented cases involving an Avalung, so data regarding its effectiveness are minimal. The downsides of the Avalung are that you must be able to get and hold the mouthpiece with your mouth during or after an avalanche, and the Avalung deals only with asphyxiation and does nothing for trauma. However, the fact remains that use of the Avalung has saved lives by extending survival times of buried people.

The Avalung has been integrated into some packs (fig. 1.41), which makes it simple to incorporate into your ski kit without adding another piece of stand-alone equipment. In the unpredictable arena of avalanches, it makes sense to stack the odds in your favor as much as possible.

ABS Avalanche Airbag System

The ABS Avalanche Airbag System works to prevent death in an avalanche from both trauma and asphyxiation. Statistically, if you are caught in an avalanche but not buried, you have a 95 percent chance of

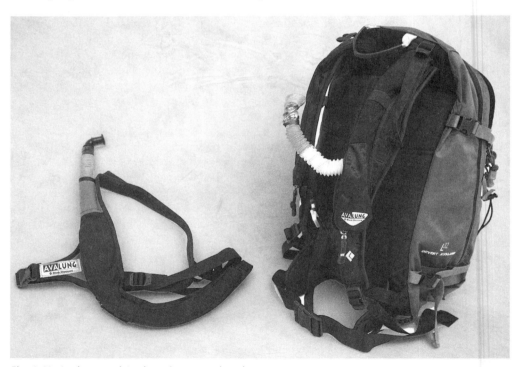

Fig. 1.41 Avalung and Avalung-integrated pack

survival (and a 5 percent chance of death by trauma).

The basic goal of an avalanche airbag is to keep the victim at the surface of the avalanche. Research has shown that the upper portions of an avalanche flow pattern are made up of larger granular particles than the deeper sections. The idea is that by inflating an airbag a person caught in an avalanche becomes a large enough particle size to stay on the surface (see "Field Experiments on the Effectiveness of Some New Avalanche Equipment" by Martin Kern and colleagues, referenced in the appendix). This also means the victim remains visible, so no beacon search is required, nor any probing or digging. Finally, in floating to the surface early in an avalanche, the skier is much less likely to go for the full ride. In the early stages of flow the surface snow moves slower than the deeper debris, so the skier's chances of being left behind on the bed surface increases.

The effectiveness of avalanche airbags is impressive: in the study by Kern and colleagues of eighty-five accidents, airbags reduced mortality by 92 percent. Research and testing related to airbags are ongoing at the Swiss Federal Institute for Snow and Avalanche Research in Davos, Switzerland.

The airbag systems available use canisters of pressurized gas to inflate the airbag. The system is integrated into a backpack (fig. 1.42) and is activated by pulling a tab when the skier is caught in an avalanche. There have been some complications with transporting the canisters—they only became legal in the United States in 2006.

Fig. 1.42 ABS pack showing the deployment handle

Packs with airbag systems also weigh a bit more than ordinary packs (2–3 pounds for a 35-liter day pack). Another downside is the cost, both to purchase the pack and to replenish the canisters. But evidence suggests the extra weight and cost are well worth it, as airbag systems seem to promise the greatest increase in survival rates for skiers caught in avalanches.

Recco System
Developed in Europe, the Recco system uses harmonic radar to locate skiers buried

in an avalanche. The system involves two components: a detector to be used by organized rescue groups and reflectors placed in skiers' clothing, boots, and helmets. The Recco system is not designed for companion rescue, but is worth mentioning here because of the increasing presence of the reflectors in ski equipment and the increasing use of the system by ski areas and mechanized ski operations (heli and cat skiing). The system is designed to fit in with all other search methods and is especially effective for use with helicopters in a search.

THE THREESOME PACKING HELPER

How much gear should you carry into the backcountry? Attitudes about this vary widely, but we'll go out on a limb and make a general statement: people tend to take too much gear with them.

We've worked for several years now on optimizing the load for ski touring and ski mountaineering. We started out like so many others—with too much. After all, you love every piece of newly acquired gear. As we grew more experienced, we tried to take as little as possible. This allows you to move faster, you have less gear to worry about, and transitions become more efficient (e.g., from skinning to skiing), but your latitude for error can become very small. After a few very chilly nights, some very hungry days, and some less than safe completions of routes, we've come to think that the truth lies somewhere in the middle.

It's difficult to say where the happy middle ground is, since so much depends on the skill and comfort level of the individual. We do believe firmly that certain items are essential when it comes to ski touring or ski mountaineering (or any form of mountain travel).

We'll state the obvious: don't skimp on items that might be vital to your safety or to completing the route. Let us explain:

The weight difference between an aluminum ice ax and a lightweight ax that still features a steel adze is relatively small. The difference in penetration power between these types of axes is tremendous. Are you sure you're not going to encounter any blue ice on that wind-scoured summit ridge? Would it be nice or necessary to have steel crampons instead of aluminum crampons? If you want to commit to superlight gear, you must be willing to deal with reduced performance. Be sure that anticipated conditions don't demand more aggressive tools. There is a lot of good gear that may not be the lightest available, but that still falls into the light category. This gear often performs much better, with only a relatively minor weight penalty.

Do you really need all that food you're bringing? Does everybody in the group really need 16 ounces of sunscreen? Work up to a lightweight cook set, light clothing, a lighter pack. Some of the new cameras are ridiculously small. Calculate your food, your fuel, bring a lighter sleeping bag, combine your clothing layers, but do not leave your first-aid kit at home.

Tip: Be minimalist, be smart, be safe.

THE THREESOME METHOD

The intent of packing in threesomes is to make you a more efficient and thorough packer, the idea being that one item of the trio will remind you of the other two. This will in turn help you be more prepared and make you a safer backcountry skier. We have tried to come up with threesomes that fit well together.

Not all of the items in the backcountry skiing and ski touring list are always required (e.g., ski crampons, goggles, sun hat, extra layer). What you take will depend on your ability to judge conditions for any particular tour. If in doubt, take it—the cumulative weight of a couple pounds should not spoil your tour on a day trip.

Daylong Backcountry Skiing and Ski Touring
- Skis, boots, poles
- Maps, compass, altimeter
- Transceiver, probe, shovel
- Skins, ski crampons, repair kit
- Food, drink, extra layer
- Bivy bag, first-aid kit, cell phone
- Base layer, midlayer, outer layer
- Hat, gloves, goggles
- Sunglasses, sunscreen, sun hat

Ski Mountaineering
- Threesomes from daylong touring list
- Harness, ice ax, crampons
- Rope, ice screws, rescue gear kit

Overnight Ski Tours
- Threesomes from daylong touring and ski mountaineering lists
- Sleeping bag, sleeping pad, shelter
- Stove, pot, fuel

CHAPTER 2

Ski touring below the Finsteraarhorn, Bernese Oberland, Switzerland

Decision-Making in Avalanche Terrain

Decisions involving potential avalanche danger can be some of the hardest to make. Often, the choices we are faced with are much more complex than a "go–no go" choice. Decision-making in avalanche terrain is an ongoing and complicated thought process that starts the moment the trip is conceived in the comforts of your home and doesn't finish until you're back at the car.

Think back to your first driver's test to earn your license. You memorized a set of rules that allowed you to pass a certain level of proficiency to get you on the road. At the time, you probably felt that passing your driving test was all you needed to know to drive safely. But looking back now, you may think it amazing that you survived your early driving years. The more driving experience you gained, the more you realized how difficult and dangerous driving can be. You didn't know it at the time, but you needed a benchmark (your driving test) to enable you to gain experience going forward without an extreme increase in your risk on the road. Without the driving test and a little prior knowledge, the roads would have been far more dangerous than they were.

Like driving, ski touring involves an experienced-based decision-making process. Being safe in the backcountry requires both a basic level of training (avalanche courses and books like this one) and a conservative margin of error as you gain experience.

"Good decisions come from experience and experience comes from bad decisions." How do you build experience without getting into too much trouble? An inexperienced user must be able to conservatively venture into avalanche terrain in order to gain real-world experience, which is easier said than done. Decisions in avalanche terrain are complicated and based on continuous analysis of information about the nature of avalanches, the snowpack and weather, the terrain, and much more.

In backcountry skiing, this analysis must often happen within a short time frame, with sometimes severe consequences if the wrong decisions are made. This is the crux of backcountry travel.

No single course or book, this one included, can completely prepare you for the complex decision-making process you'll be faced with in avalanche terrain. What we can do is provide you with a structure to help organize your thoughts that, when coupled with experience, can lead you down the path to better decision-making. The goals of this chapter are to help you:

- Learn a basic mental framework for approaching decision-making in the backcountry that allows for its complex nature.
- Understand avalanches and avalanche terrain.
- Learn the observations about snowpack, weather, and avalanches that are crucial to the decision-making process.
- Understand the role that human behavior patterns play in decision-making.
- Understand the nature and importance of tour planning for decision-making.
- Apply each aspect of decision-making in the field.

A note on sources. There are entire books written about avalanches and avalanche safety in the lexicon of skiing and mountaineering literature. For in-depth treatment of the subject, check out the references in the appendix. Our intention in this book is to focus on the information most useful to skiers in the backcountry and to present an outline for decision-making in avalanche terrain. In creating this chapter, we drew upon a variety of resources, including fellow guides and professionals, and relied heavily on the work done by the American Institute for Avalanche Research and Education (AIARE).

AIARE is a not-for-profit organization that brings together avalanche instructors from around the United States to share ideas and concepts in avalanche education. Through this collaboration, AIARE is able to provide instructors with the tools and curriculum to educate students about the knowledge and decision-making skills necessary to travel in avalanche terrain. We have chosen to model our discussion on the AIARE curriculum because of the high-quality avalanche professionals and instructors that helped create it. This chapter does not, however, cover everything you will get in a Level 1 course. Therefore, we highly recommend participating in one of these hands-on courses every few years (see the appendix for AIARE contact information).

THE ANATOMY OF A DECISION: THE DECISION-MAKING FRAMEWORK

All travelers in the backcountry use some way of processing information to help them make a decision. These decisions can be everything from gear choice to track angle to terrain selection. But how are these decisions made? What is the anatomy of the decision-making process? Are you including every important factor involved, or do you have a pattern that may get you into trouble? How do you organize and weigh the information you need to make a decision? The more deliberate and vigilant you are about the structure of your decision-making, the more you can grow and develop your decision-making skills.

A good way to approach backcountry decision-making is to view it as an ongoing process of asking the right questions. It would be impossible to list all of the potential questions you might ask during every possible tour in every possible region of the world. Every route is different, and the questions the skier needs to ask will change accordingly. To deal with this, we will describe a framework to help you organize (and understand) your thoughts, observations, and questions and that emphasizes their interconnectedness. It's called the Decision-making Framework (DMF).

As you look at the DMF in figure 2.1, notice that terrain selection plays a central role in the framework as a synthesis of all other considerations. One goal of the DMF structure is to emphasize and remind the backcountry user that all decision-making leads to choosing which terrain to move through. A second goal of the DMF is to illustrate that executing good terrain decisions in the backcountry means considering the interplay of the other components: trip planning and preparation, observations, and human factors. Starting from the bottom of the flow chart in figure 2.1, the DMF leads you through the following:

Trip planning and preparation. This is a huge part of safe decision-making in the backcountry, and we discuss the "how" of tour planning in detail later this chapter. Why is planning and preparation so important?

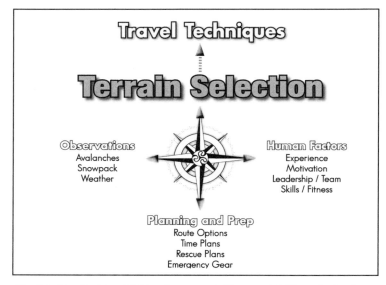

Fig. 2.1 The Decision-Making Framework (Source: AIARE curriculum)

Thorough planning and preparation sets us up for good decision-making in the field. Planning appropriate objectives and realistic alternative route options before the trip begins are key elements of this. Much of the macro-, meso-, and even micro-scale terrain selection that we do can be done in the trip-planning phase (see "Terrain Selection: Understanding and Identifying Avalanche Terrain" later this chapter).

Proper trip planning ensures that we know how long our trip will take and facilitates navigation in poor visibility. Having an emergency plan and carrying rescue gear ensures that our group is prepared to manage a situation if things go wrong and an accident occurs. Trip planning can help prevent accidents from occurring in the first place, and the process stimulates the first, and often most important, critical decision-making we do on a backcountry tour.

Observations of avalanche danger factors (avalanches, snowpack, and weather). Before terrain selection can occur, even at the planning phase, observations about avalanche danger factors must be made and considered. Observations about these factors—avalanches, snowpack, and weather—occur in all phases of a tour, as discussed in "Observations and Awareness for Backcountry Travel" later this chapter.

The backcountry user must learn to assess when observations may indicate or affect avalanche danger in the given terrain. Before the start of a trip, it is important to gather observations in each category from forecasts and weather data. Once on our trip, we must actively and constantly observe and gather information that will be useful for decision-making. The reliability of our decisions depends on the quality and quantity of our observations and on our ability to compare them to information gathered during tour planning to get a picture of current avalanche danger on the slopes we want to travel.

Human factors. This part of the DMF refers to the very important role that our human-ness plays in decision-making. The human factor refers to the nature of the group as well as to the behavior patterns individuals may exhibit on a given tour. We discuss this fully in "Human Factors and Group Dynamics" later this chapter.

Regarding the DMF and the human factor, we stress awareness, experience, motivation, leadership, levels of risk acceptance, and team skills. What is the awareness of the people involved with respect to hazard recognition, avalanche education, and human behavior? What is the experience level—avalanche training, fitness, ability, and rescue training—of each group member? Why is each person on a given tour, what is his motivation? What style of leadership exists in the group? How much of a team mentality and a shared mental model for the day does the group have? What other group or individual human factors may affect our ability to make good decisions? The answers to these questions have a strong role in shaping terrain selection, travel techniques, and almost every decision made on a ski tour.

Terrain selection, decision-making and error correction. Terrain selection is defined as the decisions we make about where we go. *This is the ultimate application of our decision-making in the backcountry.* You can't get caught in an avalanche if you're not in avalanche terrain.

Terrain selection is done on a macro, meso, and micro scale. An example of macro-scale terrain selection is when we choose to ski White Mountain instead of Black Mountain. An example of meso-scale would be to ski the north ridge of Black Mountain instead of the northeast bowl. Micro-scale terrain selection might be the decision to avoid the steep section of a slope. The backcountry skier will choose terrain after weighing the other components of the DMF and will continue to make adjustments throughout the tour.

An important part of terrain selection is the idea of error correction. Error correction is about recognizing if poor terrain selection has occurred and rectifying the situation.

Good terrain management does not come from a book, but from experience moving through terrain. There is no set of rules for safe terrain management. There are, however, a few big-picture guidelines to consider as you begin your terrain apprentice program. In order to manage avalanche terrain you must be able to identify it. We discuss the how and what of avalanche terrain in "Avalanche 101" later this chapter.

These are the steps of good terrain management:

- Understand what avalanche terrain is—be able to identify it.
- Make good observations about terrain, snowpack, weather, and human factors.
- Use some form of decision-making to make sense of your observations and select appropriate terrain.

Tip: Remember, terrain management is the art *and* science of ski touring.

Travel techniques. Travel techniques are the actions that determine *how we go.* Once we make terrain-selection decisions, we can further reduce our exposure to risk by using appropriate travel techniques. Techniques must be evaluated on a case-by-case basis to determine if they will actually have the desired risk-minimizing effect. A technique that works well in one situation may only make matters worse in another context.

It's important never to use travel techniques to justify otherwise inappropriate terrain-selection decisions. Travel techniques are secondary decisions to terrain selection. For example, if you encounter a slope that your group is concerned about, crossing it one at a time may minimize the risk to the entire group. However, each person is still at risk as she crosses the slope. Take a step back and ask, is it worth the risk, or should we select different terrain? Even when executed correctly, travel techniques don't eliminate poor stability—if a slope is unstable, it will not become more stable if you spread your group out to cross it.

USING THE DECISION-MAKING FRAMEWORK

We have described the basic components of the DMF and go into more detail throughout this chapter. As you read, think about how each part of the DMF affects the other. How does the human factor affect tour planning? What role do observations at home and in the field play in tour planning? What role does the human factor play in every aspect of the tour?

The goal of the DMF is to provide an understanding of the forces and factors involved in making a decision, to underscore the important role of terrain selection in dealing with avalanche hazard, and to remind the backcountry user that each factor can affect the other on any given tour.

AVALANCHE 101: SNOW SAFETY, AVALANCHE AWARENESS, AND AVALANCHE TERRAIN

Modern avalanche education focuses less on the science of avalanches and more on the skills for making better decisions in avalanche terrain. Knowing everything there is to know about the science of snow does not necessarily make you safer in avalanche terrain; in fact, it may even compound the problem. Having a process that leads to good decisions about where to travel is what counts.

Knowing the basics of how avalanches happen can help in making these decisions. This section is not a replacement for a snow-science textbook. It is designed to accomplish two things: first, to give you a better understanding of what ingredients it takes to produce an avalanche and, second, to give you a common vocabulary that will aid you in discussing risk in relation to avalanches.

What is an avalanche? In *The Avalanche Handbook*, David McClung and Peter Schaerer define them as "falling masses of snow that contain rock, soil, or ice." We can classify them into two main types: loose-snow avalanches and slab avalanches.

LOOSE-SNOW AVALANCHES

Loose-snow slides begin as loose, unconsolidated snow that usually starts from a point and then gathers mass as it moves down the mountain. Because of their characteristic teardrop shape they are also called point-release avalanches (fig. 2.2).

Loose-snow slides usually begin as very dry or very wet snow. In either case, the snow has little or no cohesion. These slides can range greatly in size, from quite small (referred to as sloughs) to slides containing 10,000 tons or more of moving snow. Loose-snow slides rarely come close to the size of the largest slab avalanches. They also generally have less destructive potential and fewer people are killed by them. But don't underestimate loose-snow avalanches in terrain with higher consequences. If caught, a backcountry skier is at risk from injury or worse if swept off a cliff or into a terrain trap (e.g., a gully or a crevasse).

In general, loose-snow avalanches are somewhat easier to predict than slab avalanches. Why is this? Remember that loose-

Fig. 2.2 Several loose-snow avalanches originating from the rocks above the slope

snow slides often happen with relatively dry snow or very wet snow. They also frequently occur in cold, dry weather or at very warm temperatures. The conditions that produce these slides are often easier to observe because the snow that tends to move is usually the surface or near-surface snow. This snow is affected directly by the weather, which is far easier to observe than the snow inside the snowpack. How many times have you seen the characteristic teardrop on a slope soon after the sun comes out?

Some avalanche experts believe the presence of loose-snow avalanches are actually a sign of stability deeper within the snowpack. This is because the surface snow moving down the mountain applies a load to the slope. If this does not step down into a weaker layer, thus triggering a deeper slide, it is actually a test of the slope that indicates decent stability. But again, do not underestimate the loose-snow avalanche.

In summary, loose-snow avalanches:

- Involve snow with little or no cohesion
- Are very dry or very wet
- Involve only near-surface snow upon initiation
- Usually have a teardrop shape
- Happen in conditions that are easier to predict than the conditions leading to slab avalanches

SLAB AVALANCHES

Slab avalanches start as a cohesive unit of snow. When the bonds between the unit of snow, or slab, and the surrounding snow fail, you have a slab avalanche.

Once failure occurs, the slab begins to accelerate down the mountain, breaking into smaller pieces. Instead of the teardrop shape seen in the loose-snow avalanches, the slab has angular walls where the slab broke loose from the surrounding snow. The uppermost wall is called the *crown* or *fracture line*. The lateral edges of the slab are the *flanks*. And since it was a cohesive unit of snow, it must have a lower wall; this is known as the *stauchwall*, and it's often hard to see because the slab ran it over on its way down the hill. The surface left behind that the slab slid on is the *bed surface*.

Slab avalanches (fig. 2.3) come in all types and sizes. They can range from only a few kilograms of snow to upward of millions of kilograms (see "Size Classification," below). Slabs can be made of hard snow or soft snow: so hard that you can walk across it without skis and not sink in, or so soft you can't even make a snowball. Slabs also range from wet to dry.

A slab may involve only the top layer or layers in the snowpack, or it may involve the entire snowpack at once. Because of this range, the destructive potential of slab avalanches varies greatly, but all told they often carry a much greater destructive potential than loose-snow avalanches.

Slabs avalanches can occur in all types of weather, from the nicest bluebird day to the gnarliest storm. The conditions that produce them, the stability of the snow at a given time, and the potential point of failure are relatively difficult to assess. Because of this, predicting a slab avalanche is much more complex than a loose-snow slide. Instability in the snowpack can come on

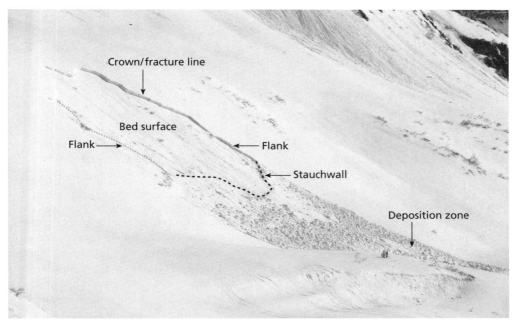

Fig. 2.3 A slab avalanche

quickly, as during a fierce storm, or it can lie teetering in balance just waiting for the right stress to send it out of balance—like a skier. When they do occur, slab avalanches often have higher destructive potential than loose-snow avalanches. As a result, avalanche research and education is focused on the assessment and forecasting of slab avalanches.

In summary, slab avalanches:
- Can be hard snow or soft snow
- Can be dry snow or wet snow
- Can involve near-surface snow or can go as deep as the whole snowpack
- Have an angular shape, with a fracture line, flanks, a bed surface, and a stauchwall
- Can be very difficult to predict and can happen in any weather

SIZE CLASSIFICATION

In North America, two main size classification systems for avalanches are used: the size relative to path and the destructive potential. Being able to recognize, communicate, and understand the size of an avalanche is important to the backcountry traveler. Later on, we'll use size classification as one of many observations to aid in the decision-making process. Both of these systems can be applied to loose-snow slides and slab avalanches.

Size Relative to Path

In a nutshell, size relative to path is the percentage of snow that moved versus what *could* have moved in the start zone. This is a good system to use on slopes that are constantly monitored—like slopes in or near ski areas and highways, or any slopes frequented by and familiar to the person receiving the information about the size of the avalanche. Highway-control workers and ski patrol are a couple of organizations that regularly use this system. As you might guess, this system has its limitations when it comes to the backcountry skier who roams around different areas and mountain ranges. Familiarity with this system will aid the backcountry skier in understanding avalanche reports posted near highways and in ski areas.

> **R1:** Very small, approximately 0%–20% of path avalanched
>
> **R2:** Small, approximately 20%–40% of path avalanched
>
> **R3:** Medium, approximately 40%–60% of path avalanched
>
> **R4:** Large, approximately 60%–80% of path avalanched
>
> **R5:** Major or maximum, 80%–100% of path avalanched

Destructive Potential

This is the most common system used in the backcountry community. It's based on an estimation of maximum destructive potential of the avalanche. The observer must take into consideration the mass of snow that moved and estimate its speed down the mountain, which gives you the destructive potential.

Here are the five levels of destruction, along with the damage each might cause and the actual mass of the snow moved:

D1: Too small to bury or injure a person. Typical mass: less than 10 tons

D2: Could bury, injure, or kill a person. Typical mass: 100 tons

D3: Could bury or destroy a car or destroy a small building. Typical mass: 1000 tons

D4: Could destroy a railway car, several buildings, or a forest up to 10 acres. Typical mass: 10,000 tons

D5: Could destroy a village or forest of 100 acres or more; the largest known avalanches. Typical mass: 100,000 tons

THE MOUNTAIN SNOWPACK

In order to understand the formation and initiation of avalanches, it is necessary to have a basic understanding of the mountain snowpack. The snowpack is made up of layers of snow, which are created as snow falls on the ground throughout the season. These layers—and the connections, or bonds, between them—can change and metamorphose over time under the effects of weather and precipitation. These layers are the basis for the formation and release of slab avalanches.

METAMORPHISM OF THE SNOWPACK

Once the snow is on the ground it immediately begins to change—a process called metamorphism. Metamorphism is neither good nor bad. It is simply the dynamic process that all snow goes through once it hits the ground. The weather and the overall climate of the region drive this change.

We care about metamorphism because it changes the structure of the layers that make up the snowpack. Metamorphism may increase or decrease the density or hardness of the layers within the snowpack. A change in layer density may increase or decrease stability depending on whether bonds between layers have increased or decreased in strength.

We break this process down into two types of metamorphism: direct weather effects and indirect weather effects.

Direct Weather Effects

Think about direct weather effects as what's happening near the surface of the snowpack. These are the four main direct weather factors:

Wind: Has the ability to transport large amounts of snow—results in rapid loading, can increase slab density, and can change grain shape.

Rain: Overall rapid loading of the snowpack (large amounts of moisture in a short time period)—rapid loading is the most common trigger of natural slab avalanches.

Temperature: Changes the settlement and creep rate of the upper snowpack.

Sun: Similar to temperature in its effects on the creep rate of the upper snowpack.

There are other direct weather factors that can change the snow surface, but these are the big four.

If the stress applied to the snowpack is added slowly enough, the snowpack can often adjust and remain in balance. When stress comes suddenly, the bonds holding the snow in place fail, which can lead to an avalanche. Picture a wad of silly putty: when you pull it slowly, you can stretch it to amazing lengths. If you pull it rapidly, it breaks instantly. This is how the snowpack responds to rapid loading due to wind, precipitation, and sudden increases in temperature and solar radiation. When light amounts of precipitation fall, the snowpack can adjust and everything stays in balance. If a raging storm comes along, look out—the snowpack might just snap.

Temperature and sun affect the snowpack a little differently than the mechanical stress of rapid loading. Instead of adding a load to the snow surface, the thermal stress of temperature and solar radiation change the creep and settlement rate of the upper part of the snowpack (fig. 2.4). Think about the top part of the snowpack accelerating at

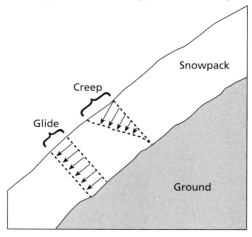

Fig. 2.4 Creep and glide in the snowpack

a faster rate downhill than the lower part. This applies a sheer stress to the snowpack. Couple this with a weak layer underneath, and you have sheer stress that exceeds the strength, and now you have snow in motion. As in every case where the stress is increased on the snowpack, this can create ideal avalanche conditions.

Melt-freeze metamorphism, a result of direct weather effects, occurs when the snow melts during the day and refreezes at night. During the later months of the ski season (although this can occur any time of year) the snowpack gets a little more sun and there are overall warmer temperatures. When snow warms past 0°C/32°F it begins to melt. This changes the structure of the grains. When the temperature drops below 0°C/32°F, as often it does at night, the water refreezes.

If this process is repeated for a few days, a corn layer exists in the day. Corn is simply a melt-freeze crust that has melted ever so slightly, forming a soft edgeable surface on the snow surface. If the crust is thick enough to support the weight of a skier, not only do we have good skiing, but stability is generally better with the added strength of the surface crust. As the sun begins to melt the frozen crust, the strength lessens and the stability can decrease. This is one of the reasons we try to ski south-facing slopes earlier in the day and pay close attention to them in the late afternoon.

At a certain point during the year, we go from a melt-freeze to a melt-freeze-a-little, then to a melt-melt cycle. The more melting there is with only a little freezing, the more free water there is in the snowpack. When this water percolates down to an impermeable layer (ice or the ground), it can provide a potential gliding surface for slabs. Eventually, the snow melts so much without subsequent refreezing that it loses most of its cohesion and becomes a rotten snowpack. These conditions can lead to a "shed cycle," where wet-snow avalanches are widespread.

Indirect Weather Effects

As the snow grains become buried in the snowpack, the snowpack insulates itself from the direct weather effects from above. People debate just how deeply direct weather effects penetrate the snowpack, but the general consensus is 10–20 centimeters. Below that boundary, snow grains experience a different series of changes.

Let's start with a little background. The first thing to understand is that the snowpack has two main boundaries: the atmosphere and the ground beneath. In most climates, the stored heat from summer solar radiation and the earth's geothermal heat keep the ground layer at or very near 0°C/32°F. The upper part of the snowpack is bounded by the atmosphere. Often in the winter, the ambient air temperature is much cooler than 0°C/32°F. Lower air temperatures keep the upper part of the snowpack cooler than the bottom part that's receiving heat from the earth.

This temperature difference creates a temperature gradient, which is defined as a change in temperature divided by the distance over which the temperature changes. Temperature gradients drive the metamorphic process because they drive moisture through the snowpack from warmer to cooler. The effect a temperature gradient has over the snowpack occurs on a longer time scale than that of direct weather effects. Metamorphism due to indirect weather can take place over the scale of days or months, whereas direct weather effects can change a snowpack in a matter of hours or minutes.

The two predominant processes that take place in the snowpack are faceting and rounding.

Faceting. Faceting is a metamorphic process in which the snow grains become more angular, less dense, and more loosely packed (fig. 2.5). In general, these characteristics lead to weak layers or weak bonds

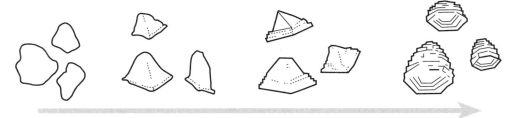

Fig. 2.5 Snow grains undergoing the faceting process (Source: AIARE curriculum)

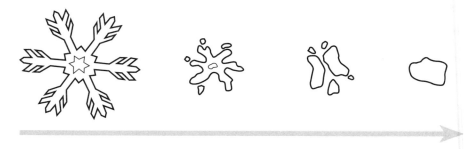

Fig. 2.6 Snow grains undergoing the rounding process (Source: AIARE curriculum)

between layers and can become one of the ingredients of a slab avalanche. Faceting is driven by the presence of a high temperature gradient in the snowpack, which drives moisture from warmer areas to cooler areas. In snow science, a high temperature gradient is one that is equal to or greater than 1°C/1.8°F per 10 centimeters. High temperature gradients are often created by cold air temperatures and shallow snow depths.

Rounding. When there is no temperature gradient or one that is less than 1°C/1.8°F per 10 centimeters, rounding of the snow grains occurs (fig. 2.6). Rounding is simply the opposite of faceting. The grains become more rounded, denser, and tightly packed together. Rounding tends to increase the strength of the snowpack. Rounding occurs in the snowpack when air temperatures warm (close to 0°C/32°F) and snow depths are large.

In summary, the two major factors that influence faceting and rounding deep in the snowpack are:

- Air temperature
- Snowpack depth

RECIPE FOR A SLAB AVALANCHE

Now that we understand the basics of the mountain snowpack, let's look at how snow conditions are related to the potential for avalanches. Three basic ingredients need to be present before a slab avalanche can be triggered:

- A cohesive unit of snow (a slab)
- A weak layer
- Appropriate slope angle

We discuss slope angle in "Incline" later this chapter, but first we focus on the first two ingredients, which are created by the metamorphism of the mountain snowpack throughout the season. Let's start simple: snow falls from the sky and is deposited on the ground. As the conditions in the atmosphere vary, so does the type and amount of snow falling, creating a snowpack with layers.

Weak Layers

A key ingredient in a slab avalanche is a weak, or failure, layer. This weak layer lies beneath the slab, providing a surface of weak bonding that can release the slab into motion. Weak layers come in all varieties, and the most prevalent are buried surface hoar, depth hoar, low-density snow, and crusts. In addition to understanding layers themselves, it is important to recognize the concept of strong over weak. If there is a strong layer (cohesive snow, i.e., a slab) over a poorly bonded (weak) layer, two of the three ingredients for a slab avalanche are in place.

Surface hoar. Surface hoar is essentially the winter mountain equivalent of dew. It forms on the snow surface as feathery crystals that range in size from less than a millimeter to over several centimeters (fig. 2.7), and these crystals don't bond well to snow that falls on top of them.

Surface hoar alone is not the problem; in fact, it's often quite beautiful and fun to ski through. The instability and danger comes from subsequent storms depositing more snow on top of this weak layer, which then becomes *buried* surface hoar.

Buried surface hoar has an amazing ability to take a lot of load in the form of compressive support—meaning a lot of snow can fall on top of it without it failing.

Fig. 2.7 Surface hoar

Buried surface hoar is a pesky and persistent weak layer that can hang around for months after being covered.

Now the problem: the compressive strength of buried surface hoar is quite good, but the shear strength is very poor. If there is a cohesive slab above it and enough of a slope angle, all it takes for the layer to fail is some trigger that adds stress to the teetering slab and, voilà, you've got yourself a slab avalanche. Overall, buried surface hoar as a weak layer contributes to a large portion of slab avalanches, especially skier-triggered ones.

Surface hoar can be persistent when it is buried in the snowpack, but while on the surface it is delicate and can be destroyed by sun, wind, rain, or a warm new storm-layer. The difficultly arises in predicting the existence of surface hoar over elevation and aspect. It may rain down low and snow up high, but it could be windy up high and calm down low...and so on. The presence or absence of surface hoar is subject to a high degree of variability.

Depth hoar. Depth hoar results from faceting deep within the snowpack. These grains have a cup-shaped look and can range in size from barely a millimeter to several centimeters. The faceting process to create these grains can take time—often days, weeks, or months. These faceted grains bond poorly to each other and to other types of grains in the snowpack, and as such they create a weak layer. Once depth hoar has formed, it takes a long time for the rounding process to occur.

Low-density snow. As a weak layer, low-density snow can act similarly to depth hoar. Low-density snow is a powder hound's dream, but only if it's the top layer. When heavier snow piles on top of a low-density layer, the change in each layer can be enough to create a strong layer (the heavier snow) over a weak layer (light, low-density snow).

Crusts. Crusts often form on the surface of the snow because of ice, rain, and sun. When subsequent snow falls on the crust, this crust becomes a buried layer. A buried crust may bond poorly with other layers and can become a good bed surface for a slab avalanche.

Crusts can promote strong temperature gradients around them, which in turn promotes faceting. In the spring, with warmer air temperatures, meltwater from the top of the snowpack trickles down through the snowpack onto the buried crust. The buried crust can concentrate the water, creating a well-lubricated surface upon which slabs might slide.

SNOW CLIMATES

Snow climates describe regions with certain general characteristics. Knowing the snow climate can help us further evaluate the snowpack in a given region. There are three main snow climates, each with its own particular characteristics of weather, snowpack, and avalanches (fig. 2.8).

In understanding snow climates, it is crucial to remember that the characteristics are general rules of thumb. When considering snow climates, focus on the results a given snow climate may have on

	MARITIME	CONTINENTAL	INTERMOUNTAIN (USA) / INTERIOR (CANADA)
Weather			
Precipitation	High rate	Low rate	Moderate to high rate
	Large accumulation	Small accumulation	Medium to large accumulation
Wind Transport	Much pre-storm	Little pre-storm	Little to some pre-storm
	Much in-storm	Some to much in-storm	Some to much in-storm
	Little post-storm	Much post-storm	Some post-storm
Temperature	Warm	Cold	Cool
Snowpack			
Depth/Distribution	Deep, uniform	Shallow, variable	Moderate to deep, variable early season, uniform late season
Layering	Uniform	Strong over weak	Variable, faceted early season, uniform and rounded late season
	Rounded	Faceted	
Temperature	Warm	Cold	Cool
Avalanches			
	Direct action:	Delayed action:	Direct and delayed action
	Many in-storm events, associated with significant storms	Some in-storm events, often associated with minor storms	
	Some post-storm events, usually ending within 24–36 hours	Many post-storm events, days or even weeks later, often associated with little or no significant weather	
Avalanche Danger			
	Quick to rise	Slow to rise	Quick to rise
	Quick to fall	Often very slow to fall	Often slow to fall early season, quicker to fall late season

Fig. 2.8 Snow climates provide guidelines for weather, snowpack, and avalanche activity.
(Source: AIARE curriculum)

the snowpack. Keep in mind also that there may be areas in a maritime climate that look continental and vice versa. A cold, dry season in a maritime range may create a more continental snowpack in an unusual year, and often an intermountain snow climate looks continental in the beginning of the season and more maritime at the end as snow accumulates.

If you are from the Sierra, the Pacific Northwest, or other maritime regions where the snow stability tends to improve fairly quickly after a storm ends, you can often ski the steeps 24–36 hours after the weather clears. In a continental snowpack like the Colorado Rockies, however, you will have a much different approach because the avalanche danger is often much slower to improve due to the climate. Be careful not to indiscriminately apply the "rules" of a region in areas where a different climate exists.

TERRAIN SELECTION: UNDERSTANDING AND IDENTIFYING AVALANCHE TERRAIN

Choosing your terrain appropriately is the ultimate goal of backcountry decision-making. There's an old saying among avalanche professionals: the three most important things to pay attention to in backcountry travel are terrain, terrain, and terrain. With appropriate terrain selection you can ski on just about any day with just about any hazard level.

What is avalanche terrain and how do you identify it? Experienced backcountry travelers develop a keen eye for the subtleties of the terrain (fig. 2.9) and know where to travel according to their knowledge of current snow stability and their risk-acceptance level. Sound complicated? It is.

In "Metamorphism of the Snowpack" we discussed the active state of the snowpack

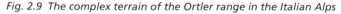

Fig. 2.9 The complex terrain of the Ortler range in the Italian Alps

and how it's constantly changing. The snowpack is dynamic and nearly impossible to predict with 100 percent certainty. Terrain, however, is relatively static. If we can learn to read and understand terrain, we can use it to protect ourselves against the uncertainties in the snowpack.

In order to understand and decide if an avalanche might affect us we need to be able to quickly and effectively do the following:

- Identify avalanche terrain
- Assess if the terrain is more or less likely to produce avalanches
- Determine if avalanches might run through the terrain
- Identify safer and more dangerous areas

Identifying Avalanche Terrain

What does avalanche terrain look like? Terrain through which avalanches may run is called an avalanche path, and there are two main types: clearly defined and poorly defined. Each type exhibits three components:

The start zone: This is the area where the avalanche begins (it must have the required slope angle for an avalanche to release).

The path or track: This is the path the avalanche takes.

The runout or deposition zone: This is where the debris comes to rest. Don't underestimate this area; it can be perfectly flat terrain.

A **clearly defined path** often looks like the classic path we've seen time and again in the backcountry or along the highway. The start zone, track, and runout are often very distinct (fig. 2.10).

Fig. 2.10 A well-defined avalanche path near Rogers Pass, British Columbia

A **poorly defined path** is trickier to identify. These paths have all three components (start zone, path, deposition zone), but one or all may not be recognizable. Your ability to correctly identify this type of terrain is paramount for your safety in the backcountry, and the more poorly defined the path the more difficult this becomes. Poorly defined paths can be found in the alpine (fig. 2.11), tree line, and below tree line sections of a mountain.

Fig. 2.11 Slopes in the high alpine can contain numerous poorly defined avalanche paths (Thompson Pass, Alaska).

Will the Terrain Produce an Avalanche?

Within both clearly and poorly defined paths, three factors of the slope help us determine if the terrain can produce an avalanche: incline, aspect, and slope configuration.

Incline

When the incline of the slope in the start zone is between 25 and 45 degrees, you're in avalanche terrain (fig. 2.12). Unfortunately for backcountry travelers, this range happens to be the ideal angle for great skiing. Slopes over 45 degrees tend to slough and purge new snow and don't tend to accumulate enough to produce a slab. Slopes under 25 degrees require extremely poor stability in order to produce an avalanche.

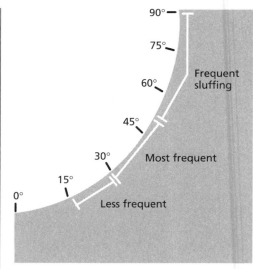

Fig. 2.12 Slope angle and frequency of avalanches

That said, the optimum angle for an avalanche can vary between the different snow climates. We've seen slabs release on slopes above 50 degrees in maritime climates, and extreme avalanche cycles can produce avalanches on slopes below 25 degrees.

When considering the incline of a slope, you must consider the angle of the start zone. The 25- to 45-degree range is what's required to start an avalanche. This doesn't mean that an avalanche can't *run through* terrain with much less angle. If your tour takes you through a low-angle path or run-out zone, but the slope above you has the appropriate angle, you're still in avalanche terrain.

DETERMINING SLOPE ANGLE

Each and every degree of slope angle plays a huge role in the physics of an avalanche. Can you *reliably* tell the difference between 28 and 30 degrees? Do you really want to bet on the slope being 28 and not 30 degrees? The key is to learn to accurately determine slope angles through practice and, when in doubt, to err on the conservative side. Here are some tools and methods for determining slope angle:

Compass. Choose a compass that has a built-in clinometer (usually in the form of an extra needle in the compass body). When standing at the top of the slope, sight down the slope; this is similar to shooting a bearing, but with the compass tipped 90 degrees (with the face of the compass pointing to the right or left) so the clinometer needle can point straight down. There are two angles to look for: average and maximum. Sighting down to the bottom (where the slope ends or has the greatest change in angle) will produce the average angle of the slope. Using the steepest portion of the slope and sighting to the bottom of it gives you the angle of the steepest section—this is often the angle you will be most concerned with. Several companies produce professional-grade clinometers that include a true sight and tend to provide a slightly better reading—the tradeoff is cost and another gadget to tote around.

Clinometer. These are small cardlike tools with a scale that reads degrees of the slope. The accuracy of the device is good, but correctly placing the tool onto the slope to get a precise reading can be challenging. To aid in this, carefully lay your pole on the snow surface and place the clinometer onto the pole and take a reading. Keep in mind the sample size you are measuring is small compared to the entire slope. Another problem with these devices is the requirement to be *on* the slope in question to obtain a measurement. Overall, these devices are best used to measure slope angle when digging a snow profile or for simply training yourself to become a better judge of slope angle. You can use the clinometer in your compass in the same fashion.

Map clinometers. These handy tools are used in tour planning and can be very helpful in determining the average angle of a slope from the map—*before* you are standing on the slope. They work by matching the scale of your map to the scale of the clinometer and then aligning the correct scale to the contours of the slope in question.

Slope Angle with Ski Poles

A very easy way to measure slope angle is to use your ski poles and take advantage of the fact that the combined inside angles of any triangle add up to 180 degrees. Here is how you do it:

First, prepare your poles before leaving home. Measure and mark the shafts of each pole 100 cm from the bottom. Make further marks on one pole (A) so that you end up with marks at 100 cm, 84 cm, 70 cm, 58 cm, and 47 cm. Label these as 45°, 40°, 35°, 30 °, and 25°.

In the field, grab pole A at the top of the handle and let it hang plumb—so that the pole tip barely touches the snow.

Hold the other pole (B) horizontally. Slide pole B along its 100 cm marking point down pole A until the pole tip of pole B touches the uphill side of the snow. Where the marking point of pole B touches pole A will be the angle of the slope (fig 2.13).

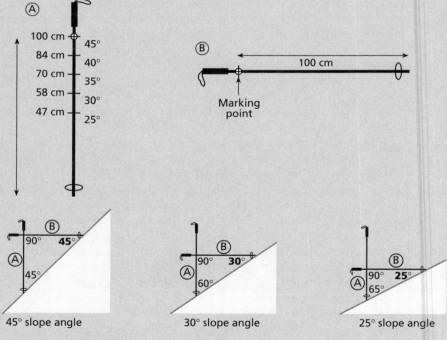

Fig 2.13 Diagram for Slope Angle Pole Trick

Aspect

In a nutshell, aspect is the overall direction the slope faces. A slope with a northerly aspect faces toward the north. Two main factors influence the snow differently as aspect changes: wind and sun.

Wind. Wind has a very powerful influence on the snowpack. Its greatest effect is its ability to transport snow from one place to another. Think back to direct weather effects: the wind can rapidly deposit large amounts of snow on a slope, thereby dramatically increasing the load on the snowpack. The slope that faces the wind is the windward side, and the slope opposite that is the leeward side. When the wind blows, it transports snow from the windward side and deposits it onto the leeward slope. This is often obvious to observe when the aspect of the slope is perpendicular to the wind. If the wind blows parallel, or across the slope, we call this cross-loading (fig. 2.14). Cross-loading can be difficult to identify, and it is often hard to evaluate the location of the resulting wind slabs.

Sun. During the winter months in the Northern Hemisphere, the sun is lower in the sky. This lower angle reduces the intensity of solar radiation. The solar radiation we do get is most concentrated on southerly aspects, while northerly aspects receive very little. On southerly aspects, even a little bit of solar radiation helps increase the ambient air temperature, which in turn helps reduce the amount of faceting; the added heat may even promote rounding within the snowpack. In general, during the winter the northerly aspects can be

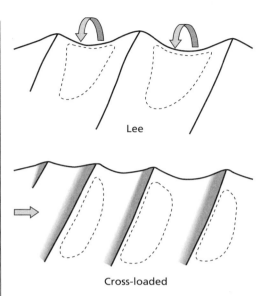

Lee

Cross-loaded

Fig. 2.14 Wind loading on lee and cross-loaded slopes (Source: AIARE curriculum)

more dangerous than the southerly aspects because temperatures and conditions on north faces are more conducive to faceting.

In the spring, the sun is higher in the sky and daytime is longer. Intense solar radiation hits southerly aspects for a longer period, adding a lot of heat to the snowpack. If enough heat is added, especially suddenly, then the bonds of the snowpack change dramatically and eventually cause the snow to move. The northerly aspects, which in winter were subject to persistent weak layers and faceting, start to consolidate in spring (because of overall increase in ambient air temperature), and these northerly slopes become the places to be. Southerly aspects are often safer in the early part of the day and can become more dangerous in the afternoon because of wet slides.

Slope Configuration

Slope configuration is the way the parts or elements of a slope are arranged and fit together. As a backcountry traveler, you want to observe all of the terrain-related nuances and subtleties that collectively make up the slope you want to ski. Some of these nuances can increase or decrease a slope's potential of producing an avalanche.

Ground cover. What is the ground surface like under the snow? A talus field of giant boulders will hold snow better than a smooth scree slope. The ground cover can provide good anchoring for the snow, or it can be predestined to make a bed surface for an avalanche.

Elevation. Is the elevation affecting snow stability? Are there weak layers or snowpack characteristics that exist at specific elevations?

Slope shape. Is the slope shaped in a way that increases the stress on the snowpack? For example, the classic convex roll (fig. 2.15) creates greater stress at the rollover point. Slope shape can change subtly and have great impact on snow stability.

Slope support. What terrain features are holding a slab in place? A slope that ends in a cliff band is unsupported, whereas a slope that eases into flat ground has support.

Anchors. What features exist on the slope that could hold a potential slab in place? Anchors can be rocks, trees, or any features that give a slab something to stick to.

Variability. Is the snowpack shallow in some places and deep in others? This becomes important in a shallow snowpack that has buried weak layers with stronger snow above, creating a bridge effect. In this case, shallower snow may mean a weaker bridge.

Terrain traps. Is the terrain configured to magnify the consequences of an avalanche? Terrain traps include gullies, creek beds, crevasses, cliffs, and any feature that could cause you increased harm if an avalanche happened above it.

Interaction with weather. Is the terrain affected drastically by sun, wind loading, or any indirect weather effects?

Trigger points. These are weak spots in the snowpack or areas of concentrated stress (fig. 2.15). A trigger point is a specific location in a start zone where a localized failure is initiated, which then becomes an avalanche. Sometimes a tree can be a trigger point (in shallow snowpack), and sometimes it can be an anchor (in deeper snowpack with no lingering instabilities). If you choose to enter avalanche terrain or you need to cross through a potential start zone, it's important to know where trigger points may exist.

In summary, you must be able to identify avalanche terrain on every scale—macro, meso, and micro—as a crucial part of your decision-making process in the backcountry. Seek instruction, education, and practice reading and evaluating terrain. Remember that terrain selection is the ultimate expression of your decision-making, and work to develop your sense and evaluation of avalanche terrain.

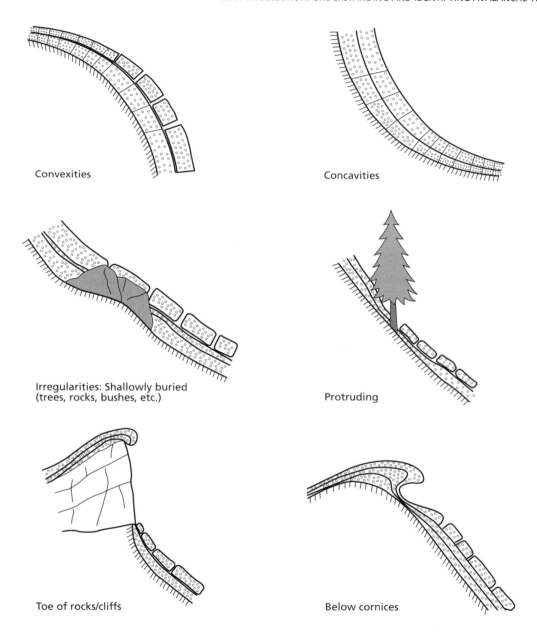

Convexities

Concavities

Irregularities: Shallowly buried
(trees, rocks, bushes, etc.)

Protruding

Toe of rocks/cliffs

Below cornices

Fig. 2.15 Common trigger points (Source: AIARE curriculum)

TOUR PLANNING

In describing the Decision-making Framework at the beginning of this chapter, we emphasized the importance of tour planning as a tool in your decision-making in the mountains. In this section we focus on how to generate an effective tour plan and how to use that tour plan when you are in the mountains.

Tour planning encompasses a wide range of activities and considerations, using a host of resources for snowpack, weather, avalanche, and terrain information. It is an extremely powerful tool in managing the risks and hazards of ski touring and ski mountaineering. You can't control all of the hazards you'll encounter, but you can better prepare yourself to deal with those hazards by trying to predict where, what, and how they might arise before you find yourself unintentionally in their midst.

As you are tour planning, you are seeking to answer this question: *What do I expect to see?* Your goal is to answer that question for every leg and every facet of your tour. What do you expect the snow to be like? The avalanche hazard? The weather? Your ski partners? The terrain? Good tour planning will take you through each of these questions and many more, and will help you generate a detailed mental picture of your expectations.

Once you have a complete tour plan, your goal is to apply it at all times during your tour. As you move through terrain, you will constantly be asking these three questions: *What did I expect to see (based on my tour plan)? What am I actually seeing? How do these observations affect my decisions?* Was there as much wind loading on lee slopes as you thought? Did the snow freeze as solidly as you predicted? Did your ski partners move as quickly as you thought they would?

This process of constant mental comparison between your tour plan and your observations in the field is your key to making decisions in the field. Armed with a detailed mental picture of every aspect of your tour plan, you can process observations and assess their impact on your route and terrain selection.

Our goal here is to show the anatomy of a tour plan. This includes how to generate route options and how to create a time plan (*What do I expect to see?*). We then discuss how to apply tour planning in the field to guide you as you move through the decision-making process of a tour (*What am I actually seeing? How do these observations affect my decisions?*).

CREATING ROUTE OPTIONS

Coming up with route options isn't that difficult; deciding which option to choose once you're in the field is the real crux. In doing so, the amount of information your brain must weigh and consider is extensive, highly varied, and may change often in a short time period. Tour planning is a way to set yourself up to be organized about all the factors you must consider in decision-making.

During the planning phase of a ski tour, create more than one option that will satisfy the goals of your group if conditions change or do not meet your expectations. These options allow a chance to change the trip if your observations indicate the ideal option is unrealistic. Without options in place, groups tend to continue onto their initial objective, even though their observations may be telling them they should not.

The information available to you for tour planning may vary depending on the region where you're skiing, but there are multiple resources out there you can use in any mountain range. These can be organized into three basic categories: history and forecasts, route resources, and human factors.

History and Forecasts: Weather, Snowpack, Avalanche

In order to know where you're going, you must first know where you've been. The history of the weather, the snowpack, and avalanche conditions are your baseline for understanding what has been happening in the mountains around you, even if you weren't out that day or that week. The forecast for these same three categories is your prediction for what will occur throughout your tour.

The amount of historical information and the accuracy and resolution of forecasts varies widely throughout the country. You may need to extrapolate information from another region to your own, or you may have highly accurate weather, snowpack, and avalanche forecasting in your backyard.

Either way, this information gathering is vital to forming an opinion about what you expect to see in the mountains. (The appendix lists weather, snowpack, and avalanche resources for mountains around the world.)

Weather. Fortunately, many other people care about the weather beyond our small portion of the population that moves in the mountains. Weather history is recorded at thousands of weather stations throughout the country and the world, and most all of that data is available on the Web.

In gathering weather history, cultivate your inner weather geek, and don't forget about your own mental weather history. Has it been warm outside your window, or cold? Precipitating or sunny? Mountain weather forecasts are available for most regions of the United States, Canada, and Europe in some level of detail. As you gather information about the weather, think about how the weather is interacting with the snowpack and what affect that interaction will have on snow stability. Often, avalanche bulletins will help you to do this—use them to guide you in interpreting how the weather will affect the snowpack.

Snowpack. Snowpack history and forecasts are slightly less numerous compared to weather forecasts. That said, any mountains that have roads, ski areas, or even industry will have someone who is monitoring the snowpack.

In tour planning, you are interested in how the snowpack will interact with the weather and vice versa, and how these factors will shape avalanche hazard in your chosen terrain. You can gather snowpack history both through your own observations out in the field and through the observations and forecasting of avalanche professionals.

Once again, the Web is an invaluable resource for this data. Information can take the form of raw data (depth, layers, grains, bonding) or narrative data regarding persistent weak layers and changes within the snowpack. It is up to you to understand, interpret, and evaluate this information for yourself. An avalanche course can be very valuable to help you gain knowledge and experience in this area.

Avalanche. The history and forecasts of avalanche activity are intimately connected to that of the snowpack and weather, but they are a separate set of observations and predictions.

Avalanche history is an excellent source of information about how the snowpack is reacting to the weather. Did any avalanches actually occur? Were they human triggered, mechanically triggered, or natural? What were their characteristics in terms of aspect, elevation, destructive potential, and so on? How does this information relate to your tour plan? This data may be available from your own observations, from avalanche professionals, and from the observations of others who have been out in the mountains.

Avalanche forecasts are the synthesis of all weather and snowpack history, with the predicted behavior the same at given aspects and elevations. Avalanche forecasts may not be available for all mountains of the world, but when available such forecasts are a valuable resource for tour planning.

Route Resources: Seeking Information About Terrain

You will ultimately be making decisions regarding terrain in your tour plan. As such, it is logical that a large part of your tour planning will involve seeking information about the terrain you will be moving through, especially if you have never been there before. This information can be in the form of photos, written or verbal info, or topographical maps.

Web, guidebooks, people. We live in the information age, and ski touring is no exception. Above, we mentioned that weather, snowpack, and avalanche data is widely available on the Web. The data stream doesn't stop there. In addition to official data sites, we now have a host of websites and blogs laden with trip reports and photos. Guidebooks focused on skiing are becoming increasingly prolific for mountains of the United States and Canada and have been in existence in Europe for years. If you live in a densely populated mountain community you can gain route information by simply talking to the people around you—guides and ski patrollers as well as recreationalists.

Terrain information from maps. Maps vary in their scale, quality, and level of detail included, but a good map will tell you more about a ski tour than all the trip reports and guidebooks combined.

Tour planning using topographical maps is an exercise in attention to detail. We outline the basics of what information can be found on a topo map and how you can use your map for tour planning. In doing so, we assume you have a basic knowledge of map and compass work, including taking and shooting bearings, reading contour lines, understanding declination, and so on. See chapter 3, Navigation, for more information regarding the application of these skills in ski touring.

The information you can expect to find in text on a topo map includes (but is not limited to) the following:

- Date created
- Date updated
- Scale
- Contour intervals
- Declination
- Grids and datums included
- Names and elevations of peaks and landmarks
- Latitude/longitude and UTM coordinates

The information you can expect to find graphically represented on a topo map can include the following:

- Ground-surface characteristics (trees, glaciers, scree, etc.)
- Water features (lakes, rivers, etc.)
- Contours (these are crucial, showing slope steepness, elevation, aspect, shape)
- Buildings and man-made features
- Trails and roads
- Potential avalanche slopes
- Aspect of terrain on your route
- On a ski touring map, ascent and descent routes with level of difficulty

Regardless of the scale and quality of your map, the most powerful information it provides is the shape and form of the terrain you will be moving through. The map contours give you a bird's-eye view of terrain. They show you the aspect and incline of slopes you may encounter, and you can see what will be above or below you. With careful map work, you can generate ideal, safer, and safest routes, highlight potential trouble spots, and plan ahead for your decision-making points.

Using maps to plan for a whiteout. In addition to tour planning for good weather, topo maps go hand in hand with whiteout navigation plans. Figure 2.16 shows a sample tour with a whiteout navigation plan in a field book, with bearings for each leg and elevations for the start and finish of each leg. When using a map to plan for a whiteout, you can pick out terrain features to use for point-to-point navigation, pick out handrails to follow, and identify trouble spots. See chapter 3, Navigation, for more information regarding these techniques.

Tour planning with a computer. This is a major time-saver and is especially useful if you are using your GPS unit as a backup for navigation, as described in "Navigation Techniques" in chapter 3. Mapping software allows you to pick points on the map, get their UTM coordinates, and upload them directly into your GPS unit. Along the way you can name them for clarity, and print them for backup use in someone else's GPS unit if yours dies. You can always hand-enter coordinates in the field if you need to, but doing it beforehand in the comfort of your home is much faster. Figure 2.17 shows an example of a whiteout navigation plan done using map software.

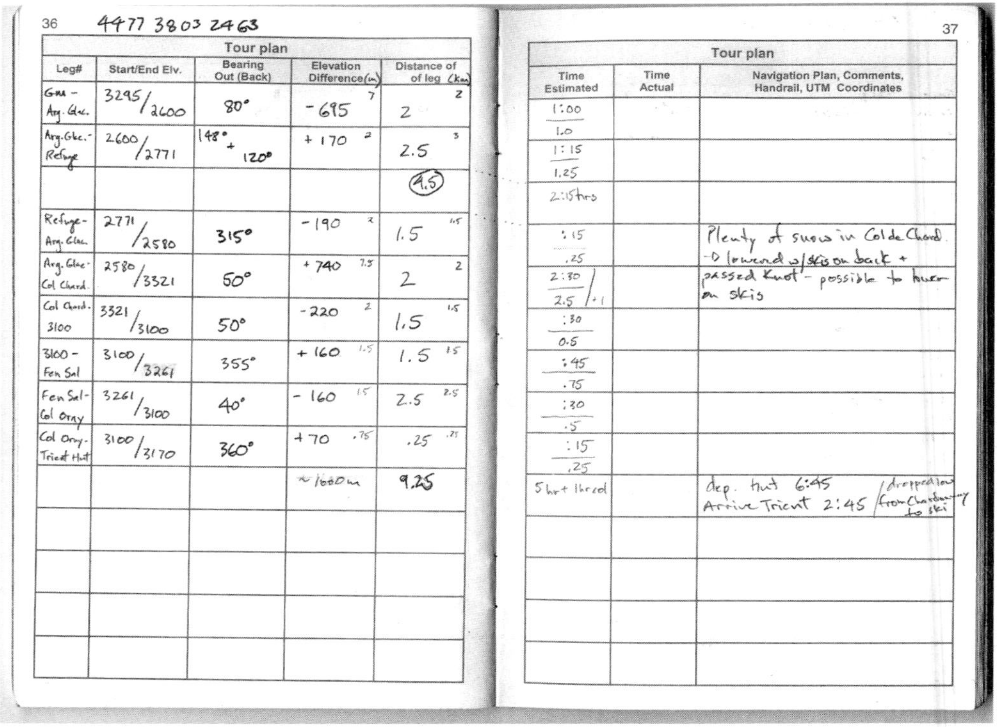

36   44 77 38 03 24 63   37

Tour plan

Leg#	Start/End Elv.	Bearing Out (Back)	Elevation Difference (m)	Distance of leg (km)
Gla – Arg. Glac.	3295/2600	80°	-695 (7)	2 (2)
Arg. Glac.- Refuge	2600/2771	148° / 120°	+170 (2)	2.5 (3)
				(4.5)
Refuge- Arg. Glac.	2771/2580	315°	-190 (2)	1.5 (1.5)
Arg. Glac.- Col Chard	2580/3321	50°	+740 (7.5)	2 (2)
Col Chard- 3100	3321/3100	50°	-220 (2)	1.5 (1.5)
3100- Fen Sal	3100/3261	355°	+160 (1.5)	1.5 (1.5)
Fen Sal- Col Orny	3261/3100	40°	-160 (1.5)	2.5 (2.5)
Col Orny- Trient Hut	3100/3170	360°	+70 (.75)	.25 (.25)
			≈1000m	9.25

Tour plan

Time Estimated	Time Actual	Navigation Plan, Comments, Handrail, UTM Coordinates
1:00		
1.0		
1:15		
1.25		
2:15 hrs		
:15		Plenty of snow in Col de Chard.
.25		-D lowered w/skis on back +
2:30 /		passed knot - possible to lower
2.5 /+1		on skis
:30		
0.5		
:45		
.75		
:30		
.5		
:15		
.25		
5 hr + thread		dep. hut 6:45 / dropprediction Arrive Trient 2:45 / from Chardonnet to ski?

Fig. 2.16 Tour plan for a day of the Haute Route with bearings for whiteout navigation

TIME CALCULATIONS

How many times have you hiked or skied out a trail in the dark? How many of those times was your dark exit intentional? If you always ski tour in the same place, you may have a very good idea about how long your trip will take. But who wants to ski in the same place all the time? Incorporating time calculations into your tour planning is a useful way of dealing with new terrain, new conditions, new ski partners…and of building intentional margins of safety into your ski mountaineering trips as you expand your horizons.

There are a number of ways to calculate how long a trip will take. The most important thing is simply to use one of them, and to do so consistently. Time calculations for a ski tour are not meant to make you a slave to the clock. Rather, they provide you with a time framework that helps you make better decisions about when you will be where during your tour.

Time calculations are more than just

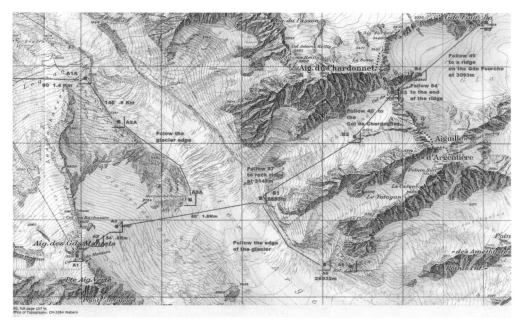

Fig. 2.17 Haute Route navigation plan created using mapping software
(Tour plan compiled by Marc Chauvin)

coming out in the daylight. They allow you to plan your tour better to manage some of the many safety issues that go hand in hand with time. Avalanche hazard late in the day, skier fatigue, daylight buffers if anything goes wrong…the list goes on and on. Time calculations also have benefits that extend beyond those of safety. Do you want to hit the corn snow when it has gone over to ankle-sloshing slop, or would you prefer to arrive at the top just as it makes that magical transition from hard snow into butter? Would you prefer to ski last night's new snow before it gets a light sun crust on it, or after?

The Werner Munter Method of Time Calculation

The time-calculation method we outline below is one of many and can be adapted to any kind of mountain travel, though we focus on travel using skis, up and down.

The basic structure is this: break your trip into a series of legs, and then consider the vertical gain or loss and the horizontal distance for each leg. The legs of your tour can be determined by a change of direction (bearing), a transition from uphill to downhill or vice versa, or a shift in your mode of travel. You can use as many legs as you see fit based on the nature of your tour. On one end of the spectrum is whiteout navigation in unfamiliar terrain (figs. 2.16 and 2.17)—lots of different legs, usually corresponding with compass bearings for point-to-point navigation. On the other end of the spectrum might be a trip to a familiar place on a clear-sky day. In that case all you need is the total vertical gain and the total distance, one leg up and one leg back. In either case, begin by setting up a chart of a sample tour plan like the one shown in figure 2.18.

Assign a name or a number to each leg of your tour, then begin filling in the start and finish elevations and the approximate distance of each leg. This information will all be coming from your map. If you are expecting bad weather, you can fill in your compass bearings for each leg, and/or your UTM grid coordinates for navigating with your GPS unit. For your time calculation, all you need to know is the start, finish, and net elevation gain and the horizontal distance for each leg.

Here is how the calculation works for each leg, using an example of a leg that travels 4 kilometers and gains 1000 vertical feet:

1. Assign units for the total horizontal and vertical distances traveled.
   Horizontal: 1 km (3281 ft) = 1 unit

LEG	Bearing	Elev. Start	Elev. End	Net Elev.	Distance	Units	Time	Comments
1	360°	7760	7200	-560	.75 Km	3	.33	
2	338°	7200	7400	+200	1 Km	3	.75	
3	360°	7400	7560	+160	.75 km	1	.25	boot over col

Fig. 2.18 Sample tour plan

Vertical: 100 m (328 ft) = 1 unit
Our example gives us 4 units for the horizontal, 3 units for the vertical.

2. Add the total number of units for horizontal and vertical. Write this in the "Units" column.
Our example gives us 4 + 3 units = 7 units.

3. Divide the total number of units to obtain the amount of time (in decimal form) for each leg. For uphill travel, divide by 4. For downhill travel on skis, divide by 10.
Our example gives us 7 ÷ 4 = 1.75 hours, or 1 hour 45 minutes, for uphill travel.

These calculations are based on the average pace made by a party moving steadily at a medium exertion and does not include any time for breaks. You may move faster or slower with any given group makeup or conditions—the important thing is to use your calculated time as a benchmark. You will know during each leg if you are moving faster or slower than your prediction, and you can then adjust your plan—or pace—if needed.

Using this example, note the following hints:

What about the math? You can use a calculator with accuracy to 2–4 decimal places, or you can do the fractions roughly and round to simplify. Whatever you do, just do it consistently. If you round up on one calculation, make sure you don't round down on the next leg. As you use this tool more and more, you will develop your personal method of dealing with the math. More importantly, you will begin to understand how that method affects your result. Experiment with it: if you always round up, do your calculations build in extra time to the day? How much?

Compare and contrast. Every time you use the system, get a little scientific about it. Write down how long it took you to do each leg or the whole tour. Make a note of who was with you and how fast your pace was. If you ran over your time, look at where: Did you have to take your skis off and boot it? Did you have to break trail? Navigate in a whiteout? All of these pieces of information will help you to plan your time for your next tour.

Be flexible in your application. Use time calculations every time you go out, but feel free to swing all over the spectrum. Run the numbers in your head when you are going to your favorite stomping grounds (how many laps can I do in four hours?). Try going somewhere totally new and map the whole tour out leg by leg. Do time calculations even when you aren't leading the group.

The Human Factor in Tour Planning

In addition to researching snowpack, weather, avalanche conditions, and terrain, there is another crucial factor to include in your tour planning: Who is going on the trip? The human factor—and the dynamics that develop among the people on your tour—play a large role in managing risk in the mountains. The more you know about the people going on the tour, the safer and more successful your trip can be.

Ask yourself these questions:

- Who is going? How many people are going?
- What is the risk acceptance level of each group member?
- What is the fitness of each member? Are there big differences in fitness among the group?
- What skills does each member bring to the group? Skiing? Backcountry travel? Companion rescue?
- What are the goals for each member in the group? Are there different or conflicting goals for the trip?
- What are the communication styles and personalities in the group?
- What equipment is the group carrying for rescue, to replace or fix broken gear, or in case of injury?

Though oftentimes overlooked relative to the other aspects of tour planning, the human factor can rear its ugly head on almost any tour. A major cause of avalanche accidents, for example, can be traced to human error and decision-making. Planning for the human factor can therefore increase your safety. It can also drastically add to a tour's fun factor and help you achieve your objectives.

Beyond the planning stage, the human factor will enter into every part of your tour. Remember from the Decision-making Framework that the human factor plays an important role in your decision-making process. "Human Factors and Group Dynamics," below, looks in more detail at this part of decision-making.

TOUR PLANNING SUMMARY

Everything discussed so far takes place before you walk outdoors. Now that you have a solid mental picture for your tour, what do you do with it? Remember, tour planning at home gives you *what you expect to see*. When you head out into the mountains you will focus on comparing what you expect with *what you are actually seeing*. The application of your tour plan means you are constantly comparing every aspect of your actual tour to your planned tour. This process begins in the parking lot and does not stop until you are back at your car at the end of the tour.

Have you ever been ski touring where everyone drives up, throws on their gear, and as soon as the first person has his skins on he takes off up the hill? Is this a race or a ski trip? On the contrary, when you and your ski partners leave the parking lot your goal is that everyone on the trip has a shared mental model for the day.

Application of your tour plan and good communication with your group will give everyone a clear idea of the following:

- That the group has appropriate rescue gear and an outlined rescue plan
- A general idea of the tour options and planned return time
- A plan for who the group leader is (and what is meant by "group leader")
- That everyone has a functional avalanche transceiver (see "Transceiver Check" in chapter 1)

The amount of up-front communication necessary for each of these can vary depending on the group dynamic, and with long-time ski partners this may all take place with a few words and a beacon check. With new ski partners it may be necessary to go through each point in more detail; this may take more time and seem a bit painful, but it can go a long way in establishing a communication style for the day and making sure everyone is on the same page.

When you start moving on your tour, you are finally in what we call "the business." You will be making decisions about track setting, pacing, snow stability, risk assessment...the list goes on. And many of these will take place more quickly than your conscious mind is aware of. In applying your tour planning you will be continually evaluating where you are, what you see in snow, weather, terrain, and your group, and if you need to change your plan based on your observations.

There will come a point in your tour planning when, "Il faut aller voir!" ("You must go see!") Ski touring and ski mountaineering demand that you "go see." Good tour planning gives you a structure and a foundation for processing comparisons between what you expect on a tour and what you find, the goal being to make informed decisions in the mountains.

A note on confidence level. Your confidence level in your tour plan is a measure of how accurate you think your predictions are based on how much information you have available to you. Ask yourself these questions: Given the amount of time and information that went into your pretrip planning, how confident are you in your expectations? How might this affect your

decision-making? If your confidence level is low, consider being extra conservative in your decisions.

HUMAN FACTORS AND GROUP DYNAMICS

Backcountry skiing occurs in a high-risk environment. Every day in the backcountry requires us to be efficient managers of this risk. In order to do so, we must first be able to identify the source and the cause of the risks we encounter. Our decision-making process involves identifying risks, quantifying them, evaluating their consequences, and then acting to mitigate them to an acceptable level for the group.

In this process, we often overlook the risk we ourselves bring to the table—the possibility that our own human behavior will increase our risk beyond what we are conscious of. We refer to this internal risk as *human factors*. Human factors come not only from ourselves, but from our interactions and decisions with our fellow skiers. Understanding human factors, how they affect our decision-making, and how to mitigate them is the purpose of this section.

A review of 1990s avalanche statistics shows human factors to be the primary factors in fatal avalanche accidents; terrain, weather, and snowpack conditions are generally contributing factors. In fact, human factors are responsible for almost 90 percent of avalanche accidents. This is especially true when it comes to people with prior avalanche education.

Human factors are impossible to completely remove from the equation—we are all human. The key to assessing the human factor problem is not our ability to observe the snowpack, weather, and terrain, but our ability to process this information and to understand what human factors can affect our decisions about terrain selection.

COMMON HUMAN FACTORS

The following list of common human factors is modified from the AIARE Level 1 manual. Think back to your last backcountry trip and see if you can identify any of the following human factors or if you can begin your own list.

Age and gender. In general, younger males (typically aged 17–27) are more willing to accept risk than older people and females.

Dependents. In general, people who have dependents (especially young children) tend to be less willing to accept risk than those with no dependents.

Technical proficiency/physical condition. Those who have a high level of technical proficiency and are in excellent physical condition are often more willing to accept risk than novices.

Blue-sky syndrome. Conditions never seem as bad when the sun is shining and the skies are blue, so people tend to be more aggressive in good weather than in bad.

Fun factor. The enjoyment derived from skiing provides a powerful urge to have fun in spite of suspecting or knowing avalanche conditions may be less than ideal. People are less apt to turn back when they are having or anticipating fun.

Goal seeking. The more important the objective, the more people are willing to ignore risks to achieve it.

Logic vs. emotion. It's common for people to make emotional decisions when anticipating a good time, when near a goal, or when in a group from which they are seeking validation. In such cases, emotion can overpower the logic that indicates conditions are marginal.

"Real" risk. At times, perceived risks can obscure real risks. For example, someone who is afraid of falling may perceive that to be the main hazard while on an unstable slope, when in fact the real risk is an avalanche. Someone may perceive the risk of avalanches to be low because she is on a small feature, while the real risk is a terrain trap into which she will be carried should an avalanche occur.

Back to the barn syndrome. The urge to simply "get it over with" and return to safety, food, and shelter is powerful. Late in the day, when people are tired and nearly home, is a time when poor decisions are often made.

Negative event feedback loop. If people are unaware of exposure to risk or if they deliberately expose themselves and nothing happens, they eventually become hardened to that risk and may, in time, expose themselves without undertaking a proper decision-making process. At that point they are simply taking chances instead of making a calculated, conscious decision to accept risk.

The "risky-shift" effect. Groups find security in numbers and tend to accept risks that no individual in that group would be willing to accept if alone.

Communications and empathy. People who do not communicate well and/or have little empathy for others may "bully" a friend or acquaintance into accepting and playing along with a poor decision.

Stress and pressure. Decision-making is compromised when people are under stress or when there is pressure to perform. Stress and pressure are often perceived to be coming from external sources (like the members on your ski tour), when in reality they often result from internal factors (desire to meet expectations, fear of failure, inexperience or uncertainty, etc.).

Low self-confidence. Lack of self-confidence can lead people to distrust their instinct and allow them to agree with a decision that they intuitively feel is wrong. In some cases, people with little formal training, or group members with less experience than the leader may observe or become aware of significant data that are crucial to the decision being made. These people are often unwilling to challenge or question the "experienced" leader or status quo in the group, even when they have information or knowledge that others do not.

Unwillingness to listen to others. In many cases, more "experienced" leaders are unwilling to listen to the concerns or feelings of "less experienced" group members who may have information or knowledge that is pertinent.

Overconfidence. Often, "experienced" and "knowledgeable" people misinterpret the data they themselves have observed and recorded. In many cases, this is due to overconfidence in one's training, personal knowledge, and/or experience.

Limited observations. Looking at one or even several variables in isolation does not account for the infinite potential combinations and permutations. In many cases accidents result not from a single variable but from a combination; the cumulative effect of one variable acting in combination with others greatly compounds the problem and increases the complexity of assessing conditions.

Lack of experience. Effective decision-making in the complex game of avalanches and ski touring relies primarily on a broad and deep experience base accumulated over time in a variety of situations. If someone lacks experience in a given situation, intuition can let even the "experts" down.

Lack of leadership. When there is a lack of clear leadership or command, the decision-making process often stalls. This is especially true in peer groups where there is no formal command structure to facilitate the process of taking in information, analyzing it, and acting. In some cases, inaction is as dangerous as making the wrong decision.

The big picture. It's easy to narrow your focus and concentrate closely on one or two factors, especially in a difficult situation, if an error is made, or when experiencing problems. This may lead to missing significant, critical factors in other areas of concern or missing the cumulative effect of several, apparently minor factors that are working in concert. It is essential that decision makers maintain a clear view of the overall situation and maintain their awareness of all pertinent factors.

HEURISTIC TRAPS IN
AVALANCHE ACCIDENTS

The human factors listed above identify behavior patterns that put us at risk. In recent years, the avalanche community has been working to understand and quantify these behaviors and to look scientifically at the mechanisms the brain uses to make decisions. One of these mechanisms is called *heuristics*.

Researcher Ian McCammon says that a heuristic is a "rule of thumb that guides most of our decisions in everyday life" and while they work most of the time, they don't always translate to good decision-making in avalanche terrain. McCammon has done significant research on the role human factors and heuristics play in recreational avalanche accidents (see "Heuristic Traps in Recreational Avalanche Accidents" referenced in the appendix). His findings show that we are most likely to fall into what he calls "heuristic traps" during times of uncertainty or when faced with the gray areas of hazard (moderate to considerable) that recreational backcountry users often encounter.

According to McCammon, these are the six most common heuristic traps:

Familiarity. People often feel comfort with areas they are familiar with, but statements like "I've never seen it avalanche here before," mean nothing. If there is unstable snow on a slope steep enough to slide and a trigger, it can avalanche no matter how familiar you may be with the area.

Social proof. Others are at the trailhead and heading out, so it must be safe!

Commitment/consistency. Stating a goal and committing to it prior to the actual day of the trip can lead to problems. We all want to be true to our word. Sometimes the commitment needs to be reexamined given the existing conditions.

Scarcity. Powder fever! The idea that all the powder will be skied up by the people we saw at the trailhead makes us rush our decisions and filter out important data.

Acceptance. The tendency to engage in activities we think will get us noticed or accepted by our peers or by people whose respect we want.

Expert halo. The tendency to assign the "expert" moniker to someone within the group who may not fully deserve that designation.

WHAT TO DO ABOUT
THE HUMAN FACTOR

Identifying and understanding the role human factors and common heuristics play in our decisions to select appropriate terrain, and the common factors and heuristic traps to look out for, are only the first steps. We must arm ourselves with the best tools possible to mitigate the chance of falling victim to an accident of our own making.

Currently, the best tool we have is open communication, which is central to the following lists of tools and questions to ask yourself and your partners. Use these tools and questions before embarking and while on your next backcountry trip. And as more research is done, pay attention to keep yourself from becoming a static backcountry user who is vulnerable to the human factor.

Tools to minimize the human factor:

■ Give yourself options in the tour-planning stage. Groups with more than one option are more likely to forgo a particular slope if a member feels unsure about it.

■ Communicate with the group (fig. 2.19). The key is to ask questions of the group. Asking questions will foster better communication.

■ Challenge and monitor all group decisions. This is a responsibility all members must accept.

■ Think out loud. Keep in mind that everyone is responsible for the outcome—if you have something to say, especially a concern, let the group know.

■ Share observations with the group. We all observe things differently. If you see something that may affect the group decision, by all means speak up.

■ Choose your partners wisely. If you can't openly communicate to your partners about your observations and feelings, then you're increasing the likelihood of being caught in an avalanche.

■ Avalanche safety equipment—*always* carry it, but travel as if you left it at home. We all have a false sense of security with technology—your brain is your best tool in the backcountry.

■ Stick to a smaller group size. Groups greater than six tend to experience communication problems and increased group-dynamic issues.

Fig. 2.19 Routefinding discussion: communication helps mitigate the human factor.

■ Increase your situational awareness. Take responsibility for your own avalanche education, and resist the tendency to fall into a skin track without looking around you.

■ Risk acceptance will differ between party members. Recognize this and weigh it when discussing options.

Questions to ask of yourself and your group:

■ Does anyone have any objectives other than the ones we discussed in our tour plan?

■ What does everyone think the avalanche danger is today? This question is a way to see who did their tour planning and possibly to assess individual risk acceptance.

■ Constantly ask the pertinent negative: What don't you/we like about this situation?

■ Ask about turnaround topics: What do we need to see today to make us want to turn around? For example, what if the wind slabs are bigger than we expected?

■ Are all the necessary ingredients present to produce an avalanche? Could an avalanche run though here?

■ Consider the premortem tactic: If an accident happened to us in this situation, what might have caused it and did we miss any key observations that may be obvious in hindsight? This can foster dialogue that may lead to missed clues and observations.

OBSERVATIONS AND AWARENESS FOR BACKCOUNTRY TRAVEL

Imagine for a moment that you need to describe to a friend all the factors that go into negotiating your daily commute. Your description will only provide so much help for your friend. Many of the decisions he will have to make during the journey will be outside the scope of your directions (if the light turns yellow, should he speed up or stop?). However, if he pays attention to his surroundings he can navigate these decisions without you. For example, cars heading directly for him might be an indicator of using the wrong on-ramp to get on the freeway. What if your friend could only make decisions based on your directions? He would be unable to deal with any unforeseen factors he encountered on the way. Without the ability to make his own observations, your instructions would be useless to your friend.

In the avalanche world, like the world of commuting, you'll need to make your own observations. In certain situations these observations are blindingly obvious—when you see an avalanche occur you have a good indicator of the stability of that slope. Most of the time, however, you will not be dealing with an easy decision based on one observation. The nature and type of observations includes awareness of a host of information. Until you have built up experience, it may be helpful to use a system to help you remember all the factors involved. The system described here is intended to get you asking the right questions.

There are three main factors that affect or influence avalanche danger: weather, snowpack, and avalanche activity. In each of these categories, look for specific information about the following:

Weather: precipitation, wind, temperature, and solar radiation

Snowpack: snow cover, layers, bonding, whumphing

Avalanche activity: when, where, what, and how

OBSERVING THE WEATHER

What observations will you make about the weather?

Precipitation: type, intensity, and accumulation

Wind: speed, direction, and duration

Temperature: current, max/min temp, and trends/storm trends

Solar radiation: cloud cover, intensity, and duration

Weather observations can be informal (e.g., "It snowed all day"), but it can also be very helpful to understand the language used by members of the scientific and avalanche-study communities. The international snow science and avalanche communities have developed some specific methods of observing and recording the weather; this allows for open communication of weather data across international borders. For resources regarding weather observations, please see the appendix.

OBSERVING THE SNOWPACK

What can you observe about the snowpack?

Snow cover: height, strength, and variability

Layers: strength, temperatures, and grain characteristics

Bonding: strength, plane characteristics, and failure layer

Whumphing: initiation, propagation, and extent

Snowpack observations are valuable pieces of information we gather along the way to help compare and contrast the current snow conditions with the information accumulated during the planning phase. Observations about the snowpack fall into two main categories: snow profiles and active tests.

Snow Profiles

Snow profiles can be performed using informal or formal observations. In making formal observations, the goal is to gather detailed and specific data about one or all of the following: snow crystals, layers, temperatures, and the bonds between layers. The techniques and methods used in doing so—crystal and layer identification, measuring temperature, bonding tests (compression and Rutschblock)—are quite specific. To learn how to correctly make formal observations about the snowpack, we highly recommend taking an avalanche course offered by a provider that is part of a national or international organization (see the appendix).

What about snow pits? How often have you heard the phrase, "We dug a pit, then we decided to ski it"? A snow pit—or snow profile—is a way of looking directly at the snowpack. It is important to understand that not all snow profiles are created equal—they can be a quick check for a known weak layer, or a source of extensive data taken twice daily and used for avalanche forecasting.

As a backcountry skier, once you learn how to dig a snow profile you will probably fall somewhere in between. Regardless of what kind of profile you dig, the most important thing to understand is that *the data you collect tells you what is happening in that exact spot only.* This is called snowpack variability: specifically, it means that snowpack depth, composition (crystals and layers), and characteristics vary drastically and unpredictably across terrain.

What are the implications of snowpack variability for the backcountry skier? It means that data gathered in a snow profile should be used for information gathering to test hypotheses formed during the tour-planning process (*what do you expect to see?*). Information from a snow profile should *not* be used to make a go–no go decision. If you decided to ski a slope, it should be part of the decision-making process that began with your tour planning, not a quick choice based on one piece of information.

A note on snow science. Keep in mind that less technical information can be easier to gather and requires less training and experience to correctly interpret. As such, it can be useful to decision makers of any experience level. This is not to discourage you from pursuing the science, looking at grain types under a magnifier, or doing shear tests; just approach decisions conservatively using this data until you have appropriate experience and training in its interpretation.

Active Tests

Active tests are techniques you can use to gather information about the snowpack as you are moving through terrain. Many of these tests can be quickly performed without getting out your shovel or digging a pit. The results of these tests are not scientific data. Rather, they are indicators you can use to check against your expectations from your tour plan: *what am I actually seeing?*

The more information you can gather, the better—active tests can provide you with many small pieces of information across varied terrain (e.g., is there wind loading on this aspect as we move up in elevation?).

Ski Pole Test

The ski pole test is one of the quickest tests a backcountry skier can do, so it can be done many times over the course of a tour without interrupting the flow of travel.

The objective. To determine relative layer densities.

How to perform. Push your pole into the snow. Next, move the pole off-center in the hole you just created. Now, carefully pull the pole up and out of the snow, feeling for the different layers in the snowpack. Can you feel a specific layer? Are they stacked as you expected? Is there a strong layer over a weak layer? You can also use this test to gauge the depth of surface snow over a crust.

Hand Shear Test

The hand shear test is a nonstandardized test similar to a shovel shear test requiring nothing more than your hand (see *Snow, Weather, and Avalanches* referenced in the appendix for more detail on the shovel shear test).

The objective. To determine cohesiveness of surface snow, bonding strength between layers, or to check for the presence of a hidden weak layer.

How to perform. On the uphill side of the track, isolate a column of snow using your gloved hand (the ski track removes the compressive support of the column). The column can be any size, given that this is a nonstandardized test, but a column with the surface area of your shovel is a good place to start. Next, place your hand behind (on the uphill side of) the column and give it a pull downhill—try to do this with an even force that progressively becomes greater. Note how easy or hard it is to slide the block. Did the block come off with relative ease, or did you have to pull hard to get it to move? Note the plane of failure: does it look smooth, or is it rough and uneven?

Observations While Skiing/Skinning

This test requires nothing more than your senses, feeling and looking at the snow as you ski or skin through it.

The objective. To note anything and everything in regards to the snow as you travel through it and to compare the findings to your pretrip research.

What to look for. Snow-surface changes, depth and characteristics of the snow. As you move through different areas, do you notice density changes of the layers? Do you see any evidence of wind effect?

Signs of instability are *cracks* and *whumphing*. As you move through the snow, be on the lookout for cracks that shoot out from your skis. Whumphing—so called because of the noise the snowpack creates—occurs when a portion of the snowpack collapses suddenly. These can be visual and auditory indicators of instability (a slab over a weak layer).

OBSERVING AVALANCHE ACTIVITY

What can you observe about avalanche activity?

When: current, recent, past

Where: area, terrain configuration, terrain traps

What: natural triggers, human trigger, other triggers

How: destructive potential, propagation, failure layer

One of the best clues in evaluating stability is the presence of avalanche activity. As you might expect, observing an avalanche on a slope is an indicator of the poor stability of that slope. What about the slope across the valley, or those with similar aspects and elevations? As you move through the mountains, constantly look for the signs of previous and current avalanche activity. The more recent the activity is and the more closely the slope matches the one you're on, the more relevant the information becomes.

INTERPRETING YOUR OBSERVATIONS

The final question is how you interpret your observations. Think of quantifying your observations as critical to snow stability or not. *Red flag values* are observations that meet or exceed critical parameters in each observation. Red flags indicate that avalanche danger may be increasing. The greater the number of red flags you observe, the greater the potential avalanche hazard may be. Make sure to connect your observations of red flags with your tour-planning process—often you will have a mental list of red flags you expect to see (based on the weather and avalanche forecast).

The observations and red flag values discussed here are a significant part of the decision-making process. Few or no special tools are required to make many of the observations or determine if red flag values have been attained. Many of the observations require only that you be looking around you with a keen awareness. In making observations, remember your goal is information gathering—observations will help you evaluate the expectations and hypotheses formed in your tour planning and preparation.

RED FLAG VALUES FOR WEATHER, SNOWPACK, AND AVALANCHE ACTIVITY

Weather

Precipitation:

Type: rain or heavy snow

Intensity: greater than 1 inch per hour

Accumulation: greater than 12 inches in the last 12 hours

Wind:

Speed: strong enough to move snow (about 15 miles per hour)

Direction: loading snow on aspects where you will travel

Duration: several hours or more

Temperature:

Current: at or greater than 0°C/32°F

Max/min temp over last 12 hours: at or greater than 0°C/32°F

Trends/storm trends: colder to warmer temps during a storm

Solar radiation:

Cloud cover: intensifying radiation or allowing high radiation

Intensity: strong

Duration: long—greater than an hour or two

Snowpack

Snow Cover:

Height: less than 5 feet

Strength: weak

Variability: high—deep in some areas, shallow in others

Layers:

Strength: strong layer over weak layer

Temperatures: near 0°C/32°F

Grain characteristics: large, loosely packed, angular/faceted

Bonding:

Strength: test results from CTV (Compression Test Very Easy, fractures during the cutting of the column), CTE (Compression Test Easy, fractures with between 0–10 taps), or CTM (Compression Test Moderate, fractures with between 10–20 taps); Rutschblock less than or equal to 4

Plane characteristics: smooth, clean shears at failure

Failure layer: large, loosely packed, angular grains

Whumphing:

Initiation: natural or human trigger

Propagation: far, greater than 10 feet

Extent: widespread

Avalanche Activity

When:

Current: observed or occurred in last 12 hours

Recent: 12–36 hours maritime climate, 12–48 hours continental climate

Past: greater than 36/48 hours, do conditions still exist?

Where:

Area: widespread

Terrain configuration: terrain similar to where you travel

Terrain traps: traps exist where avalanches are running

What:

Natural triggers: any natural triggers are observed

Human trigger: any human triggers are observed

Other triggers: remote triggers are observed

How:

Destructive potential: greater or equal to a D2

Propagation: wide fracture lines that run far

Failure layer: failing on weak layers

(Source: AIARE curriculum)

Analyzing the effects of red flags, assessing current danger ratings, and evaluating how much or how fast the danger will change requires a higher level of training than can be provided in a book or even in a course. Over and above training, analysis and assessment of avalanche danger requires a depth of experience that no one source can provide. Even for experts, analyzing and forecasting snow stability and avalanche danger is an inexact science loaded with extrapolation and probability.

Many of the most experienced decision-makers will allow for a margin of error, with margins being greater when uncertainty is higher. Those with lesser training and experience should always err on the side of caution when learning to select terrain as part of the decision-making process. This is especially true when conditions are ambiguous, when you feel uncertainty, or when conditions are beyond the scope of your training or experience.

Twenty-five degrees and still scary in a touchy snowpack in the Canadian Rockies

DECISION-MAKING APPLIED

How can you keep track of all the information and observations that make up your decision-making process? How can you apply the decision-making process in any region, be it your home mountains or on a trip? Below is a series of questions designed to assist the backcountry traveler in decision-making, organized into the acronym STOP, which stands for: *Snowpack and Weather, Terrain, Options, People.*

Use this acronym in three ways: as part of your pretrip decision-making, at the trailhead, and throughout the tour.

PREPARATION STOP: PRETRIP PLANNING

Planning and preparation is the foundation for your decision-making process in the backcountry. Your first STOP occurs at home before the trip.

Snowpack and Weather: Check the avalanche bulletin, the weather forecast, and the snow report.
- Record snowpack info: What are layers of concern? Are there weak layers, or strong over weak? What aspects and elevations?
- What are the forecasted weather trends for precipitation, wind, temperature, and solar radiation?
- What is the hazard rating, and is it trending better or worse? Why?

Terrain: Use guidebooks, maps, photos, online trip reports, information from friends or guides.
- Identify potential avalanche terrain on the proposed route.
- Could this terrain produce an avalanche in the current or forecasted conditions?
- Identify potential safer terrain on the proposed route.

Options: Choose alternatives in the terrain.
- What is your ideal route?
- What is a backup, safer route?
- What and where are potential hazards on each option?
- Where are potential observation and information-gathering points en route? What are potential decision-making points en route?

People: Assess the skills and dynamics of the group.
- How compatible is the group?
- What are each skier's ability, experience, and fitness?
- Are there group decisions, or does one person dominate?
- Is the group prepared and trained for rescue, repair, and first aid?
- Is the group agreed on potential decision-making points en route?

TRAILHEAD STOP: IN THE PARKING LOT

Things often change at the trailhead—the group changes, the weather changes, or the gear changes. In doing all of your planning and preparation, your goal was to put together an idea of *what you expect to see.* The trailhead is an excellent place to stop a moment and evaluate how your day is shaping up, and to begin to compare *what you expect* with *what you are seeing.*

Snowpack and Weather: Was the weather forecast correct?
- What were the actual precipitation amounts overnight?
- What is the wind speed and direction?
- What have the temperatures been overnight? What are they now?
- What is the cloud cover? Is it sunny, or raging snow?

Terrain: Does the terrain match your expectations?
- Is the snow cover what you expected?
- Is the visibility good enough to see the terrain?
- Are the potential avalanche start and runout zones what you expected?

Options: Is the group clear on the options and decision-making points?
- Do the options line up with the goals and makeup of the group?

People: Check to see how well the actual group matches the planned group and how well prepared the group is.
- Do you have the necessary group gear—rescue, repair, first aid?
- Individual rescue gear—does everyone have a shovel, beacon, and probe?
- Beacon check—is everyone's beacon functioning correctly in the three-part check?
- Emergency plan—what are emergency phone numbers, where are the car keys?

EN ROUTE STOP: IN THE TERRAIN AND ON THE TOUR

As you move through the terrain, you are continuing to make observations and considering their effect on your terrain selection. Is the avalanche hazard trending higher or lower? The en route STOPs will occur throughout the day, both at points you have picked out as part of your tour plan and as the terrain presents the opportunity.

Snowpack and Weather: Based on your observations, what are current conditions and trends? Are they what you expected them to be? Are there red flags there?
- Can you see any evidence of avalanche activity?
- Do active tests show any signs you had anticipated? Cracks, whumphs, layers in pole tests, hand shears?

- If you do a field pit, do your results confirm your expectations? Are there strong layers over weak layers? Do you find them widespread in the terrain, or only in specific locations?
- Is there a significant amount of new snow or precipitation? Is wind transport occurring?
- How good is the visibility and how strong is the solar radiation?
- Are the temperatures warming or cooling?

Terrain: What is the nature and extent of avalanche terrain?

- Are you making observations in areas of terrain similar to those you want to ski?
- Does your route take you into potential start zones or runout zones?
- Could this terrain initiate an avalanche in the current conditions?
- Can you select terrain to protect yourselves from the avalanche hazard?

Options: What options do you have to mitigate the hazard at this point?

- What alternatives do you have for your route through this hazard?
- Can you use travel techniques to mitigate the hazard? Would spreading out be effective?
- Are you on your time plan?

People: How are people functioning as a group?

- Is the group keen on making observations, or do they just want to ski it?
- What is the group's experience level in making and interpreting observations about the snowpack?
- Is communication working among the group? Does everyone know what the plan is?
- Is the group aware of potential human factors/heuristic traps at work?
- Is everyone eating/drinking/warm enough? Is anyone getting tired or falling behind?

(Source: Colin Zacharias, UIAGM guide, CAA and AIARE avalanche instructor and examiner for the ACMG)

CHAPTER 3

Plateau de Géant, France

Navigation

Navigation is important for ski touring and ski mountaineering. Travel on skis takes place on snow, which means you aren't likely to be following a trail all the time. Your tours may also lead you to the high alpine or glaciated terrain, both of which can magnify the difficulties of moving in poor or nonexistent visibility. The value of doing your own navigation on skis is even greater than in other disciplines, like hiking or mountaineering: if you're always following someone else's tracks, how will you ever find the untouched powder stashes you seek?

This chapter focuses on those elements of navigation that are most useful for ski touring and ski mountaineering. For more in-depth treatment of navigation, see the resources in the appendix.

Fig. 3.1 Navigation tools: map, compass, GPS unit, and altimeter

NAVIGATION TOOLS

The tools used for navigation are map, compass, altimeter, and Global Positioning System (GPS) unit (fig. 3.1). Of all four tools, the GPS unit is the most likely to run out of battery power. For that reason, we

emphasize parallel navigation: use your map-compass-altimeter set, and use your GPS unit for backup. If your batteries die and you have no map-compass-altimeter navigation tools, you'll promptly find yourself in a pickle!

Map. "Tour Planning" in chapter 2 discusses the information available on topographical maps. Here are some basics for choosing and using this tool:

- Obtain the most accurate maps you can, and make sure they are readable. Squinting at a poorly printed map is a great way to start off on the wrong foot.
- Get a good map case or print the map on waterproof paper. One of the keys to navigation is accessibility of your instruments. Whether you wear the map around your neck or stuff it in your pocket, you must have a protective layer of some sort to keep it from being destroyed when you're navigating in the elements.

Compass. The necessary characteristics of a good compass are as follows:

- Adjustable declination. This is crucial for on-the-fly navigation.
- Flip lid with a mirror for shooting bearings. This is important for accuracy in shooting bearings.
- Magnetic. If you have a compass in any other gadget, use it as a backup. Your compass should not require batteries to function correctly.

Declination is the difference between true north and magnetic north. If you drew a straight line from where you're standing to the geographical location of the North Pole, that line would point to true north. However, when you look at your compass to find north, the arrow points in the direction indicated by the earth's magnetic fields. These fields vary over time and space and don't always point in the same direction as your true-north line. Declination accounts for this difference and allows you to move between your compass, which shows magnetic north, and your map, which shows true north.

Following a bearing means setting a bearing on your compass dial, rotating your body until the compass needle aligns with magnetic north, and then proceeding in the direction indicated by the compass.

Taking a bearing in the field means pointing your compass to a landmark and aligning the needle to magnetic north in order to obtain a compass heading. Key points in this process are keeping the compass level, using the sights and/or mirror so you can take a bearing with your arm extended, and aligning the needle correctly.

Plotting a bearing on a map happens once you have a bearing from the field. Place your compass on the map with the front-side corner touching the known landmark. Rotate the rest of the compass until north on the compass face lines up with north on the map. Draw a line along the edge of the compass; you are somewhere on that line.

Taking a bearing from a map means placing your compass on the map, pointing from one point to another, and aligning north on the compass dial (NOT the needle) to north on the map. This gives you the bearing to get from one point to another.

You can then follow this bearing in the field, provided your compass has an adjustable declination that is set correctly.

Altimeter. This is a crucial piece of equipment for navigation in any conditions. Make sure you have at least one altimeter that is connected to a barometer (versus those linked to your position in a GPS).

GPS. Entire books have been written about selecting, purchasing, and using a GPS unit (see "Navigation" in the appendix). In general, seek out a GPS unit with a good, intuitive user interface, plenty of memory for storing waypoints, and a good interface with the available electronic mapping programs.

NAVIGATION TECHNIQUES

Once you have the basic knowledge of how to read maps and use a compass, you can begin to apply your navigation in the field, bringing all tools to the mix—map, compass, altimeter, and GPS. In every case, navigation with map-compass-altimeter requires that you start navigating *before* you're lost. If you don't know where you are, you have no reference point to use for navigation. This is one of the main strengths of the GPS unit: you can get completely lost and turn it on, and instantly you'll have your location as a reference point.

PINPOINTING YOUR LOCATION
Also called resection, this technique requires that you have some visibility, as you will need at least two pieces of information

to locate yourself, plus your elevation for verification. If you are on a ski tour and the visibility begins to deteriorate, make sure you have time to gather bearings before you lose sight of your landmarks.

Pinpointing using resection is often (incorrectly) called triangulation. Shoot a bearing on at least two different landmarks that also exist on your map. Plot each bearing on the map, making sure the front of your compass is correctly oriented. The intersection of the two lines you plot will give you your location; use your altitude to verify this intersection and increase your accuracy.

Tip: When pinpointing your location, try to use landmarks that are close to 90 degrees apart.

WHITEOUT NAVIGATION USING MAP AND COMPASS
In ski touring and ski mountaineering, you are often forced to navigate in a full-blown whiteout above tree line (fig. 3.2). Whiteout navigation is a skill that requires attention to detail and planning, and planning beforehand is essential: it is much easier to plot whiteout navigation *before* you are in a whiteout (as discussed in "Tour Planning" in chapter 2). Ideally, you will have landmarks, bearings, elevations, and distances already plotted on your map, ready for use.

Walking a Bearing on Skis
Human error is often the crux of whiteout navigation. Humans are not symmetrically

built, and as a result it is difficult for us to walk in a straight line if we have no reference points to guide us.

Point to point. This method can be used if you have just enough visibility in your near field to pick out objects ahead of you. While standing still, set your bearing and pick an object that falls on the imaginary line leading ahead of you on your bearing. Skin along with your compass out and your eyes on the object. When you reach the object, pick out another object ahead of you and continue leapfrogging from point to point. As you go, check behind you to see how straight your ski track is.

Using a moving point. There are times when the whiteout is total, and you are peering into what looks like the inside of a ping-pong ball. In this case you can use a person to provide your reference point.

- Send one person out front, as far away from you as possible, but close enough that you can still see him, and he can still hear you.
- Stand still and orient your skis to point exactly along your bearing.
- Direct the point person to move left or right until he is standing exactly in line with your bearing. Make sure his skis are pointing in the same direction as yours.
- Begin skinning forward together, watching your compass all the while. As soon as your point person begins to deviate, instruct him to correct his direction. The point person needs to adjust only slightly to stay in a straight line. Ideally, he will do so by rotating his skis slightly, then moving ahead again. This method

Fig. 3.2 Whiteout navigation in the Bernese Oberland, Switzerland

requires patience and good communication between the point person and compass holder, but with practice you can settle into steady movement.
- If you are on a glacier, you can use this technique with a rope between the point person and the navigator.

Handrailing

No matter how good you are, you will deviate somewhat from your bearing given a long enough distance. To set yourself up for success, you can incorporate the technique of handrailing into your tour planning and whiteout navigation. Handrailing is when you use large or distinct terrain features in your whiteout navigation plan as reference objects. The following are a few ways you can use handrailing to your advantage:
- Stay close to a large feature—like a cliff or a ridge—that borders a glacier or snowfield.
- When you shoot a bearing across a wide-open space, aim for a big feature, then follow that feature to find smaller features or more difficult spots. For

instance, if you are crossing a glacier to find a col, aim for the cliffs to the side of the col, then follow the cliffs until you reach the col. The cliffs are your handrail.

Contour-Tangent Method

In convoluted or technical terrain, it can be difficult to determine the correct descent route in a total whiteout. Before you set your group up for a skin back out of the wrong drainage or put them at risk of skiing above unknown hazards, check the aspect of the slope you are about to descend to make sure you are going the right way:

- Stand in the snow with your skis totally flat and perpendicular to the fall line. Imagine that you are lining your skis up so they are tangent to a contour line on the map.
- Use your compass to shoot a bearing perpendicular to your skis, straight down the fall line.
- Your bearing gives you the aspect of the slope you are standing on. Check this aspect with your map: does it match the aspect of the slope you think you are on?

Creating Visibility as You Ski

Skiing blindly downhill in a whiteout can be extremely dangerous; you have no way of knowing if you are about to ski off a wind lip, into a crevasse, or off a cliff. Whether you are on a glacier or a snowfield, you can mitigate these hazards by creating visibility in front of you as you ski. There are several ways to do this:

- Use a tightly wound prusik or cordelette (or a tree branch) as your "mouse." Roll the bundle down the hill in front of you as you ski. The mouse will show you if there is a change in slope angle or a sudden hole.
- Throw a snowball. It often gives enough contrast to make out the slope right in front of you.
- Go fishing. Tie a long cordelette to the end of your ski pole with a weight (knots or a carabiner) at the end of it. Cast your fishing line out ahead of you to provide depth perception and make sure the way is clear.
- The probe sweep. Assemble your probe and use it to sweep an arc in front of you as you ski. Doing so will show you what the snow surface ahead of you is like.

These methods can all be used moving up, down, or sidehilling. Traveling in a whiteout—especially on a glacier—is dangerous business, and using these techniques can drastically increase your ability to travel safely.

NAVIGATION USING GPS

Going into full detail about navigating with GPS is beyond the scope of this book. Instead, we discuss the philosophy of navigating via GPS and the powerful tool of combining mapping software and a GPS unit for tour planning. See the appendix for additional resources.

A GPS unit is an indispensable tool for whiteout navigation. At the same time, relying solely on your GPS unit is risky because of the battery issue: no battery power, no tool. Further, if you spend six hours following the arrow on your GPS, how many sets of batteries will you need to bring with you on a tour? What, then, is the best way to incorporate GPS into your navigational toolbox?

There is a balance here. A GPS unit can be used as a check and a backup. If you program all the waypoints of your tour into the unit before you leave the house, you can turn it on and check your location—and your position relative to any of the waypoints—at any time during the tour. Navigate using map and compass, and if you are ever uncertain,

double-check with the GPS unit. In this way you avoid using all your batteries by having the unit on all day (particularly useful if you are out for more than one day). You also minimize the time it takes to use your GPS unit in the field—pre-programmed waypoints prevent head scratching in bad weather. Finally, if you need to you can use the GPS unit to obtain your position and plot it on your map as a last check. See "Tour Planning" in chapter 2 for information on using a computer, map, and GPS unit to plan for whiteout navigation.

TEST HOW STRAIGHT YOU CAN WALK

You can do this exercise with several friends. Find a frozen, snow-covered lake, pond, or any wide-open spot with a uniform surface. Line everyone up on one side of it, skis and skins on, separated by 40 feet or so. When everyone in line is in place, have them cover their eyes with a scarf or hat. Send one point person (not blindfolded) out to the middle of the space, a few hundred yards away if possible, and have them stand still. The person without a blindfold then yells to everyone, so they can all hear the direction from which her voice is coming.

Now for the fun part. All the blindfolded parties walk toward where they think the point person is. That person remains silent as the skiers move. Each blindfolded person is directed to walk the direction and distance they think is correct to reach the person, then to stop and wait. When the point person sees that everyone has stopped, she gives permission for everyone to open their eyes. Inevitably, people have skinned to the left, to the right—anywhere but in a straight line to where they thought they were going.

This exercise is a great visual reminder of how hard it is to walk straight in a whiteout, and it allows you to figure out which direction you tend to curve when walking blind.

CHAPTER 4

Touring for powder in the Canadian Rockies

Uphill Movement

How many times do you learn to walk in a lifetime? Most of us might immediately answer, "Just once." But pause a moment and think about walking in broader terms. What about learning to walk in heels, or learning to walk in crampons? Anyone who has tried either would agree that each requires a special set of movement skills above and beyond a normal stride. If you wish to move successfully through the backcountry, it's time to learn to walk again—this time, with skis and climbing skins attached to your feet.

Why learn new walking techniques for skiing? Safety, efficiency, style, or simply the desire for perfection are all possible answers. Good technique while moving uphill can increase your safety as you move through terrain and can help prevent injury. It can extend your range by creating efficient use of your finite energy supply, and it can turn your uphill experience from

a punishing slog into an enjoyable and challenging aspect of the tour.

In this chapter, we discuss two aspects of movement uphill with skis: first, the act of skinning itself, and second, the setting of a skin track.

SKINNING: THE MOTION

Skinning uphill should ultimately be a smooth, even, and efficient movement. Your legs and hips should be doing all the work, and your upper body should be relatively calm, hinging smoothly at your hips with each step. In this section we break this movement into its basic elements: body position, the step, the stride, ankle position, and shoulders and arms. We also discuss the uses—and abuses—of heel lifters in skinning technique.

BODY POSITION

When skinning uphill you should be coming to an upright stance as you weight each step. Good posture—head up and shoulders back—will keep you from leaning forward.

Before you take a step, try standing with your skins on, skis pointing uphill on a slight incline. Keep your back straight with your knees slightly bent, and focus on pressing your weight down through your heels. Pick a stance that allows you good balance, with your feet and skis slightly less than shoulder-width apart (fig. 4.1). You should be able to stand without putting any weight on your poles; efficient skinning is not an upper body exercise.

THE STEP

When taking a step with skins on, your ultimate goal is to use as little energy as possible. This is accomplished by using your frame as much as you do your muscles.

Fig. 4.1 Have a good upright stance with weight in your heels.

1. Begin with your hip/hip flexor, and draw your leg forward from the point where it attaches to your body. Imagine snapping a whip in slow motion from behind you to out in front of you—your hip bone is the handle of the whip, and your foot is the end of the whip. By moving the handle of the whip you cause the motion to propagate along the length of the whip until it reaches the end.

   You should be able to set your leg forward using only a slight rotation of your hip and hip flexor. The key to doing this successfully is to resist the urge to lift your foot—and ski—off the ground (fig. 4.2a shows incorrect motion). Lead with your hip and draw the ski forward from your boot toe—the end of the whip—keeping

Fig. 4.2b Lead with your hip and draw the ski forward with your boot toe.

Fig. 4.2a Incorrect step – don't lift the ski off the snow.

your skins in contact with the snow surface throughout the movement (fig. 4.2b).

2. Once you have "snapped" your foot out as far as you want it to go (fig. 4.3a), shift your weight forward onto that foot (fig. 4.3b), bend the knee, and stand up using your leg muscles (fig. 4.3c). In the motion of standing up, lead with your hips instead of your shoulders; doing so will help you hinge upright with each step and will keep your center of gravity in the correct place over your skis (fig. 4.3d).

   With each step, make sure to check in with the rest of your body. Are you ending your step upright, head up? Or have you bent at the waist and begun to lean forward? (fig. 4.4.) Making sure your torso

Fig. 4.3a "Snap" your foot forward in front of you.

Fig. 4.3b Shift your weight forward onto front foot.

Fig. 4.3c Bend the knee and stand up using your leg muscles.

Fig. 4.3d As you stand, hinge your hips forward so you come upright with each step. At the same time, begin your next step by leading with your hip and drawing the back ski forward.

Fig. 4.4 Make sure you are not staying bent at the waist for the whole step, especially in steeper terrain. You may need to bend forward as part of the step, but focus on hinging upright as you weight each step.

hinges upright in gradual terrain will set you up for success when you move into steeper territory.

Tip: If you find you are not hinging upright with each step, pick a point ahead of you and keep your eyes on it as you walk. Focus on the scenery, not on the skin track!

THE STRIDE

What is the best stride to use—long or short? There is no absolute rule on this. You will find that strides vary—person to person, in steeper or mellower terrain, on a long day or during a ski mountaineering race. For most people, their ideal stride is their most efficient stride. Your most efficient stride will vary based on the terrain and pace at which you are moving. In steeper terrain it is more strenuous to take large steps, and until you have excellent technique it is difficult to maintain efficient movement during high-speed skinning.

How do you find your most efficient stride? Pick a slope with a constant angle, and experiment. Put your boots in walk mode and loosen your upper buckles. Make the longest step you can and feel how much energy you are using. Now gradually step shorter distances until you feel you are on the line perfectly between a long stride and an efficient stride. Now try taking the shortest strides you can (see how much energy that can waste, too!), and then gradually lengthen them to that efficient point.

The bottom line: your ideal stride is unique to your body. It will be dictated by a combination of your technique, flexibility, and the proportions of your muscle groups and bone structures. Remember, a long or short stride isn't necessarily faster or slower. An efficient stride will use the least amount of energy to move through given terrain at a given pace.

ANKLE POSITION

You want to keep the surface of your skins in contact with the snow whenever possible. This applies when you're traversing a slope as well: when traversing, your skins lose some contact with the snow, and you must use your technique to correct the situation.

With each step, roll your ankle slightly downhill to bring your skis in maximum contact with the snow surface (fig. 4.5). Most backcountry boots will give you enough lateral range to do this, provided you are in walk mode and have your upper buckles appropriately loose. This becomes particularly important on ice and hardpacked snow (we will revisit this in "Skinning in Difficult Conditions," later in this chapter).

Fig. 4.5 Use your knees and ankles to roll your skis slightly downhill. This brings more of the skin in contact with the snow.

SHOULDERS AND ARMS

What are your arms doing when you are skinning? The answer varies depending upon terrain. Are you skinning up the fall line, or traversing a slope? It also depends on your pace. At an efficient speed, your arms will be doing very little, whereas at a race pace you may be using them a lot.

From an efficiency standpoint, the primary thing your arms should *not* be doing is pushing you uphill; if you come home from a ski tour with sore wrists or triceps, you need to work on your skinning form. When walking on flat ground or moving directly up the fall line, do whatever is most efficient for you—gentle pole plants with each step, alongside the same or alternating foot.

When traversing a slope, make sure to keep your shoulders on a horizontal axis. Do this by sliding your uphill hand down on the shaft of the pole until your shoulders are relaxed and your hands are at about equal height (fig. 4.6). This will keep you balanced, will protect your shoulders, and will keep your uphill hand warmer, since gravity does not force blood out of your hand.

> **Tip:** If your uphill glove slides down your pole too easily, tape the top part of your pole like a hockey stick, or buy poles with a grip coating.

HEEL LIFTERS

In the world of backcountry skiing, heel lifters (aka heel elevators) are a polarizing issue. Half the population will immediately pop up to the highest setting and set a steep

Fig. 4.6 Good upper body technique when skinning. Notice hand position on uphill pole.

skin track straight up the hill. The other half will flat-out refuse to use their elevators, no matter how steep the track or how bad the pain in their Achilles tendons. Perhaps the best way to think about lifters is as an available tool, and there are pros and cons to their application.

Pros:

- Heel elevators ease some of the stretch on your heels and calf muscles, especially in a steeper track.
- They can save you energy in a steep track by allowing you to use fewer muscles to make a step (see the "What's Your Angle?" sidebar later this chapter).
- They are very useful for breaking trail in deep snow because they keep your ski tips from diving under the snow with each step.

Cons:

- Heel elevators shift your center of balance forward over your skis and cause your skins to slip if conditions are tricky, just as they would if you were bending at the waist and leaning forward.
- They make it more difficult to roll your ankle and keep the skin surface in contact with the snow surface.
- They can make kick turning more challenging, especially at the highest lift setting.
- Using them will shorten your stride, which can make it less efficient (see the "What's Your Angle?" sidebar later this chapter).
- Setting them up and down frequently during a tour can waste time and interrupt your pace.

In summary, use your elevators when the pros outweigh the cons. At the same time, remember that you can often set a track that doesn't require them.

SKINNING: TURNS

Have you ever watched someone on skins work their way up a zigzag skin track, struggling through each kick turn? Perhaps you have experienced this yourself: wobbling precariously on one foot, with the other foot partway around and the tip or tail stuck in the snow, wondering which knee or hip is going to give out first.

Turning with skins on, whether in a gentle curve or a sharp angle, takes more energy and technique than walking up a straight track. However, a good turn—well staged and smoothly executed—should cause only the slightest blip in the rhythm of your step or the number on your heart-rate monitor.

THE AVA TURN

Before describing kick turns, it is important to understand another method of turning with skins on in low- to medium-angle terrain. The AVA turn—so-named after the shape your skis make doing it—uses less energy than a kick turn and consequently should be used whenever the terrain and slope are appropriate.

To execute an AVA turn, you simply change the orientation of each ski slightly with each step.

The AVA Turn to the Right

1. For the first turning step, rotate your left leg and foot to alter the angle of your ski, making an A shape with your skis instead of the parallel lines of a relaxed stance.
2. For the second turning step, rotate your right ski so that your tails are now together, making a V shape with your two skis.
3. For the third step, turn your left ski tip to the right, making the A shape again with both skis.

You are essentially rotating in place, stepping around in a tight circle whose center is behind you by the tails of your skis. You can begin with either an A or with a V, and using small A's and V's—smaller distances between your ski tips or tails—uses less energy than larger ones.

The AVA Turn Moving Forward

Now you are ready to execute an efficient AVA turn while moving forward. With each A or V step you will move in two directions: forward and to the side.

1. From a parallel stance, move your foot forward as per a regular step, but rotate your leg inward from the hip to place your ski on the snow to make the A shape (fig. 4.7).
2. For your second turn step, move your foot forward and rotate the second ski so that it completes an V (fig. 4.8).

Fig. 4.7 AVA turn: rotate your leg to make an A.

Fig. 4.8 AVA: move the other leg forward and make a V.

3. Keep repeating the process—A, V, A—
until the track behind you traces a
gentle arc in the snow.

Experiment with the steps—you will
discover that you can trace a wide or tight
arc depending on the width of your A or V
relative to the length of your step forward.
To execute a tight turn you don't need to
make huge angling steps—that's a waste of
energy! Instead, decrease the length of your
stride forward and maintain a modest angle
with your skis for each step.

The AVA turn is a powerful tool for moving efficiently through gentle terrain, and
once you are conscious of it you will find
yourself applying it any time you want to
put a curve in your skin track. The curves
you make should be smooth and even, with
a constant radius. This keeps your pace and
stride constant (think efficiency) and gives
a clean line (think style). We discuss this
further in "Track Setting," later this chapter.

On steeper slopes, the AVA turn becomes
strenuous and the efficiency of movement
begins to drop away. While the advanced
skinner can probably continue using it for
steeper turning locations, beyond a
comfortable slope angle it becomes more
efficient to use kick turns.

THE KICK TURN

What are the different kinds of kick turns?
How do they differ? And why do we care?
As we say again and again in this book: in
the mountains, it is vitally important to use
the right tool or technique at the right time.

The skis, boots, and bindings you can
use in the backcountry are many and
varied. Some alpine touring bindings have
springs in them, which cause the ski to
return to the heel when the ski is lifted in
the air, and some do not. Dynafit bindings
have an almost frictionless hinge point.
Some telemark bindings have high resistance in the boots and cables, and some are
designed with a low-friction pivot point that
allows the ski tail to drop.

There are also many variations in the
terrain through which you'll be moving.
You'll attempt kick turns in steep terrain as
well as flat; on hard or icy snow as well as
floundering in powder. Frequently you'll
be tucked up against a tree or some other
terrain feature that catches your tips or tails
during your turn.

The goal is to have a variety of kick
turns in your bag of tricks. In doing so,
you'll be able to select which technique to
apply at which time. Developing a bag of
tricks takes practice, so don't be afraid to
find a mellow spot to hone your skills. Keep
in mind that doing kick turns shouldn't
hurt, so if something is painful, stop! Untie
the knot you've tied your body into and
consider alternatives.

The Kick Turn Setup

What do all kick turns have in common?
The setup for any kick turn is the same
across the board, and good setup is crucial
for a good kick turn.

Before executing any kick turn, you
must first establish a platform level enough
to keep yourself from sliding backward mid-
turn as your body weight shifts over your
ski. Laying a track up the slope with good

platforms will give the track a wishbone shape (fig. 4.9), and the folks following in your footsteps will thank you for it.

The sequence of a good kick turn setup:

1. Be conscious of your track as you approach the turn. Ease the angle of your track over the space of a few steps before you reach your turn location.

Fig. 4.9 Good platforms for kick turns give the track a wishbone shape. Take a few steps past the turnaround point and then do your kick turn.

2. When you stop to make your turn, do so with your skis at a low angle. If your skins have been slipping at all, set up with your skis perpendicular to the fall line and with your tails at the same elevation as your tips.

3. Once you have arrived in this position, stomp out a ministance for your skis—this is especially important in hard snow conditions.

> **Tip:** Take a couple of steps beyond the place you have chosen to do your kick turn. This will set you up for a low angle upon leaving the kick turn.

Executing the Kick Turn

For the AT skier, how you execute a kick turn depends slightly on whether you're using bindings with springs (like the original Diamir Fritschi binding) or bindings without springs (like the Fritschi Freeride or Dynafit bindings). Bindings with springs keep your ski with your boot when your ski is lifted in the air; whereas when using bindings without springs, the tail of your ski drops when you lift your ski off the snow.

For the tele skier, your kick turn will depend on if you are using a binding with strong return (cable bindings with strong springs) or a binding with a low-friction pivot point.

In any case, for AT and tele setups the first three steps of a kick turn are the same. There are several techniques for finishing your kick turn—choose how to do step 4 depending on the binding you're using.

Making the turn:

1. Begin with a good setup, as described above. In difficult conditions, check the following: if you had no skins on your skis, would you slide forward or backward? If the answer is yes, adjust until your skis are flat (fig. 4.10).

2. Shift your weight to your downhill ski, and use your downhill pole for balance. Place your uphill pole above you and off to the side, high enough on the slope so that your ski can clear it as it swings by (fig. 4.11a). Swing your uphill foot forward, rotate it outward while bending your knee slightly (fig. 4.11b), and draw an arc in the air with your ski tip (fig. 4.11c). You can do this as a flipping motion; use your muscles to get momentum, with your ski going forward and rotating, then let gravity do the rest once the tail of your ski has cleared the snow by your standing foot. After the kick, place both of your poles on the slope above you for balance.

3. Check to make sure that your feet are close together and your skis are almost parallel. The closer your feet are to each other, the smaller the effort required to shift weight from one to the other. If you can get your

Fig. 4.10 Kick turn Step 1: Set up with a low-angle platform.

Fig. 4.11a Kick turn Step 2: Pole positions for the first kick.

Fig. 4.11b Kick turn Step 2: Swing foot forward and rotate it outward with your knee bent.

Fig. 4.11c Kick turn Step 2: Draw an arc in the air with your ski tip.

skis almost parallel and flat, you can prevent a skin slip when shifting your weight to the uphill ski (fig. 4.12). Make sure both poles are on the slope above you, and then shift all your weight from the downhill foot to the uphill foot. This is a simple, subtle motion, and should require minimal effort.

4a. **With binding springs or low-return tele bindings:** Now it's time for some finesse. You must time the motion of your leg with the kick you give your ski. To begin, lift your downhill ski a few inches off the snow and straighten your leg so

your downhill boot drops below your standing boot. When looking down at your feet, your kicking boot should be hidden behind your standing boot.

Now you must kick and rotate your hip simultaneously. You will rotate your kicking foot inward in a motion starting at your hip, keeping your kicking leg below your standing leg and almost straight. Now the finesse: give a quick kick through your heel as you begin to rotate your kicking leg. This will pop the tip of your ski up and drop the tail, thereby allowing you to continue rotating your ski clear of the slope above (figs. 4.13a–c).

Fig. 4.12 Kick turn Step 3: Stand in the 'ballet' stance with both feet close together and ski tips pointing in opposite directions. Place your poles on the slope above for balance.

Fig. 4.13a Kick turn Step 4A (with springs or low return tele bindings): Transfer your weight to the uphill ski and lift the downhill ski several inches off the snow. Important: do not rotate your ski tip into the snow as you lift it, and make sure the ski remains parallel to the snow surface.

Fig. 4.13b Kick turn Step 4A (with springs or low return tele bindings): As you kick, rotate your hip and leg inwards.

Fig. 4.13c Kick turn Step 4A (with springs or low return tele bindings): Continue rotating your leg until your skis are parallel.

Fig. 4.14 Kick turn Step 4B (no springs or with pivot tele bindings): Transfer your weight to the uphill ski and place the inside edge of the floating ski against the inside of your standing boot and rotate the ski around until parallel.

4b. **Without binding springs or with a pivot tele binding:** With all your weight on your uphill foot, lift the downhill ski a few inches off the snow and straighten your downhill leg. This motion will drop your floating foot below your standing foot. Pause and allow your ski tail to drop and your ski tip to come free of the snow and lift up.

Place the inside edge of your floating ski so it touches your standing boot and rests on the heelpiece of your binding. Keep the floating ski in contact with your boot like a pivot point while you move your downhill leg in an arc around it, bringing your skis parallel (fig. 4.14).

4c. **Tele binding with strong return:** With these bindings it can be hard to get your ski around with the final kick because your ski is stuck to your heel. There are several options. One, in some tele bindings you can loosen the springs so the return of the spring is not so strong and you can clear the kick described above. Two, you can modify the kickless technique (step 4, without binding springs or with a pivot tele binding above): shift your lower foot so the inner side of that ankle touches the outside of the ankle on your standing foot (fig. 4.15). Then rotate the ski using your hip and leg to

Fig. 4.15 Kick turn step 4C (Telemark bindings with strong return): Transfer your weight to the uphill ski and drop your lower leg downhill. Bring the inside ankle of your lower foot to touch the outside ankle of your standing foot.

clear the snow and bring it parallel. Your third option is to use the downhill-initiated kick turn described as a variation below. Finally, you can bring your leg around in stages above you.

Troubleshooting the kick turn:

■ **Problem:** In the uphill kick (step 2), your ski gets stuck on the snow because you can't lift it high enough to clear the hill above you. This can include getting your tail stuck on your downhill binding.

   Solution: The key is in the arc. If you try and rotate your foot straight from your stance, there is no clearance for your ski. Move your ski *forward* first,

and then up and around. Doing so in a dynamic motion can be helpful.

■ **Problem:** You are having trouble getting your feet close to each other in step 3.

   Solution: Try shoving the tail of your uphill ski into the snow up to the binding (fig. 4.16). This trick only works if the snow is soft enough.

■ **Problem:** In step 4, your ski tip gets stuck in the snow or won't lift out of the snow in the first place (fig. 4.17).

   Solution with binding springs or low-return tele bindings: Adjust the position of your kicking leg. Drop your kicking leg below your standing leg, make sure it is almost straight, and then

Fig. 4.16 Troubleshooting: Shove the tail of the uphill ski into the snow.

Fig. 4.17 Troubleshooting: If you find yourself in this position, return the ski to the snow in the ballet stance (Step 3). Make sure your ski tip is clear of the snow before you try the kick/rotation.

rotate it outward. From that new position, try the kick/flip again.

Solution without binding springs or with tele pivot binding: Allow your kicking leg to drop below you, so your floating ski touches your boot as close to the tip as possible. It may help to flex your standing leg slightly. Press the inside edge of the floating ski against your boot or binding as you pivot your leg around.

Variation:
Downhill-Initiated Kick Turn

This variety of kick turn is very useful on steep terrain or in tight quarters near a tree or rock. It's also a good alternative for anyone who has trouble doing the high-kick part of the basic kick turn or for use with cable tele bindings with strong return.

1. Set up similar to the basic kick turn: create a good platform and set your skis at a low angle. The difference is you will be executing the turn on the snow *below* your initial stance. If you are doing the kick turn on steep ground, stomp out a platform and then move slightly above it. Plant both poles in the slope above you for stability and balance.
2. Lift your uphill foot a few inches and set the inside edge of your uphill ski at ankle height against the inside of your standing boot (fig. 4.18a). Keeping boot-edge contact, slide your floating foot backward, bringing your ski tip close to your standing boot. With your floating leg almost straight,

Fig. 4.18a Downhill-initiated kick turn Step 2: Lift your uphill foot and set the inside edge of your uphill ski against your boot.

rotate your floating foot all the way around your standing foot (fig. 4.18b). Keep the floating ski in contact with your standing boot—this gives you the leverage you need to keep the tail of your floating ski out of the snow as you rotate it around.

3. Once you have rotated your floating foot around to the downhill side of your standing foot, bend your standing knee and lower your floating foot to the ground (fig. 4.19). Maneuver until you are in the ballet position, with your feet within a foot of each other and your skis close to level. Once you are in a stable stance, shift your weight to the downhill foot. Use both poles and the slope above you for balance.

Fig. 4.18b Downhill-initiated kick turn Step 2: Slide your floating foot backwards against your boot while pivoting the ski.

Tip: Use your pole basket to grab the tail of your ski and pull it up to parallel.

4. With all of your weight on your downhill foot, slide your uphill ski diagonally up and away from your body (fig. 4.20a). With as little excess movement as possible, bump the tail of your uphill ski from above your standing foot to just below it. Set the inside edge of that ski near the ankle of your boot, and slide your uphill ski backward along your boot (fig. 4.20b). Continue this motion until your floating leg is almost straight and directly downhill of your standing foot. Swivel

Fig. 4.19 Downhill-initiated kick turn Step 3: Once you have rotated your floating foot around your standing foot, bend your standing knee and lower your floating foot to the snow.

Fig. 4.20a Downhill-initiated kick turn Step 4: Slide your uphill ski diagonally up and away from your body (1). Move the tail of your uphill ski from above your standing foot to below it (2).

Fig. 4.20b Downhill-initiated kick turn Step 4: Slide your uphill ski backwards along your boot to clear your ski tip from the snow.

Fig. 4.20c Downhill-initiated kick turn Step 4: Swivel your hip to rotate the floating ski and bring your skis parallel.

your hip to rotate the floating ski around your standing ankle and bring it parallel with the standing ski (fig. 4.20c).

Troubleshooting the downhill-initiated kick turn:

- **Problem:** In step 2 the tail of your floating ski gets stuck in the snow as you try to rotate it.

  Solution: Rest your ski on the heelpiece of your binding as you rotate the ski around.

- **Problem:** In step 3 you can't get the floating ski all the way around to level and near enough your standing ski because the tail wants to drop.

  Solution: Use the heelpiece trick from above. If you still need more help, use a dynamic motion, forcing your ski tip down as you swivel it.

- **Problem:** You can't shift your weight to the downhill foot in step 3 without losing your balance.

  Solution: Bend your standing knee and make sure your weight is centered, not leaning too hard into the hill or on your poles. See "Skinning in Difficult Conditions" later this chapter for more tips when doing this in steep or hard-packed terrain.

Variation:
Downhill-Facing Kick Turn

This technique is most often used in downhill mode, with skins off and skis and boots in ski mode. We mention it here in the uphill section primarily because folks still use it as an uphill technique. If you come from an alpine or Nordic skiing background, you may have used this turn to change direction on flat ground or when facing downhill. As we'll see in chapter 7, Downhill Skiing Techniques, this turn works very well in both of these circumstances in ski mode.

For uphill travel in walk mode, it can be useful in deep or difficult snow conditions, but it can be treacherous on steep or hard slopes when you're facing downhill. Overall, using this turn in uphill mode is generally less efficient and more awkward than the other kick turns in your bag of tricks. (**Note:** photo sequence shows downhill mode.)

1. The motions of this kick turn are the same as those in the basic kick turn—the setup is the same and the sweeping kick is done facing downslope (figs. 4.21a and b).

2. Shift your weight to the downhill foot (fig. 4.22). This is the difficult part; on a slope of any angle you step down to shift feet, which makes the somewhat awkward ballet position very uncomfortable as gravity pulls you forward.

   The danger here is that in maintaining balance, the tendency is to lean back, which causes the skis to lose their edge in hard snow. The fall from this vulnerable position—either forward or backward—can be a real knee twister.

Fig. 4.21a Downhill-facing kick turn Step 1: Stand on the uphill ski and begin swinging the downhill ski around.

Fig. 4.21b Downhill-facing kick turn Step 1: Bring your skis as close to parallel as possible, perpendicular to the fall line.

Fig. 4.22 Downhill-facing kick turn Step 2: Shift weight to the downhill ski using your poles to balance.

Fig. 4.23 Downhill-facing kick turn Step 3: Finish the turn by lifting and rotating the uphill ski and bringing it parallel.

3. From this stance, finish the turn by lifting and twisting your uphill leg to bring your skis parallel (fig. 4.23).

Kick Turns in Steep Terrain

Once you have mastered all the kick turns, you will find you can apply them in increasingly steep or difficult terrain. Here are some basic techniques to increase security for yourself and your ski partners.

Stomp or chop a platform with your ice ax or shovel. Even the steepest hill can provide a flat space to execute a kick turn with a little work (fig. 4.24).

Spotting. You can provide a good spot for someone doing a kick turn by standing below his stance. From below, use your poles to support the edge or back of his

Fig. 4.24 Be aggressive and use force to create a good platform in steep or frozen terrain.

Fig. 4.25 Spotting a kick turn from below

downhill ski as he moves his uphill ski (fig. 4.25). When spotting, make sure you are secure enough in your stance to be able to hold and support your partner!

SKINNING IN DIFFICULT CONDITIONS

Skinning uphill is not always characterized by efficient movement over consistent snow. The snow surface can be too warm or too cold, too deep or frozen solid. In these conditions your forward progress can grind to a slow crawl while your exertion level sky-rockets. Ever tried to skin up refrozen corn without ski crampons? You find every muscle in your body clenched tight to keep from sliding backward with each step. Or what about breaking trail through deep, heavy snow, floundering at such a snail's pace that you are forced to abandon your tour?

Fear not. There are ways to deal with the tricky conditions that the mountains—or the skin track—may throw your way. Using these techniques might not bring you back to your most efficient pace, but they will save you valuable energy and can help you manage risk in the mountains.

DEALING WITH
SNOW TEMPERATURES

Snow consistency can vary greatly in temperature depending on season, aspect, elevation, and region. What's more, snow can vary drastically in temperature over a relatively small area. Each snow condition—cold or warm, or both—creates its own set of difficulties.

Cold Smoke

Problem: When snow is very cold and powdery, it can be very slippery to climb.

Solution: Practice so that you are able to apply perfect skinning technique and body position. It only takes a nominal amount of force in the wrong direction to dislodge the static friction holding your skis to the snow. Consequently, you must do everything you can to keep the direction of force you apply to the skin exactly downward.

As you weight each step, make certain of the following:

- You are weighting your skins through the heels of your boots.
- Your body is hinging upright, with your hips coming forward.
- Neither skin leaves the snow as you draw it forward with your leg.

You may need to shorten your stride slightly in order to maintain perfect downward force from your center through your skins with each step. As you refine your skinning technique, you will be surprised at how much difference the slightest shift in weight and balance can make.

In addition to all this, you can add a small prestep, a slight stamp of your foot through your heel, which sets the nap of your skins in the snow before you weight them. In using this technique it is crucial *not* to lift your ski off the snow. The stamp must apply extra force to your skins when they are *already in contact* with the snow in order to be effective. Slamming each ski down from the air to the snow is a waste of energy and can make your skins less effective because the nap has no chance to grab during the impact of your ski on the snow.

Warm and Sticky

Warm snow makes for easier walking... until it starts to stick to your skins. This happens when you move from cool snow to warm snow, or vice versa. It can also occur if you are skinning for a long period of time in wet snow and your skins become saturated with water.

Problem: Snow sticks to your skins in thick clumps until you are dragging a rough uneven platform 4 inches thick under each foot that weighs five times what your skis do (fig. 4.26). This is irritating after two or three steps and becomes exhausting if you don't deal with the situation.

Solution: Use skin wax. Clear all the snow from the skin surface and apply the wax to the entire surface of the skin. If your skins are still dry you can usually apply wax in the direction of the nap and solve the problem. However, if the skins are beginning to get wet, go ahead and rub the wax in with and against the nap—the more, the merrier. The idea of the wax is to coat the hairs of the skin nap to prevent

Fig. 4.26 This would be a good time to get out the skin wax.

snow from sticking, and wet skin hairs are particularly sticky. Keep the wax handy in a pocket to reapply if necessary. Also keep in mind that older skins will get wet more quickly as the waterproof coating on the nylon wears off over time.

Tip: Carry a standard ski wax scraper to remove snow from your skins before applying skin wax.

SKINNING IN DEEP SNOW

If you are standing in 18 inches of new snow there is no way around breaking trail, and there is no way around working hard to do it.

Problem: When breaking trail, your tips dive into the snow as you push your skis forward. Once this occurs, the effort required to push forward against all that snow goes way up.

Solution: First, wear your wider skis that day. Second, put your heel lifters in a high position. Your wide skis will float better, and heel lifters prevent your skis from diving deep in the snow. With each step, move your ski forward and flick the tip up with a kick through your heel, keeping the ski at an angle relative to the ground and clearing the snow surface with your ski tip before each step.

Finally, if the snow becomes so deep that you can't lift your leg enough to free your ski tips, it's time to stash your poles on your pack and get out your shovel. With each step, use the shovel to remove the snow that has spilled over and is covering your skis, then kick your ski tip free and move forward.

SKINNING IN FROZEN OR UNEVEN SNOW

At some point in your ski touring career, you will encounter a frozen snow surface that resists your attempts to skin up it (fig. 4.27). Your first and best defense against slipping in hard conditions is a properly cut skin for your ski (see the "How to Cut Skins" sidebar in chapter 1). However, even the most flawless skin-cut job will only help so much without the right skinning technique and ski crampons.

Scribe, Stamp, Roll

Problem: Hard or frozen snow makes it difficult for skins to catch.

Fig. 4.27 Melt freeze crusts provide challenging skinning and often call for the use of good technique and ski crampons.

Solution: *Scribe, stamp, roll.* When skinning in hard snow conditions, everything mentioned above with respect to the importance of good body position applies. But you need more than body position. With each step you must create a sticking surface, then set the nap of the skin in the snow of that surface, and finally roll the skin surface onto that surface.

1. The *scribe* creates a narrow (1–2 centimeter) platform for your skins to grip. To scribe your ski into the snow, you must actively push your ski edge in a horizontal direction into the hill as you slide the ski forward, keeping the edge in contact with the snow (fig. 4.28).

2. To set your skins before you commit your full weight to the ski, *stamp* your foot lightly through your heel, being very careful not to lift the ski or unweight it even slightly. Several light stamps may work better than one large stomp.

3. After the stamp, transfer the remainder of your weight to the ski—*roll* your ankle slightly downhill to rest the skin onto the surface created by the scribe. This is totally counterintuitive for the downhill skier who holds the edge by rolling the ski into the slope.

Throughout all three steps, it is crucial to keep a constant pressure down on the

Fig. 4.28 Correct scribing technique. Note the track left in the snow.

Fig. 4.29 Your scribed track should look like this.

Fig. 4.30 Use a ski pole by your foot to self-belay in hard snow skinning conditions. Push the pole all the way into the snow up to the basket for best security.

Fig. 4.31 Ankle roll in low-angle terrain. In steeper terrain, the ankle roll is less pronounced.

ski—this helps hold the tenuous contact between the skin and the snow (fig. 4.29).

Problem: Even with the scribe, stamp, roll, and perfect body position, you are still slipping or losing your edge.

Solution: Give yourself a spot with your ski pole. Place your downhill pole below the edge of your downhill ski, midway between your boot and your ski tip (fig. 4.30). Scribe, stamp, and roll the ski, and when you commit your weight to it the pole should be near your boot.

SKI CRAMPONS

Ski crampons are a crucial tool for ski touring and ski mountaineering. They create added security in conditions where even the best skinning technique fails. However, taking them on and off for every steep or slippery spot adds unnecessary transitions and can waste a lot of time on a tour (see chapter 5, Transitions). The key is to understand when good technique will suffice versus when ski crampons are the better option.

The technique for walking with ski crampons is almost identical as for regular skinning. A few points to note with ski crampons:

- Rolling your ankle downhill will allow more of the crampon teeth to come in contact with the snow (fig. 4.31).
- In some models, using heel lifters will prevent the teeth from even reaching the snow and defeats the purpose of putting ski crampons on.
- Ski crampons limit your stride length slightly because the teeth catch on the snow before your foot can reach full stride.

TRACK SETTING

Track setting is both a skill and an art. Learning to set a good track can be a maddening experience that alternates between clear-cut concepts and hard-to-express ideas about intuition and feel. In its execution you will encounter endless nuances of terrain and a continuous flow of decisions to be made. Logging hundreds of days in the mountains isn't enough to achieve good track-setting skills. As an aspiring artist, you need an understanding of some basic concepts to guide you and a keen sense of self-evaluation when applying your skills. In setting a line up a mountain you lay your signature upon it, and the track you create is a record of your relationship with the terrain.

How do we approach this complicated challenge? First let's look at the ideas of *intention* and *consistency*.

The idea of intention is to encompass a broad view of your tour. What is your intention for the day? What are your concrete goals for the day? How to want to achieve

Fig. 4.32 The beauty of a perfect skin track

them? Who is with you? Why are you all together? On one day you may be looking for a workout on a half-day tour. On another, you may be introducing a friend to ski touring. All of these intentions will shape your experience—and your track—differently (figs. 4.32 and 4.33).

Once you are you clear in your intention, your next challenge is to apply that intention as consistently as possible to all aspects of your tour. Are you consistent in how much risk you are accepting throughout the tour? Are your track angle and pace consistent? Is your objective well suited to your group and the conditions? Seek always to be clear in your intention for the day,

and strive to create a track that consistently reflects that intention.

SAFETY, EFFICIENCY, SPEED: THE BASICS

In setting a good track, there is no dogma, no right-or-wrong list. Rather, there are guidelines to help you in decision-making as you ascend. These guidelines are organized around three basic concepts: *safety*, *efficiency*, and *speed*. The decision-making process that takes place using these three categories is dynamic and continuous throughout the course of a tour, and the three categories interact with each other on a larger scale.

Safety

Safety means freedom from danger, risk, or injury. In the context of track setting, safety determines the direction and location of your track based on the presence of objective hazards. In the safety-efficiency-speed sequence, safety occupies the first position for a reason. It is always your first consideration as you make terrain choices for your track, and it carries the highest consequences if poor decisions are made. This may seem obvious, but it is important to emphasize as a mental reminder every time you move through the backcountry. If you set an inefficient track, the consequences are far less dire than if you set an unsafe track.

As discussed in chapter 2, Decision-making in Avalanche Terrain, good terrain selection means paying attention to things like the interaction of snow stability with slope aspect and incline, and recognizing terrain traps, among other observations. Now take a step back: when considering safety in setting a track, you may be dealing with an even longer list of objective hazards than those associated with avalanches. For example, there may be exposure or falling hazards, potential rockfall and icefall, crevasses, and more.

Fig. 4.33 Steady-angle track through meandering terrain near the Icefall Lodge, Canadian Rockies

In setting a track, you must ask yourself the same questions over and over: What are the objective hazards, and how can I set my track to avoid them or minimize them to an acceptable level? Am I safe here, and what can I do to increase my safety moving forward?

Efficiency

A dictionary definition of efficiency is "the ratio of the effective or useful output to the total input in any system." Efficiency in ski touring is the overarching goal of using the minimum amount of energy ("total input") to achieve the maximum rewards of your ski objective ("effective or useful output"). Think of miles and vertical elevation traveled per amount of fuel burned. You can go from A to B using two energy bars, or you can go from A to B using eight. Which is more efficient? Clearly the first option. The energy your body burns getting from A to B is the common thread in considering efficiency gain and loss.

Earlier this chapter we discussed seeking efficiency of motion within your stride. Now we expand this idea to include efficiency of motion through terrain. Think about factors that might decrease your efficiency, making you burn through eight bars instead of two:

- Steep track. Two things happen here. First, your muscles are working harder so your exertion level goes up. Second, as the track angle increases, your stride length decreases. As a result, your cadence must be faster and you need to take more steps to cover the same amount of ground (see the "What's Your Angle?" sidebar).
- Track is too flat. Conversely, if a track is too flat you lose efficiency because you've decreased the angle so much that you need to take 30 percent more steps to cover the same ground.
- Fast pace.
- Poor consistency in track angle or speed (see "Pacing" later this chapter).
- Stopping and starting too much.

Now think about using only two energy bars. Efficiency can be introduced into your track in many ways:

- By maintaining a constant track angle and pace, thereby keeping your heart rate steady throughout the tour.
- By choosing an efficient line—not too direct, not too circuitous.
- By carefully selecting the location and number of your kick turns, and even by choosing the most effective turn in any given situation.

Why seek efficiency? Efficiency in track setting will enable you to move quickly through easy terrain and to save your physical and mental resources for the difficult aspects of a tour. It will also equip you to deal more successfully with difficult or convoluted terrain when you encounter it. If you are efficient on the uphill, you save leg power for the enjoyment of the downhill...and isn't that the point of going up in the first place?

WHAT'S YOUR ANGLE?

So there we were…the slope steepened and the terrain was treed and variable. We came upon a ruddy, sweat-soaked pair climbing in a very steep, preexisting, uphill track. After a congenial "howdy-do" we crossed the steepening track and continued on our merry, and lower-angle, way. The two fellows paused for a moment to assess the options of following us or continuing in the established track. Then they flicked their heel lifters up to "stiletto" and continued upward. Our group crossed the steep track several times on the way up to the top of the slope, and each time we found we were farther and farther up the slope from the high-heeled duo. The pace of our steps was not any faster than theirs, yet we had casually left them far behind. We hadn't even made more than a few kick turns all day.

How could it be that on that day a shallow, sinuous track was faster and more efficient than a straighter line that climbed more elevation with every step? The secret is in the mechanics of stride. The most efficient stride makes good use of your body's biggest hinge, your hips. Your hips are the junction between your largest bone, your femur, and your largest muscle, your gluteus maximus. An efficient stride uses larger muscles in short spurts and maximizes rest in the brief moments between steps. A shallower track with less heel lift allows greater stride length than a steeper track with maximum heel lift. Although in very steep tracks you can gain more elevation per step, each step moves you forward less. Steep tracks require more force per step to move a person upward against gravity, and they generally increase the use of smaller muscles in the body's core and lower legs for skin traction and stabilization.

That said, if your track is too shallow, you could waste even more time and energy than if your track is too steep. A track angle that is overly shallow can add many unnecessary steps and additional mileage, and often creates more energy-depleting uphill turns. An efficient track must gain both elevation and distance toward your destination as quickly and steadily as possible.

How steep is the perfect track? The most efficient track angle is simply one that is not too steep and not too shallow. Uncommonly steep tracks often increase efficiency in narrow terrain features, in short sections where you want to avoid kick turns, or in very firm snow with excellent skin traction. Flatter tracks often make sense when they allow you to travel more directly toward your objective or allow you to access a terrain feature that is easier to lay a track on. Finding the perfect angle takes practice and will vary significantly according to the terrain, the snow conditions, and the group.

Howie Schwarz is a UIAGM mountain guide based near Bishop, CA and owner of Sierra Mountain Guides, as well as an instructor and examiner for the AMGA Guide Training and Certifications Program and an instructor for AIARE avalanche courses.

Speed

Speed is the distance traveled divided by the time this travel takes. In track setting, speed means exactly the same thing: how much time it takes to get from one point to another. When evaluating the element of speed in setting your track, you will be asking yourself, is this the fastest way I can get to my objective?

Your speed can be affected by many variables: pace, track angle and line, even your method of travel. You may be able to reach your goal faster by simply increasing your pace, or you may get there just as fast by setting a steeper track or a more direct line. Picture a wide, steep couloir: is it faster to skin or to take your skis off and boot straight up it?

Throughout the course of a tour, you will encounter a hundred decisions that will either increase or decrease your speed. Your task is to be aware of these and to make the most of them according to your intention for the day and your track.

SAFETY, EFFICIENCY, SPEED: PUTTING IT ALL TOGETHER

You now have the mental checklist for track setting, in order of importance: safety, efficiency, and speed. You have a basic understanding of what each category involves and how it will affect your track setting. The next step is to think about how they interact with each other and how to shape that interaction to consistently meet your intention for your ski tour.

When you are setting a track, use the safety-efficiency-speed checklist constantly. At every point in your ski tour, ask yourself about safety:

- Am I safe where I am now?
- Will I be safe where I am going?
- If not, how can I increase my safety in the given terrain using my track?

Once you have decided that your track meets your safety criteria, move on to efficiency:

- Am I being as efficient as possible?
- Is my track angle constant, or am I going from steep to flat and back to steep again?
- Is my line efficient, or have I missed opportunities to gain elevation and built in too many kick turns?
- Have I chosen the most efficient line from A to B?

When you are satisfied that you are being as efficient as possible, move on to the final item on your checklist, speed:

- Is my track getting me from A to B as quickly as possible?
- Can I alter my track or my travel techniques to increase my speed?

As you work through your checklist, you will find that *your decisions in one category will almost always affect those in each of the other two.* The most efficient track may not be the safest track. The fastest way from A to B may not be the most efficient track. Sometimes safety will rule like a tyrant over your skin track, forcing you to set a steep track to avoid avalanche slopes or to sprint full-bore to escape deteriorating conditions.

Then there will be other days when avalanche conditions are rock solid, or the terrain is mild, or your ski partners are good enough to skin up blue ice if you led them to it. There are countless factors, countless consequences, and countless decisions to be made. This is the power of the safety-efficiency-speed progression: it enables you to recognize and prioritize all of the factors you encounter and to create a track that consistently meets your intention for the day.

THE SKILL SIDE OF TRACK SETTING: APPLYING TECHNIQUE

We've talked a lot about what you want to achieve in setting a track, and that skill and art are both involved. What follow are some specific techniques you can use to achieve these goals, from both the skill and artistic sides.

Contouring. Once you have your mental setting of how steep your track will be, think about holding that angle and wrapping around hills and features, rather than always going straight up and over them (fig. 4.34).

Fig. 4.34 Contouring around terrain in the North Cascades

Look ahead. Resist the urge to focus on the terrain immediately in front of you. Look at the long view instead, and you will find yourself planning a track for the whole slope instead of just a 30-foot section of it. This will help you keep from skinning into a corner that is difficult to escape.

Approaching hills. Again, plan ahead! Set up your approach to a hill so you don't bump headlong into it. Swing wide and, if possible, begin gaining elevation before you get to the hill (fig. 4.35).

Applying turns. Use the most efficient turn possible for a given terrain configuration. Use an AVA turn instead of a kick turn whenever you can, and be conscious of the most efficient way to use that AVA turn. In mellow terrain, a long, smooth turn may be the most efficient, whereas in steeper terrain a quick AVA turn in place limits

the number of steps you must make at a steeper angle.

Locating turns. Be conscious of how many kick turns you're doing. They use a lot of energy—could you get by with fewer of them (fig. 4.36)? When it's time to put a turn in, seek the easiest place to make a turn—small areas of lesser steepness, or areas without trees or rocks to catch on skis.

Gain elevation. Never miss a chance, no matter how small, to gain elevation. If the terrain angle eases off for just three steps, you can adjust your track to take advantage of this. There are two benefits here—you maintain consistency in your track angle, and you gain elevation in an easy spot, thereby setting yourself up well for the next steep terrain you encounter. Remember the last time you got "stuffed" by a tree—stopped from your ideal track

Fig. 4.35 Good setup for approaching a hill with a track that swings wide

Fig. 4.36 Track with too many kick turns

because you couldn't get your track above the tree? Four feet of elevation is the difference between getting stuffed and clearing the tree, and most likely you could have gained that 4 feet somewhere back in your track, long before you were even thinking about that tree.

Tip: The angle dial. Picture an imaginary dial on your skis with which you can select the angle for your skis. Choose an angle on that dial and focus on keeping your skis set to it.

THE ARTISTIC SIDE OF TRACK SETTING: SEEKING THE LINE

Figure 4.37 shows an example of a beautiful line down a mountain—a glimpse of how a skier's experience and intuition can create beauty while interacting with the terrain.

The line in a downhill context is the skier's best way down—whether for good snow, the right-sized cliff, or simply to leave the most aesthetic signature on the mountain. This same concept applies to a skier moving uphill through terrain and is every bit as complicated and artistic.

The artistic line uphill is the one that best meets your intention and does so with style. At first, you may only see one line when you stand at the base of a slope. As you progress in your track setting, however, you will find that from any given spot a variety of possible lines will present themselves. Further, those lines will constantly shift and change as you move through space.

Finding the line in track setting means not only being able to see the possibilities (fig. 4.38), but also constantly making decisions about which line to follow based on your intention for the tour and your desire for consistency. In undulating terrain, this can be the path of least resistance through a variety of pitches. In steep terrain, it can be a sequence of segments, punctuated by kick turns, which will bring you to the right places at the right elevations. In any terrain, it should be the most beautiful track you can weave.

Pacing

Pacing is a vital part of uphill movement and plays an important role in managing your track in all three categories of the safety-efficiency-speed progression.

Pace and safety. Regarding safety, pace can be used to minimize your exposure to

Fig. 4.37 An aesthetic line down the mountain. Think about your uphill track in the same fashion: can you make a beautiful line with your skis going uphill?

an objective hazard. You can set a pace to move quickly below an icefall on a glacier or to escape avalanche terrain in deteriorating conditions. A fast pace can deliver you to a south-facing slope before it warms up and wet slides begin running. On the other end of the spectrum, you can apply a slow and steady pace to help a skier who has bonked to conserve energy for the ski down, thereby minimizing his risk of injury.

Pace and efficiency. Pace maximizes your efficiency by helping you get the best mileage out of your body's engine. Your car's engine has a most efficient RPM and speed, and your body works the same way. Your heart rate is an indicator of your engine's RPM, and if you travel at a pace that matches your ideal RPM, you'll use your available energy much more efficiently. Revving the engine wastes gas, as does stopping and restarting the engine all the time. You can improve your body's efficiency by improving your level of fitness, which means being able to travel at a faster pace using the same amount of energy. In short, managing your pace is one of the most powerful ways to manage your efficiency in walking uphill.

Pace and speed. It's easy to think about pace and speed as equivalent, but be careful—they're not. Pace is your *rate of travel* moving from A to B, and speed is *how long it took* you to get from A to B. A fast pace can certainly increase your speed, but it's by no means the only way to do so. In fact, a medium pace might be the fastest way to get to your destination. Often, a pace that is too fast means you'll burn through your available fuel or redline and need to stop for a break. Setting exactly the right pace—one that is above your most efficient pace but below your redline—can maximize your speed in track setting.

TROUBLESHOOTING THE PITFALLS OF TRACK SETTING

These are some common mistakes that happen again and again when track setting.

Missed opportunities to gain elevation. If you are looking ahead and maintaining a constant track angle this won't happen...but somehow, missed opportunities seem to sneak into your track the moment you stop paying attention.

Elevation-gain optimism. It takes practice to develop an eye for where your track will take you. Again and again you'll find that your track doesn't reach the spot you were hoping it would, and you must change your plan or put a kick turn in somewhere you'd rather avoid. You must work at it until you can develop an eye for this spatial knowledge.

Hesitation or uncertainty. You have your intention, you have your progression...now all of a sudden you see so many possibilities for a line that you can't pick one. The resulting track is disjointed and erratic because you can't decide which line to take. Once you see a line, commit to it; you can change it as you go, but try to avoid shifting your whole plan all the time.

We've talked about how to approach track setting, about the importance of having a clear, consistent intention for your track and your tour, and about the safety-efficiency-speed structure for evaluating your decisions. Now what? The rest is up to you. Experiment with applying all these theories, and practice them every time you go for a ski tour. Self-evaluate on every track you set, and examine any skin track you encounter. Every time you set a skin track, make sure you look back behind you...the hindsight offers a wealth of information if you look for it. Track setting is a skill and an art that you can continue to develop for your whole ski touring career.

Fig. 4.38 Two track options to gain the same col. Track A has a few kick turns but keeps the track angle low. Track B has no kick turns, but is steeper overall.

CHAPTER 5

Margaret Wheeler making a quick transition above Thompson Pass, Alaska

Transitions

In ski touring and ski mountaineering, a transition can be a change in locomotion, travel techniques, or equipment. For example, changing from skinning to skiing and back again, from moving uphill to skiing down, stopping to change in and out of ski crampons, and the like. A lot of time can be gained or lost when you make transitions. Do we care whether we get going ten seconds faster or not? No. But planned transitions keep the stress level down, and efficient transitions during a difficult tour can actually save hours and make us safer.

Think of a five-minute water break that turns into a twenty-minute backpack explosion. If you do this several times a day (4 x 20 = 1 hour 20 minutes!), you could jeopardize your objective or put yourself in the wrong place at the wrong time. In addition to affecting trip duration, good transitioning is also about location and timing. Switching your gear or mode of travel at the wrong time or place, or using the wrong

application, can quickly turn into a dangerous situation.

Apply the proper technique at the right time and you will be a safer mountain traveler, will save your energy, and will end up at your destination more quickly—the holy trinity of safety-efficiency-speed, our mantra for understanding mountain travel.

TRANSITIONS AND SAFETY

Let's think about what it means to make safe transitions when you are in more technical terrain than an easy ski tour. What are your considerations? The key word here is *anticipation*. As you move through terrain, you should be constantly looking ahead and thinking about why, how, and where your next transition will occur. Often we transition specifically to mitigate hazards in the mountains. Being able to recognize hazards—such as a slope too steep to cross on skis—is essential to safe transitions.

You're touring along and see that the

Fig. 5.1 Transition time on the Boston—Forbidden Col in the North Cascades: a quick transition from skinning to booting where the couloir becomes too steep and exposed

gradually steepening slope ahead of you appears frozen. If you're a technically strong skinner you might be able to move up the slope without transitioning at all. Alternatively, you might be able to keep going with the use of ski crampons. At some point it may be safer to move up a 40-degree frozen slope with boot crampons than on skis.

If you know you'll have to put your ski crampons on, plan your transition for the bottom of the slope. There it will be easy; no gear from an open backpack will roll downhill, and you can do things in a relaxed fashion. Putting your ski crampons on in the middle of a frozen slope can be quite dangerous if there are consequences to a slip and fall.

Maybe it's obvious from the bottom of the slope that you'll need boot crampons higher up on a slope, but not down low. For example, the slope above bottlenecks into a couloir too steep to skin (fig. 5.1). You might still skin up the lower portion, but set up for your transition at the bottom: put your crampons and maybe a rope at the top of your pack for easy access.

If you think you might have to rope up higher toward the bottleneck, make sure that your rope is not going to turn into a bird's nest of tangles, that the little bit of gear on your harness is ready for action, and that you have a plan for strapping your skis onto your pack. Also try to avoid turning transitions in steep terrain into rest breaks. These kinds of transitions should be anticipated and prepared for.

Remember that effective anticipation of proper transitions is actually a part of planning your tour in the first place (see chapter 2, Decision-Making in Avalanche Terrain). Plan your transitions and plan your breaks as much as possible: they are not necessarily the same thing, and transitions turn into breaks too often. Too many unplanned transitions and breaks can slow you down and affect your safety. The flip side of this is knowing when you need to take an unplanned break, for example, to pinpoint your location. Hesitation to take a short break in order to establish your location can turn into a serious safety hazard and/or a substantial time loss.

A note on the quality of transitions: in order to be safe, you must first be skilled and quick in your transitions. You might have to transition quickly because of objective hazards above or because the temperatures are turning dangerously warm. If you work on your technique, you might even avoid stopping all together. But you should only consider speeding up your transitions if safety doesn't actually suffer—being rushed can be dangerous.

TRANSITIONS AND EFFICIENCY

What does it mean to make efficient transitions? In general, efficient transitions are planned, well timed, and are also a matter of choosing the right gear and having that gear accessible. This helps you conserve your energy for the length of your tour. If you have planned your tour well, have the right gear, use it at the right time, and anticipate the right transitions, you will most likely end up being faster *and* more relaxed. That's efficiency. More specifically, you can consider efficiency when deciding to use a particular technique, as in the following examples.

Continuing with the ski crampon example, some folks think ski crampons are useless because boot crampons could accomplish the same thing. We couldn't disagree more. Many a snow surface is too hard for skinning without ski crampons, but doesn't support the weight of a person without skis on. Part of efficient transitions is choosing the right tool (fig. 5.2).

Very often the terrain is varied—from flat to steep, frozen to soft, and back to flat

Fig. 5.2 Hard skinning surface called "Firnspiegel" created by a strong melt-freeze cycle. An ice crust too thin for booting required ski crampons for the entire tour up, then delivered epic corn on the descent.

again. You can certainly just put your ski crampons on and leave them on, but this is probably not the most efficient solution. Touring with ski crampons in flat terrain is surprisingly exhausting. Conversely, touring on frozen moderate to steep terrain with ski crampons can be the most efficient way of traveling up a hill. Again, choose the right tool for the conditions, and you'll make only necessary transitions.

Another consideration for efficient transitions is to think about thermal stability. Folks are usually a bit overdressed and therefore overheat. The proper transition would be to anticipate your exertion level and needed layers in advance, setting your pace appropriately.

Admittedly, it can be unpleasant to dress down at the end of a break when you're already shivering. Keep your transitions short and fluid, packing your gear so that all the tools and clothes you anticipate using are easy to access—you'll warm up soon enough. Overall, remember that the ultimate transition efficiency can include reducing the number of transitions by employing good technique and good planning.

TRANSITIONS AND SPEED

How and why would you seek speed in your transitions? Fast transitions are a result of successfully anticipating the kinds of transitions you will encounter—pack smart and be dialed in with your gear. If you are transitioning efficiently, you will save time as well. There are many reasons for speedy transitions: you might want to get to your destination 20 percent faster than planned and you're willing to expend a disproportionate amount of energy to accomplish this. So you move over to a steeper line, use heel lifters, and go full steam up an incredibly steep track. You might have to do this in order to get out of harm's way...or you might need coffee so badly that all means are justified.

TRANSITIONS FROM SKINNING TO SKIING

For safety. Take off only one ski at a time, deskin this ski, put the ski back on, and then deskin the other ski.

This is especially important in glaciated terrain. You are more likely to fall into a crevasse if you take both skis off. If you are traveling in a group, do not bunch up for this transition, unless you are certain that the particular spot offers absolute safety.

For efficiency. This simple one-ski-at-a-time technique is actually a great energy saver in deep snow conditions, since you avoid sinking and wallowing in deep snow and the resulting extra effort to get back onto your skis.

For speed. If your ski descent is very short, simply fold up the skins and loop them through the hip belt of your backpack (fig. 5.3). This way, you don't have to take off your pack at all, let alone open it up. *The best speed considerations have nothing to do with hurrying.* You know you're getting good at transitions when you're going fast and haven't hurried once all day.

Fig. 5.3 Quick skinning—skiing—skinning transition—loop skins in the hip belt of a pack

Tip: In windy conditions when it is difficult to stick your skins together, use the toe of your boot to hold the skin while you fold it (fig. 5.4).

TRANSITIONS FROM SKIING TO SKINNING

For safety. Make sure you choose a safe spot for skinning up. This is obvious and yet is often ignored. For example, if you ski a run one at a time and finish grouped up in a potential avalanche runout zone, move out of the slide path before putting your skins on.

For efficiency. If you're shivering while putting your skins on, it's hard to remember that you'll be hot once you start climbing. But try to anticipate how warm you'll be a few minutes into the touring effort. Try to reach thermal comfort equilibrium—where you're neither too cold nor overheating—as

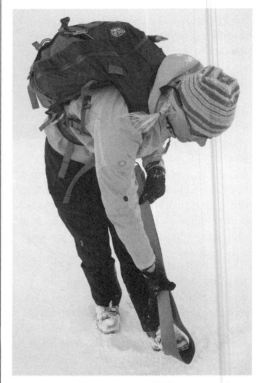

Fig. 5.4 An efficient way to fold up your skins in windy conditions

quickly as possible. This saves energy because your body is not struggling to cool itself. You also save time by avoiding the layer break that so often comes 20 minutes into the skinning effort. A good rule of thumb is to be slightly cold standing still before you start skinning.

For speed. Some ascents are very short, and it might not be worth the trouble to adjust your layers and rebuckle your boots when you'll be readjusting all over again in just a few minutes. Maybe just unzip your jacket and walk a bit slower—you'll be faster in the end if you avoid unnecessary gear manipulation.

Tip: If you have trouble separating your new sticky skins, put your back into it—step on one end and pull the other.

TRANSITIONS FROM SKINNING TO BOOTING

This transition can occur for a variety of reasons: booting unroped up a couloir, working through a section of terrain using belayed climbing, or setting up a rappel from a summit.

For safety. If you're making a sport out of skinning all the way to the top of a steep feature, you need room. Cutting back and forth on a steepening and gradually narrowing slope up to a col (a classic terrain feature) can be dangerous for several reasons, and a transition to booting in the right place can be an excellent way to manage the hazards.

For example, a portion of the ridge on one side of the col could be corniced. If you're too focused on transition efficiency and decide not to transition at all, you might find yourself under the cornice ridge unnecessarily as you cut your skin track. Figure 5.5 shows an approach and transition that mitigates the cornice hazard at the top of the couloir. If snow stability on this steepening slope is suspect and you're cutting back and forth on it, you could risk releasing the slope. In this terrain you might be better off transitioning to a quick boot track that goes straight up the hill, which will disturb the slope far less and will avoid objective hazards (the cornice).

When to take your skis off or when to leave them on is a difficult question to answer and is often completely situational. Look around, consider the hazard, and use your judgment.

For efficiency. Which technique is the most efficient, skinning or booting, is also situational—it depends on the conditions, your skinning skill, and the terrain. As your skinning technique improves, you'll most likely choose to keep your skis on longer. Booting may be faster in some cases, but can take more energy than skinning. There is one constant element: your judgment. It's up to you to decide what technique will be most efficient for you.

For speed. If the booting-up section is short, you might not have to bother putting your skis on your pack. Put them over your shoulder like you've done a thousand times in the ski area parking lot. Improving your basic movement skills will save you time

Cornice hazard

Boot track

Transition

Approach
ski track

Fig. 5.5 Complicated track setting in terrain where a fine line between efficiency and safety needed to be found

here: if you feel comfortable kicking a few steps into a 40-degree slope with your skis slung over your shoulder, you'll save yourself the time of strapping your skis to your pack. Alternatively, tuck your poles behind your head, between your shoulder blades and your backpack, and ascend with one ski in each hand (fig. 5.6).

Tip: To improve your transition speed, buy a pack that allows for attaching skis quickly and that carries them solidly.

TRANSITIONS FROM SNOW TO GLACIATED TERRAIN

For safety. As a general guideline, it's a good idea to have your harness on if you're traveling on a glacier of any size. It's surprisingly common to find ski tourers without harnesses or crevasse rescue gear on glaciers in North America. We've found this to be especially prevalent in the Pacific Northwest and parts of the Canadian Rockies. Though it's *not always wrong* to forgo a harness when traveling on glaciers, it's safe to say that it's *never wrong* to have it on.

Fig. 5.6 Save transition time: stow your poles between your back and your backpack, and carry a ski in each hand instead of strapping them to your pack.

For efficiency. In putting on your harness for safety prior to traveling on a glacier, you have avoided possible inefficiency: you won't be pausing midglacier to don your harness if conditions change.

For speed. Use a harness that you can put on without taking your skis off. Have your glacier-travel gear neatly bound and clipped to your harness (fig. 5.7).

Fig. 5.7 Ready for glacier travel, clean and simple—make sure cords and slings hang short and will not come unbound as you travel.

TRANSITIONS FROM UNROPED TO ROPED TRAVEL IN GLACIATED TERRAIN

For safety. Going from unroped to roped travel is another tricky topic, and the proper execution of this judgment call is completely situational.

Though it can be highly inefficient and unnecessary to rope up on glaciers while touring uphill, it is not wrong to do so. It can be tough to choose the right technique, especially if there is crevasse-fall hazard in steep and potentially frozen terrain. For a complete discussion of roping up, see "Roped Travel" in chapter 6.

If you're transitioning from unroped to roped travel in a downhill skiing situation, be prepared to reduce your speed downhill. Roped skiing technique has to be impeccable, flawlessly coordinated, and you must be aware of the limited holding power you have in the event of a fall (especially in hard-snow conditions)—gravity will be working against you. Navigating crevasse-fall hazard in downhill mode can be very tricky. Skiing downhill while roped is most often done with each person snowplowing or sideslipping. Also see "Advanced Skiing Techniques: Skiing on Belay" in chapter 7.

For efficiency. A certain amount of prerigging is highly advantageous in the event of a crevasse fall (see "Prerigging for Glacier Travel" in chapter 10). However, the prerigging should be kept clean and efficient. This means that your harness should be set up to allow for efficient multifunctioning and unencumbered movement in case of an incident (e.g., your harness is set up for crevasse rescue and self-rescue with the same gear). Practice your system so that you can create it quickly and cleanly.

For speed. The key to roping up quickly is having good rope-handling skills. This includes creating a neatly coiled rope and being able to quickly put on and take off Kiwi coils (see "Roped Travel" in chapter 6).

TIPS FOR TRANSITIONING

- Always analyze where the hazard is coming from and what the net effect of it will be. It will help you make good decisions and proper transitions.
- Try to anticipate your transition. Doing so will help you plan and execute each transition more smoothly.
- Purchase a backpack that let's you organize your gear and has a well-functioning ski carrying feature.
- Try to keep things simple when transitioning, for safety's sake. Ask yourself where the hazard is coming from and make sure that the result of the transition will reduce the hazard.
- Try to accomplish as much as possible with as few movements as possible. This will teach you to purchase tools that have multiple functions, to properly pack your pack, and to time your transitions.
- A certain level of efficiency comes from simply realizing that thermal comfort equilibrium at all times is a grand illusion. Learn to become okay with being a bit cold or hot at times. Adjust your movement rate and try to redefine your perception of discomfort.

CHAPTER 6

Mike Hattrup rappelling into the Couloir Poubelle, Argentiere, France

Ski Mountaineering Techniques

Ski mountaineering encompasses many elements of the mountaineering world and the ski touring world all wrapped up in one outing. This may seem like a tall order, but it happens quite frequently in a moderate form. There are thousands of ski mountaineering summits all over the world, and they all have a few things in common. They are skinnable to a point high up on the mountain, where the terrain changes drastically from snow to rock. Skis get deposited, the rope comes out, crampons go on, and suddenly you're climbing on an easy but exposed ridge to the summit. Quintessential ski mountaineering summits include the Finsteraarhorn in the Swiss Alps (fig. 6.1), Mount Shuksan in the North Cascades of Washington State, and Diamond Peak in Alaska's Chugach Range.

Fig. 6.1 View from the ski depot (at Hugisattel) of the Finsteraarhorn toward the mountaineering portion of a classic ski mountaineering objective (Bernese Oberland, Switzerland)

PROTECTION IN SKI MOUNTAINEERING

During the course of attaining a ski mountaineering objective, opportunities for building anchors and placing protective gear abound. Entering the top of a steep couloir, rappelling over an unexpected cliff band, rescuing a partner who's fallen into a crevasse, and negotiating the steep icy pitch to make the summit are all possibilities in the ski mountaineering realm.

Unlike the climber at the local crag, the ski mountaineer travels through a variety of mediums: rock, snow, and ice. Understanding how to protect each type of material is essential to your safety during a ski mountaineering tour.

Placing gear or protection is done to protect the lead climber by creating a means for attaching the rope to the rock or ice as the climber leads up and away from the belay. You also place gear to make up the different points of an anchor, used for either belaying a fellow climber or for rappelling. For ski mountaineering, we recommend carrying a small rock rack, ice protection, and a rope suitable for your objective (fig. 6.2).

Fig. 6.2 Rope and basic ski mountaineering rack

Using protection in ski mountaineering differs from other forms of mountain travel. When placing protection in a pure rock climbing environment, you might assume a high likelihood of falling regardless of the consequence. In ski mountaineering, you encounter situations where the fall likelihood is low to moderate, but the consequence of a fall is extreme.

As a ski mountaineer you need to be able to calculate this balance of likelihood vs. consequence (fig. 6.3). And to make this evaluation you must be able to assess your own ability in the terrain and then determine the consequences of a fall. Safety,

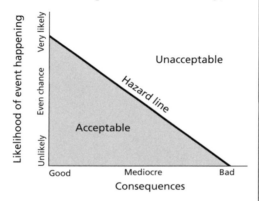

Fig. 6.3. Be aware of the likelihood to consequence ratio when reaching decisions. The more dangerous the potential results of your decision, the less likely those results should be. If a particular result is very likely, you want it to have minimal negative consequences. Where the line falls will vary from person to person, but be aware when you are approaching the zone of unacceptable hazard and rethink your decisions if they cross your personal hazard line.

efficiency, and speed also must play a role in your decisions: overprotecting a route may blow your time calculation, adding another set of hazards.

Knowing how and when to place protection will come with experience—along the way it is useful to employ the concept of likelihood vs. consequence and apply the guidelines that follow.

In this chapter, we discuss the basics of anchors and gear placement for ski mountaineering—basic setup and likely applications, their pros and cons, and things to consider. We assume a certain level of climbing knowledge; further reading and experience are essential (see "Climbing and Mountaineering" in the appendix).

ANCHOR BASICS

An anchor must be strong enough to hold the force applied to it. In other words, *it cannot fail under the applied load.* In ski mountaineering, you will be building anchors of varying strength to hold various loads—remember: likelihood vs. consequence and consider your anticipated load. Use this concept anytime you choose to build an anchor in the mountains, whether during an alpine climb or on a ski mountaineering trip.

The mountaineering world has several acronyms to help in evaluating anchors. We will use **EARNEST** and cover some anchor basics.

Equalized. Each and every component of the anchor should have the load distributed evenly between them. In ski mountaineering, you may often have a single anchor point—obviously this rule doesn't apply in those cases.

Angle. When building a multipoint anchor (two or more points sharing the load), consider the angle of the sling or cord joining the points. The goal is to have the smallest angle at the master point between the pieces of protection (angles greater than 90 degrees will actually increase the load on the anchor).

Redundant. We often use more than one point in an anchor so that if one point fails, the whole anchor doesn't fail—redundancy. It's okay to use a single-point anchor (like a sizeable tree) if you are positive that it won't fail when you apply your load.

No **E**xtension. In a multipoint anchor, if one piece should fail, other pieces of the anchor should not get shock loaded.

Strong. The anchor should be strong enough to support the load applied to it. Consider the forces involved and build accordingly. Overbuilding every anchor by a great deal may not be necessary and can waste a bunch of time. In rock climbing, building extremely strong multipoint anchors is the norm. In ski mountaineering, consider building your anchors *strong enough* to hold the potential load applied to it. Practice your anchors in a controlled environment so you understand the holding power of a particular anchor in different conditions.

Timely. In the mountains, speed can equal safety. Become proficient at building adequate anchors so you don't introduce other safety concerns due to a blown time plan.

Tip: Terrain anchors made of rock, snow, or ice can save you the time of building your own anchor. By looking around your environment, you may be able to find a suitable anchor that will satisfy the EARNEST criteria. (See "Snow Terrain Belays" and "Rock Terrain Belays" later this chapter.)

ANCHORS ON SNOW

Anchors on snow can be built using your skis, using just the snow itself, or using features present in the terrain.

THINX ANCHORS

Anchors made with your skis can be some of the strongest anchors you can build. A helpful acronym to remember these anchors is **THINX**. Note that this acronym does not necessarily list the anchors in order of strength. Each letter represents the shape of the anchor made with your skis.

Factors such as snow type and consistency, on-hand materials, time available, and possible consequences of a fall are all considered when determining which anchor to build. Strength is the main consideration when choosing one of the THINX anchors. In general, one way to remember the relative strength of each anchor (shy of testing it to failure) is to observe how much snow the anchor is pulling against—the greater the amount, the stronger the anchor is.

T-anchor. The T-anchor (fig. 6.4) is one of the strongest snow anchors you'll be able to come up with. It's also known as the T-trench, T-slot, and the deadman.

The strength of the T-anchor, as with all snow anchors, varies greatly with snow density and type. The top of the T is made with a ski, and the bottom part is a sling or cordelette pointing toward the load. The load applied to the anchor pulls against the snow on the downward side of the ski.

To build a T-anchor, first determine the direction of pull. The top part of the T is dug first and is perpendicular to the direction of pull. The length of the slot should be slightly longer than the ski going in to it. The depth of the slot is determined by the strength of the snow. If the snow is dense wet snow, a very strong anchor can be built with a slot only one foot deep. Lighter dry snow doesn't have as much cohesion and won't provide near as much strength; therefore several feet may be needed to provide a strong anchor, and a backup anchor may be required. Undercutting the slot by 15 degrees will help keep the ski in place

once loaded. Keep in mind that strength is achieved by pulling against a mass of snow; if you disturb this snow, the strength will decrease—so try not to walk on this snow when building.

Create a second slot centered on and perpendicular to the top part of the T and in line with the direction of pull. It's important that this slot be at least as deep as the ski slot so as not to lever the ski out of place. This slot allows the cord to come from the ski to the surface and becomes the attachment point for the anchor. The strength of the anchor comes from pulling against the mass of snow, so try to create a narrow slot just wide enough for the cord.

Attach the cord or sling to the center of the ski, keeping in mind its sharp edges, and place the ski into the trench. If using only one ski, face the edges toward the pull and pad or wrap the ski with something like a climbing skin or a glove. Both skis together, base to base, usually protects the sling well enough, but a little padding doesn't hurt. Backfilling the trench with the ski in it does not add strength to the anchor, but it does improve the anchor by reducing the chance of the ski being levered out of the slot upon loading. Certain bindings with a connecting bar between the toe and the heel (e.g., Fritschi) can be damaged if the sling runs over the bar—feed the sling under this bar instead.

The end of the sling is the master point for the anchor where you attach the load. You can dig a trench in the snow underneath the master point to allow for clearance.

Fig. 6.4 T-anchor

Tip: The T-trench can be made with many different objects. Ice axes, pickets, stuff sacks filled with snow, and even sticks or rocks found nearby are all suitable for burying in a T-trench. The smaller the object to be buried, the more carefully the T-trench needs to be constructed.

H-anchor. The H-anchor (fig. 6.5) is a reasonably strong and quick-to-build anchor for firm snow. The H-anchor is best suited for consolidated spring snow and firm summer snow. The snow should be firm enough to require a fair amount of effort to push the skis into the ground, but not so hard that you require a hammer to get them in.

To create the H, place both skis side by side, 1 to 2 feet apart, tail-first into the snow, and at an angle between 10 and 15 degrees uphill from plumb. Force the tail of each ski into the snow at least down to the binding (**Note:** When using bindings such as the Fritschi, unlock the binding from the downhill mode and allow the binding bar to stay above the snow as the ski is pushed into the snow). If the snow is too hard and you can only get the ski in a foot or so, the anchor may not even support body weight and you should consider an alternative.

Once both skis are in place, use your ice ax or something similar in strength to go between the skis on the surface of the snow—this is how you will attach the sling to the anchor. Girth-hitch or clove-hitch the sling to the center of the ice ax. The end of the sling is the master point. Make sure your ice ax is perpendicular to the load and

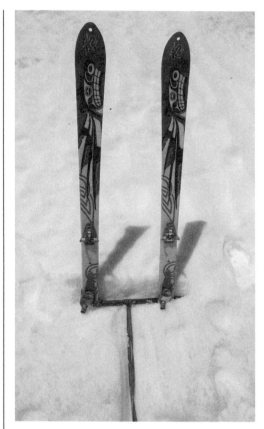

Fig. 6.5 H-anchor

that your sling is centered in the middle of the ax with the pick in the snow.

I-anchor. The I-anchor (fig. 6.6) is the quickest to build and the weakest of the ski anchors. Firm snow is required for this anchor, and it may be best suited for a small load or a situation in which the consequences are low. This is a good anchor to augment a seated body belay.

Fig. 6.6 I-anchor

Force a single ski or a pair of skis base to base into the snow, up to the bindings, as for an H-anchor. If only using a single ski,

face the base downhill toward the load to reduce the chance of the sling being cut by the edges. Pad the edges with something like a skin around the ski.

Girth-hitch or clove-hitch a sling around the ski at the snow surface, being careful to not wrap the sling around the binding bar. The end of the sling toward the load is the master point.

N-anchor. The N-anchor (fig. 6.7) is a modified I-anchor. Once again, this anchor requires firm consolidated snow in order to be effective. The N-anchor provides more strength than the I, but it requires that your ski tips have holes. It also takes more time, equipment, and fiddling to get it right.

To build the N, first start by building the I-anchor with a single ski. Next, place the other ski uphill 3 or 4 feet, in line with the direction of pull. Fix one end of a cordelette to the base of the uphill ski. Run the cord through the hole in the tip of the downhill ski. Tension the cord to create a slight bend in the downhill ski—a truckers hitch works

Fig. 6.7 N-anchor

well for this. The second ski is simply keeping the first ski from moving and bending toward the load.

Girth-hitch or clove-hitch a sling to the downhill ski at the snow surface, being careful to not wrap the sling around the binding bar. The end of the sling toward the load is the master point.

X-anchor. The X-anchor (fig. 6.8) improves upon the I by creating a greater surface area of snow to pull against. Firm snow is also needed for this anchor.

To begin, push the tail of a ski into the snow at a diagonal, with the tip facing uphill by 10 or 15 degrees. Push the second ski into the snow, base to base with the first ski, creating an X.

Fig. 6.8 X-anchor

Wrap both skis at the snow surface with some padding to protect the sling from the sharp edges. Girth-hitch the sling around both of the skis, creating a master point at the end toward the load.

> **Tip:** If any of the THINX anchors don't provide adequate security, consider placing yourself in a seated belay anchor, attaching yourself to your ski anchor, and belaying off your harness. Your body and bracing gives the seated belay anchor a little bit of shock absorption and reduces the load on the ski anchor.

SNOW BOLLARDS

The bollard can be an extremely strong anchor with a huge advantage that many other anchors don't have: you can rappel off them and leave no gear behind. The concept of the bollard is to dig out a teardrop-shaped trench in cohesive snow or ice, resulting in a teardrop-shaped mound that you can wrap a rope around (figs. 6.9 and 6.10). The bollard works best with strong, consolidated snow. The stronger the snow, the smaller the bollard needs to be. There is no rule of thumb for the size of the bollard; this is a good anchor to practice and test prior to using in an actual situation. The only real disadvantages of the bollard are that it takes a fair amount of time to construct and ropes can get stuck on it.

First, score the outline of the bollard in the snow in the shape of a teardrop. The thicker part of the teardrop faces uphill or away from the direction of pull. The side

Fig. 6.9 Digging a snow bollard

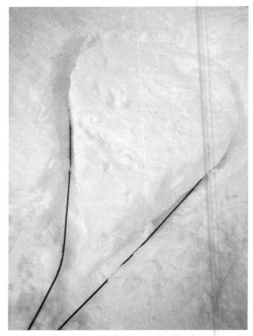

Fig. 6.10 Rope around a snow bollard

facing the direction of pull is the point where the two parts of the trough come together. Depending on the snow, the size of the bollard can range from 1 foot across for ice to more than 10 feet across in softer snow—at a certain point, the snow will not be strong enough and the rope will simply cut through the bollard. Be careful not to disturb the snow inside the teardrop; the strength of this snow is what gives the bollard its strength.

Once the size has been determined, begin excavating the teardrop-shaped trough with a slight undercut to prevent the rope or cord from slipping over the lip. In general, the

depth of the trough should be around 1 foot; when in doubt, make it deeper.

If you are using the bollard to rappel, find the center of your rope and place it on the uphill side of the teardrop. Now you will have both ends of your rope of equal length and ready to rappel.

You may choose to back up the bollard for the first few skiers. To do this, you can simply use your skis and create any one of the THINX anchors above the teardrop, or use a quick ice ax backup (fig. 6.11). Use a sling from this ski anchor and attach it to the rope at the apex of the teardrop. The key here is to have a slight bit of slack in

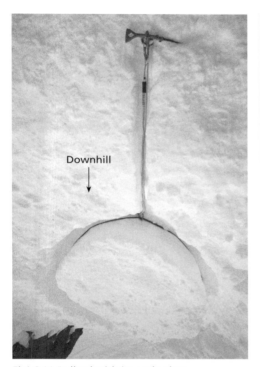

Downhill

Fig. 6.11 Bollard with ice ax backup

the sling so the bollard takes all the weight and so you can test the strength of the bollard. Careful though— too much slack and failure of the bollard may shock-load the second anchor, causing it to fail.

Tip: In softer snow, consider padding the rope around the top side of the bollard with skins, packs, clothing. Rocks and even tree branches can be used and left behind. This will increase the surface area of the load on the bollard, minimizing the potential for the rope to cut through the bollard.

Tip: You can also use a cordelette placed around the bollard, joining the ends with a flat overhand or double fisherman's knot. With a large bollard, this may give you more rope to get you to your destination, especially when using shorter ski mountaineering ropes. This can also help keep your rope from getting stuck. The only downside: this cordelette will be left behind.

SNOW TERRAIN BELAYS

The mountains present many opportunities to provide security for yourself and your partners. Many of these opportunities require thinking outside the box of conventional anchor and belay stations. Terrain features made out of snow and ice can provide exceptional security and require little time to construct.

Moats. A moat is the gap between the steep part of the mountain and the snowpack, formed as a result of the entire snowpack creeping slowly downhill. The general concept of a moat belay is for the belayer to get inside the moat and to become a counterbalance for the climber (fig. 6.12).

For the belay to be effective, you must ensure a stance that allows good control of the rope and no chance of you being pulled out of the moat. Shallow crevasses can be used in the same manner as moats, just make sure you're on a solid surface when you go in.

Snowy knife-edge ridges. For the alpinist, sharp ridges of snow are aesthetic and provide exciting exposure (fig. 6.13).

Fig. 6.12 Belayer in a moat

Fig. 6.13 Summit ridge of Eldorado Peak in
Washington's North Cascades

Often, ski mountaineers come upon these features unsure of how to effectively protect themselves.

If the ridge allows for members of the party to travel on either side of the ridge, protection is straightforward: one person travels on each side of the ridge with a short rope-length between them (see "Rope Handling and Roping Up" later this chapter for tips on tying in short with a Kiwi coil). The rope should have no slack in it and should be just long enough to allow reasonable travel on both sides of the ridge. In the event of a slip, each person is protected by the counterbalance weight of the people on the other side of the ridge.

For the complex ridge that doesn't allow for members to travel on either side, you may need to blend several techniques to adequately protect it. Some of these techniques (short roping and short pitching) can be found later in this chapter, and some techniques are beyond the scope of this book. A good reference is *Alpine Climbing* by Mark Houston and Kathy Cosley, and the appendix has additional recommended reading.

ROCK PROTECTION AND ANCHORS

Many ski mountaineering objectives require climbing on or near rock. Sometimes you'll be able to use natural features for anchors, other times you'll need to place protection.

ROCK PROTECTION

Carrying a small rock rack can give you many more options for security and more chance of success in safely getting to and from your chosen summit. Certain routes may only require one or two pieces of gear, while others may have much more extensive and exposed sections on rock, requiring an alpine rack. What follows are general guidelines for rock protection in a ski mountaineering environment—see "Climbing and Mountaineering" in the appendix for additional resources.

In your tour planning stage, gather as much information on your objective as possible and adjust your rack accordingly. Rock gear is heavy, and a ski mountaineer is always concerned with weight. That said, a small rock rack can be an excellent safety net when skiing into the unknown. We've all taken a rock rack for a ski tour and never used any of it, but knowing we had it allowed for continued exploration and, ultimately, a safe and successful tour.

Nuts

Nuts are considered passive protection and can be used to create intermediate protection for part or all of an anchor. Nuts are inexpensive and provide great security when placed correctly, and they can be a cheap way to build rappel anchors if you need to descend.

Carry a small set (three to five) ranging from sizes 3 to 7 (fig. 6.2 and 6.14a). Nuts are slotted into a crack or flake in the rock; therefore you need to have nuts that correspond to the sizes of cracks in the rock.

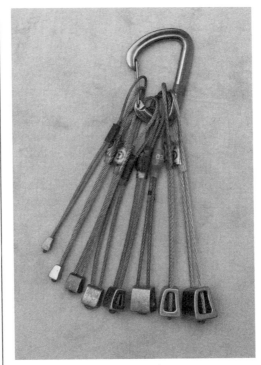

Fig. 6.14a A selection of nuts

Basics of nut placement:

- The placement is only as strong as the rock around it—seek solid rock.
- Anticipate the direction of pull—orient the cable of the nut toward the direction of pull.
- Use the nut that most closely resembles the shape of the crack.
- Seek placements that have a lot of rock contact with the metal of the piece.
- Seek placements with a constriction below the piece in the direction of pull.
- Give the piece a firm tug to set it in place.
- Attach a sling or quickdraw to the piece so the rope doesn't loosen the placement.
- Practice placing the gear on the ground at the local crag prior to using it.

Cams

Cams are considered active protection because the springs in the cam are actively holding it in its location. Cams are expandable and therefore versatile, fitting in a range of crack sizes. Cams weigh more and cost more than nuts. They do however, give you many options and offer quick-to-place protection in smooth-sided cracks, where nuts may not be suitable, often making cams worth their extra weight and cost.

A typical ski mountaineering rack may consist of two or three cams ranging in size from 0.5 to 2 inches (fig. 6.2 and 6.14b). Depending on the route, you may want to carry cams on the smaller or larger size of this range. Cams bigger than 2 inches weigh a fair amount and usually don't fall into the standard rack for ski objectives.

Fig. 6.14b A selection of cams

Recently, a new style of cams with greatly extended range became available. Some of these can cover the crack sizes of three standard cams. The new cams cost a little more but allow you to carry a couple of cams in place of the five or six previously needed to cover the same range in crack sizes.

Tip: Carrying only two cams gives you only two points of protection. If your route requires longer pitches of harder climbing, two cams and three nuts may not be enough points of protection to adequately protect yourself—you'll need to increase the amount of rock gear in your rack.

Basics of cam placement:

- Solid rock must surround the cam—the placement is only as strong as the rock.
- Snow, dirt, ice, and moss in a crack can compromise placement strength. Clean it out!
- Cracks that flare (become wider toward the direction of pull) may not provide a good placement—seek other options.
- Choose the right size cam for the crack—cams have a range in which they achieve optimal strength and can still be removed. If the cam is overcammed (too big for the crack), it may become stuck. If the cam is undercammed (too small for the crack and tipped out), it won't provide enough holding power.
- Anticipate the direction of pull and face the stem of the cam toward this direction.
- Practice placement and removal on the ground at the local crag prior to using.

Pitons

Pitons are an invaluable tool to the ski mountaineer. Pitons are inexpensive pieces of protection made of steel, soft iron, or titanium. Think of pitons as nails you can attach a quickdraw to that come in a variety of shapes and sizes (fig. 6.15).

These nails need to be hammered into cracks in the rock to achieve their strength, so you'll need some sort of hammer for the job. Many modern ice axes and ice tools have a hammer in place of an adze, and you should consider carrying one of these if you expect to use pitons. Because of the hammering needed for placement, a fair

Fig. 6.15 A selection of pitons

amount of time is needed to evaluate and make a good piton placement.

In ski mountaineering, pitons are most often used as rappel anchors in descent, but they may also be used as anchors for upward travel or as intermediate pieces of protection. The placing of pitons is truly an art form, and with recent advancements in equipment the craft is not as widely used as it once was. That said, we feel it's an important skill to have in your bag of tricks. What follows are basic things to consider when placing pitons—this should not be the only thing you read about piton placement (the appendix has some recommended reading).

There are many piton shapes and sizes available that go beyond the scope of this book. Often, the names given to the different styles resemble the shape of the piton. Each rock type is unique and cracks will have different characteristics in terms of shape and form. If you're carrying a handful of nuts and cams, treat the pitons as the tool for protecting smaller cracks, leaving the nuts and cams to protect larger cracks. We recommend carrying two knifeblades and one or two angles.

Tip: We recommend hiring a guide or teaming up with an experienced partner who can pass along the craft of piton placement to you.

Basics of piton placement:
Position—Look—Listen

- *Position* the piton in a crack that runs perpendicular to the direction of pull. Place the piton by hand into the crack; the correctly sized piton should fit snugly into the crack with two-thirds of the piton showing. The eye of the piton should face towards the direction of pull.
- *Look* at the crack of the surrounding rock while you are pounding the piton in. The size of the crack should not expand as you pound.
- *Listen* to the sound as you pound the piton in: each blow should increase the pitch of the ring. Ideally you will hammer until the piton eye is flush with the rock. Any decrease in pitch as the piton goes in is an indication of a weakened

placement. **Warning:** if the tone stabilizes before the piton eye is flush with the rock, the piton placement is limited in its strength.

Tip: If you cannot bring the piton eye flush with the rock, but you feel the placement is solid otherwise, you can girth-hitch a sling around the shaft of the piton, just as you would for an ice screw (fig. 6.19).

If you want to remove the piton, leave enough room on either side of it to hammer it back and forth to loosen and remove it.

Practice, practice, practice—once again, on the ground at your local crag, preferably with an experienced partner or instructor.

ROCK TERRAIN BELAYS
Natural rock formations occur throughout the mountains and can be used as belay anchors, intermediate protection, and rappel anchors. The basic principle of a terrain belay is to find solid lips and horns of rock that provide adequate friction for the rope and that will keep the rope in place under the direction of the load. Using terrain belays is one of the quickest, simplest, and purest forms of moving in rocky terrain in the mountains.

When traveling in the mountains, look closely at the features around you and think outside the box when it comes to protection on rock. Start to develop an eye for finding adequate horns and lips that allow you to move more quickly through the terrain (fig. 6.16).

Fig. 6.16 Rock horn used in belaying a climber

- Rounded edges of lips and horns
- Position of the rock relative to the belayer to give the belayer a good stance for maintaining control of the rope
- Position such that the rope runs around the rock and falls in line with the direction of pull

Tip: Practice on the ground at the local crag, seeking out lips and horns to get an idea how much friction is needed to hold the rope with different loads.

ICE PROTECTION AND ANCHORS

Knowing about ice protection and anchors is important in ski mountaineering. You may encounter ice in numerous situations on your ski tours. Without skills, these encounters can be turnaround points or potentially dangerous.

ICE SCREWS

Carrying a couple of ice screws on your harness is a good idea anytime you're traveling in glaciated terrain or may encounter hard and icy slopes. Even if you don't plan on climbing any steep ice, carry one or two ice screws on your harness for rescue purposes. For example, you may be able to reduce the weight on your partner who's holding your fall by placing a screw in the wall of the crevasse and attaching it to your harness. See "Crevasse Fall: Self-Rescue" in chapter 10 for more information about ice screws in rescue.

Remember: An anchor is only as good as the rock it is made of. Choose carefully, test your anchors, and be conservative.

Features to look for:
- Solid rock that's attached to the bedrock
- Enough surface on the rock to provide enough friction for the job

What follows only covers techniques that deal with the modern ice screw design. These have the more high-relief thread design—consult your local gear shop if unsure which ice screws you have.

How to Place Ice Screws

Most of what we cover concerning ice screw placement relates to ice conditions found on common ski mountaineering routes, not on ice climbing routes. As ski mountaineers, we often encounter ice that is more glacier ice than pure water ice. The techniques of modern ice climbing are beyond the scope of this book, and there are several good sources for this information (see "Climbing and Mountaineering" in the appendix).

Ice screws are only as strong as the ice that holds them. Once you've decided to place a screw, evaluate the quality of the ice where you want to place it.

Ice characteristics to look for:

- Solid and dense ice
- Clear blue ice (no air bubbles). White ice tends to be more aerated and not as strong.
- If the ice is near rock, make sure the ice is well attached and thick enough.
- If the ice is not smooth and flat, seek the concavities and avoid the convexities. Use your ice ax to make a smooth (concave) spot.

Preparing to place an ice screw. If there is a lot of white aerated ice (aka party ice), use the adze on your ice ax to remove as much as necessary to get down into the solid ice (fig. 6.17). You need to remove enough of this party ice to allow the hanger of the screw clearance as you spin it to place it. This can take some doing and on steeper terrain can take up a lot of energy—so get a good stance.

It takes a fair amount of force to get the screw started. When climbing vertical or near-vertical ice, the recommended height to place the screw is around the level of your hip—this allows you to get more leverage to get the screw started and doesn't

Fig. 6.17 Removing bad ice for screw placement

push you back off your stance. When you're in steep terrain, try to get a solid stance that allows you better leverage on the screw.

> **Tip:** Invest in good ice screws, and try to keep the teeth and surface from getting nicked. This makes a big difference in how easily a screw can get started and turn during a placement.

Angle of ice screws. For most ski mountaineering applications, we recommend placing the screw perpendicular to the direction of pull (fig. 6.18). Placing the screw above perpendicular can potentially break the screw or help lever it out of the ice. Current techniques for ice climbing recommend placing screws 10 to 15 degrees below perpendicular—this only works in solid water ice with modern screws.

Depth of ice screw. Place the screw so that the hanger comes flush against the ice and faces the anticipated direction of pull. In thick ice and glacial ice, doing this is not a problem. If the ice is thin and against the rock, try to use the shortest screw you have so the minimum of the screw shaft is left exposed. If the hanger is greater than 10 centimeters from the ice (and you can't find a better/deeper placement), girth-hitch a sling to the screw against the ice—this reduces leverage on the screw if it's loaded (fig. 6.19). If the tip is hitting rock and the screw has less than 10 centimeters exposed, go ahead and attach a quickdraw to the hanger.

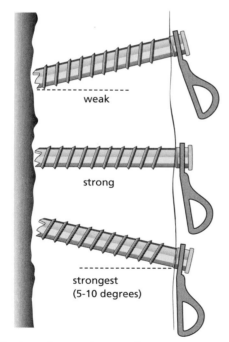

Fig. 6.18 Diagram showing the angles of a screw placement

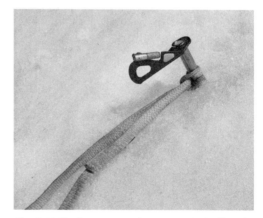

Fig. 6.19 Shallow screw placement tied off with a girth-hitched sling

Tip: When ice screws are placed correctly, they can take an unbelievable amount of force. When they're not, they may not even hold your body weight. Judging the strength of screw placement takes experience and even then can be difficult. So anytime you're relying solely on this protection, as in the case of an anchor, place two screws and equalize them, or consider a V-thread.

V-THREAD
(ABALAKOV ANCHOR)

The idea behind the V-thread anchor is to create two intersecting holes (the V) with an ice screw so that you can thread a piece of cord through the V and tie it off.

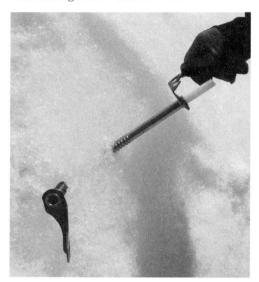

Fig. 6.20a Leave the first screw in partway to help judge the angle for the second screw.

V-threads are common in ice climbing for rappelling off a route without leaving ice screws behind. As long as the ice is solid and doesn't contain holes or cracks, V-threads can be extremely strong. A good way to determine if the ice is good enough for a V-thread is to ask, would the ice hold a screw? If the answer is yes, then it should produce a strong V-thread anchor.

The longer the ice screw used to drill the V, the greater the amount of ice you can pull against, ultimately increasing the strength of the anchor. A 22-centimeter ice screw works best.

First, clean off any party ice on the surface. Take the screw and screw it into the ice at 45 degrees from plumb on a horizontal plane. Screw it all the way into the ice and then reverse direction and remove it. From the hole you just created, measure (using the screw) horizontally for the next hole. This hole will become the second half of the V. Place the screw, aiming to connect with the first hole at the end of the screw. If done correctly, and this takes some practice, you will have two equal-length holes joining each other in the shape of a V.

Tip: If you have two ice screws, leave the first one partway in to help you eyeball the angle of the second screw (fig. 6.20a).

Take a piece of 6- or 7-millimeter cord and push it into the first hole. Take your V-thread tool and reach into the second hole and snag the cord. Pull the cord out of the second hole (fig. 6.20b). Next, join the two ends with either a flat overhand or a double

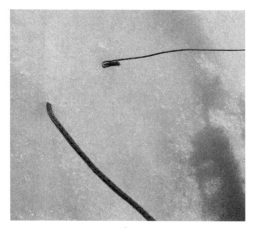

Fig. 6.20b Use the V-thread tool to pull your cord through the hole.

fisherman's knot fig. 6.20c). You now have a suitable master point to either belay or rappel from.

ICE BOLLARDS

Constructing an ice bollard is the same as making a bollard out of snow, only ice bollards are smaller. Ice bollards can be quite strong and only need to be about 1 to 2 feet in diameter (fig. 6.21). If you don't have ice screws to build an anchor or to make a V-thread, this may be your only option in ice. The big limiting factor is the time and energy ice bollards take to construct. It takes a considerable amount of effort to build one, and you will most likely need an ice tool to do so.

Fig. 6.20c A V-thread anchor

Fig. 6.21 Rappelling off an ice bollard

Caution: The strength of ice can be hard to judge. The more aerated the ice (white in color), the weaker the bollard may be. Practice making ice bollards before you commit to one.

SEATED BELAYS

The need for a rope as protection depends on the angle of the slope, the consequence of a fall, and you and your partners' comfort level. With belays as with anchors, it's helpful to keep in mind the idea of a security progression: given the likelihood and consequences of a fall, how much security do you need to provide? We discuss belays in a progression of increasing security.

Sometimes, natural features that can be used as anchors, such as moats and rock, don't exist on your route. So building an anchor made with your skis and belaying off it may be a good idea. If you feel some protection with a rope is needed, but it's not necessary to construct a full anchor, you may choose to use the seated belay. You can also use a seated belay in conjunction with a ski or other anchor.

A seated belay can be quickly constructed using the belayer's body weight and stance to provide the security, and it is an effective anchor on both snow and rock. The key to a good seated belay is the solid and well-braced position of the belayer.

Situations when a seated belay is useful:

- Anticipated loads will be low. If a high impact dynamic leader fall may be encountered, choose a higher level of protection.
- Speed is of the essence. Seated hip belays move large amounts of rope quickly, and setup time is minimal compared to building a multipoint anchor. Example: a long moderate couloir when you feel a belay is prudent.
- If the ropes are snow covered or icy. Icy ropes can be hard to hold or can jam up if you're using a conventional belay device. The hip belay is less affected by icy ropes.
- You wish to add some dynamic absorption capabilities to your existing anchor. Placing yourself in front of an anchor with a seated stance and flexed legs allows you to take some load from your anchor.

A seated belay can be achieved any one of three ways: with the rope wrapped around your lower back (the hip belay), by belaying off your harness using a Munter hitch, or by using a belay device off your harness. Each is described below. See "Climbing and Mountaineering" in the appendix for additional resources.

With seated belays, the art is in the application. Learning how to perform any of these procedures is only part of the equation—the other half is the knowing when to apply them appropriately. Become comfortable with all of these seated belays by practicing them in a controlled environment and testing them to get a feel for their holding power. Use the safety-efficiency-speed mantra when applying any of these techniques to your situation, and remember that safety always trumps the other two. When in doubt, increase the level of security so you're comfortable knowing you can adequately protect yourself and your partner.

THE HIP BELAY

The hip belay—with the rope around your lower back—is one of the quickest belays to set up.

Face the direction of pull. Place the rope coming from the climber around you,

Fig. 6.22 Good hip belay technique

at the lower-back level. The rope going to the climber is on the opposite side of your belay hand (the hand holding the rope in a forward position when giving out rope; see fig. 6.22).

When rope needs to be taken up, as when belaying from above and the climber is ascending, your belay hand moves across your body and your other hand pinches the rope. Your belay hand slides on the rope toward your body, grabs the rope, and pulls in the slack.

In the event of a fall by the climber, or any time friction needs to be added to the rope, firmly grasp the rope in your belay hand and move it across your body to increase the friction of the rope around you.

Pros. Very quick to set up—no harness, no carabiner needed; provides a fair amount of friction; you can feed rope quickly.

Cons. Hard to escape the belay; can be uncomfortable on your back if a load is applied to the rope (as in a fall) and has limited holding power.

BELAYING OFF YOUR HARNESS WITH A MUNTER HITCH

The setup is similar to the simple hip belay. Instead of wrapping the rope around your back, the rope goes through a carabiner off the main points or belay loop on your harness (fig. 6.23). Belay the climber with the standard belay technique using a Munter hitch.

Pros. The highest friction of the seated belays; simple and does not require a belay device; easier to tie off and escape the belay than the hip belay.

Fig. 6.23 Belaying off the harness in a seated belay

Cons. Can twist the rope; difficult to feed as quickly as a hip belay.

BELAYING OFF YOUR HARNESS WITH A BELAY DEVICE

Set up as you would with a Munter hitch belay. In place of the Munter hitch, use a belay device off your harness using standard belay techniques.

Pros. Doesn't twist rope; rope feeds quickly through the device; easier to tie off and escape the belay than the hip belay.

Cons. Can be harder to tie off than a Munter hitch; need to carry a belay device; can be hard to lock off in tight spaces; some devices provide very little friction with skinny ski ropes (which are often used in ski mountaineering).

BASIC SEATED BELAY: SKIS OFF

There are several positions for seated belays that offer increasing levels of security. The first is the basic bucket seat that is often used in alpine climbing. This works great in the couloir that you're booting up. It also works best with softer snow—possibly better than the THINX anchors in really soft snow (see "Anchors on Snow" earlier this chapter for details on THINX anchors).

The basic idea is to create a bucket seat for the belayer that faces downhill. Do this by digging or scooping a deep bucket for your bum. Next, settle into this with your legs wider than shoulder-width apart and a slight bend in your knees. Try not to disturb the snow between your legs—this is adding resistance to you being pulled downhill. Kick your heels deep into the snow, creating a solid and deep platform for your feet to push against—this allows you to turn into a human shock absorber. Finally, you'll want to be set up to lean your back into the hill (away from the direction of pull).

Once the belay position is built, you can either wrap the rope behind your back for a classic hip belay, or you may choose to belay off your harness using a Munter hitch.

SEATED BELAY: BOTH SKIS ON

You can add security to the basic seated belay by using your skis on your feet. This is a great technique for short sections when your skis are still on (i.e., you haven't switched to boots only)—for example, when your partner feels less confident than you do when entering the top of the couloir and wants the added security of a rope.

Start by excavating the bucket for your butt, just like the basic seated belay. Sit down into the bucket with your back leaning uphill, facing downhill. Force the tails of your skis into the snow until your heels are in contact with the snow: make sure that you stick the tails of your skis in at a perpendicular angle to the slope. We've found that having your ski tips slightly wider apart than your heels is a more comfortable position. Your feet should be wider than shoulder-width apart and your knees slightly bent for better shock absorption (fig. 6.24).

You can choose how you want the rope to run, either off your harness or around your back. Use caution: the sharp edges of your skis can damage or even cut the rope.

Fig. 6.24 Seated belay with both skis on

SEATED BELAY: ONE SKI ON, ONE SKI BRACING UPPER BODY

A potential weakness to a seated belay is your upper body rotating and being pulled forward when the rope is loaded. To reduce this you can use one of your skis to help support your upper body.

Begin as with the above belays by creating a deep bucket to sit in. Before you take one of your skis off, first consider which side the load will be on. The direction of pull dictates which side the load (climber) rope is on. It's best if you can position yourself directly above the climber—then the choice of left or right load side is up to you. Your only consideration should be the side you're most comfortable with and the one that allows the best chance of maintaining good control over the rope in the event of a fall. This tends to be the dominate hand holding the rope, with the load side opposite the dominate hand.

Once you've determined the load side, remove the ski from your load-side foot and sit into the bucket. Wiggle yourself into a solid seat and force the tail of the ski that's on your foot downward into the snow—just as in the two-ski seated belay—with a slight bend in the knee to help absorb the load. Kick your other foot into the snow, creating a solid platform to push against, also with a slight bend in the knee.

The remaining ski now gets used as a brace for your upper body. Force it tail-first into the snow near your groin on the load side (fig. 6.25). The top of the ski should be uphill of plumb and slightly touching your chest when you're in position. Careful

Fig. 6.25 Seated belay with one ski on, one ski bracing upper body

of the ski's sharp edges. Also, the binding type may dictate whether the base or top sheet touches your thigh—you may want to experiment with this.

When performed correctly, this anchor provides more security than skis off or both skis on by minimizing rotation and the forward drifting of your body. The only cost is that it takes slightly more time to construct.

SEATED BELAY: CLIPPING THE BELAYER TO THE ANCHOR

If you want to add even more security to your seated belay, you may choose to attach yourself to another anchor. The situation,

conditions, and consequence of a fall will dictate the strength of the anchor you use.

If you're near a solid natural anchor like a tree, simply run a sling or cord around the tree and clip it to a structural part on the back of your harness. You may not have any natural anchors, and the seated belay anchors don't provide enough security alone to adequately protect the fall. In this case, any of the THINX ski anchors can be built uphill of your seated belay stance and affixed to the back of your harness with a sling or cord (see "Anchors on Snow" earlier in this chapter for a description of THINX anchors).

> **Tip:** Use this technique anytime you need to add strength to your seated belay or to your natural anchor.

SEATED BELAY ON ROCK

The rock environment provides many opportunities to use seated belays. Similar to the seated belay on snow, the solid stance and positioning of the belayer is the paramount consideration to provide a secure belay, and holding power should be matched to expected load.

Find a good stance that allows secure placement and good bracing for your feet. Sit down with a slight bend in the knees to give good shock absorption. Keep a low center of gravity to minimize the chance of you being pulled with the load. If you feel you may be pulled off your stance, consider attaching yourself to the rock via a sling or rock protection, or completely change your position.

LIMITATIONS AND BENEFITS OF ALL SEATED BELAYS

LIMITATIONS:

- Harder to escape the belay when compared to belaying directly off the anchor
- Risk of the belayer being pulled downhill (if you aren't attached to an anchor)
- Not suitable for high dynamic loads
- Belayer can get cold and wet from sitting in the snow

BENEFITS:

- Reversible—you can quickly switch to a lower from climbing
- Quick to set up
- Allows for rapid feeding of the rope
- Dynamic—may be used in conjunction with a marginal anchor

ROPED TRAVEL

Traditionally in the mountaineering world, you often rope up for glacier travel. Ski mountaineering is the exception to that rule for a couple of reasons:

- Most ski mountaineering on glaciated terrain happens in the winter and spring, when the seasonal snowpack is the greatest and snow bridges over crevasses are at their thickest.
- Skis distribute your body weight over a much larger surface area, so you're less likely to break through snowbridges.

In ski mountaineering, deciding when to rope up while traveling uphill on a glacier can be a tricky decision. Here are some basic situations where you should at least consider roped travel on glaciers:

- Poor visibility
- Shallow and/or unconsolidated snowpack
- Known areas of high crevasse hazard
- Sun-affected spring snowpack
- Fresh, strongly wind-transported snowpack that could have obscured crevasses
- A little bit of all of the above

Tip: On the uphill when in doubt, put a rope on; it's rarely wrong to do so.

ROPE HANDLING AND ROPING UP

A properly coiled rope stays together when you're carrying it and comes apart easily when you want to use it. Quite often a rope doesn't fit into a backpack, so it gets stowed under the top lid of the pack or draped over the top of the pack (this simple technique requires a butterfly coil).

At some point the rope needs to come out of the pack. Often the terrain is simple enough that roped travel, in one shape or another, is possible. So how do you rope up? The basic progression of roping up doesn't really change from ski mountaineering to alpine climbing, ice climbing back to rock scrambling.

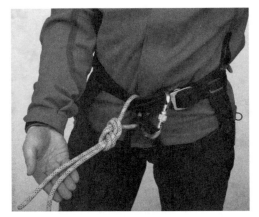

Fig. 6.26 Basic tie-in with a figure eight follow-through

Tie in. First, tie in with a figure eight follow-through (fig. 6.26).

Store excess rope. Next, unless you are doing pitched-out climbing, you probably won't need all the rope you have. Terrain transitions are likely, so the basic Kiwi coil is probably the most effective way to store the excess rope (figs. 6.27 a–f).

People get into nasty accidents because they have failed to tie off the Kiwi coil properly. If the terrain is transition-intensive enough, constant rope-length changes can seem tiring, and if one rope section is super short, you might be tempted to not tie off the coil. In a fall this can lead to disastrous accidents where you actually strangle yourself.

Fig. 6.27a The first loop of the Kiwi coil. Stand up straight and make sure to pull the slack out of the rope.

Fig. 6.27b Note the perfect length of the coils.

Fig. 6.27c Take a bight of the leading rope and push it through the original tie in loop.

Fig. 6.27d Take the bight and pull it behind the coils.

Fig. 6.27e Grab the bight and...

Fig. 6.27f ...Tie a double overhand knot around the leading rope.

The coil's tie-off knot can actually open up on its own for a few reasons: the rope is new and slippery because of its dry treatment, the rope is slippery due to icy conditions, or transition-intensive terrain causes you to hurry and do a sloppy job with the tie off.

You can tie the coil off using a barrel knot (fig. 6.27f). Alternatively, apply the simple carabiner technique (fig. 6.28). Slide the carabiner though the tie-off knot. Then clip the carabiner through the resulting bite and around the single strand of rope that connects you to the other climber.

Fig. 6.28 The multi-function finish. Clipping through the tie-off knot makes it easier to open if loaded. Use the same carabiner to finish the tie off and prevent the knot from untying as you travel. Note: you can also clip your pre-rig system in here to keep it from sliding down the rope.

This ensures that the knot doesn't untie itself and, on the opposite end of the spectrum, that you'll be able to untie the knot when you want to. If you have to arrest a fall and the knot gets loaded very hard and suddenly, you might have a hard time undoing it once the load has been transferred to the anchor. The carabiner can also act as a component in any system used for self-rescue.

> **Tip:** Consider tying knots in the rope between each person when you're in glacier-travel mode. If someone falls in a crevasse, the knots will dig into the snow and help catch the fall. This can be a big help in crevasse rescue (discussed in chapter 10), and is particularly useful if you are in a party of two, because the knots take some of the load off your harness. Tie a figure eight on a bight or a butterfly knot every 3–4 feet in the rope. (Important: *If you tie knots in the rope you must be able to rig a drop-loop system for rescue.*)

PRERIGGING FOR GLACIER TRAVEL

If you spend time traveling on glaciers, it is important to understand how to help yourself and your partners if a crevasse fall occurs. Prerigging for glacier travel has two potential uses: one, if you fall into a crevasse you can use the cordelette/hitch as your waist loop—part of your ascending system in self-rescue; two, if someone else falls into a crevasse, you can use the cordelette/hitch to transfer the load to the anchor (this becomes your load-transfer cordelette). In both cases, having the cordelette/hitch prerigged on the rope can save you time and energy when you're experiencing the stress of a crevasse fall.

To prerig for glacier travel, put a cordelette on the rope near your tie-in point (using a friction hitch or device) and clip it loosely to your harness. Regardless of what hitch or device you use to set up your prerig system, be aware of the following:

■ Make sure your prerig clip-in is not tight to your harness. You need enough cord to allow a bit of slack when it's clipped to your gear loop. Without this slack, your prerig cordelette can get stuck clipped to your harness if the rope gets loaded (fig. 6.29).

Fig. 6.29 One option for a pre-rig setup: short cordelette attached to the rope with a prusik and clipped to harness (note slack in the cord)

■ Use a locking carabiner to store your prerig cordelette. If you need your prerig cordelette for self-rescue or load transfer, you will need a locker.

WHAT ABOUT THE TEXAS KICK?

The Texas kick is a traditional prerigged system involving two loops for your legs. The benefit of the two loops is easier climbing on a free-hanging rope for long ascents, but the disadvantage of this system is that it is complicated to learn and rig. It also gets in the way during glacier travel. Often you will have a crevasse wall to brace on as you ascend, so using one leg loop (as described below) works great.

ROPED UPHILL TRAVEL WITH SKIS

Why would you *not* have skis on when there is crevasse-fall hazard? Don't skis distribute your body weight more evenly on snow?

Think about how an actual crevasse fall might come about. Would it result from popping through a snowbridge (crevasse-fall hazard) or from sliding into a crevasse after falling on steep frozen terrain (falling/sliding hazard)? Consider where the objective hazard originates and most likely your decision to keep your skis on or take them off will become easier. If the hazard is a direct fall into a crevasse because of a failed snowbridge, being on skis is the smarter way to go because the skis will distribute your body weight over a relatively large area.

Although a lot of time on glaciers is spent unroped in ski mountaineering, the need for a rope can arise quickly (fig. 6.30). That is why we recommend that in most cases you have your harness on and your basic crevasse rescue gear in place when you're on a glacier.

Once you deem it unsafe to be moving unroped, stop and rope up in a spot that you consider safe from crevasse falls. Remember from chapter 5, Transitions, that you must anticipate this transition so you can find a safe area to put the rope on. If you feel that you have to rope up in an unsafe area, it's best if your teammates stay in their places and only one person moves backward in order to distribute the rope.

More often than not you will be using a Kiwi coil to store excess rope on either end of the team. This allows you to adjust rope length—a Kiwi coil is very easy to change, so you'll be more apt to react to ever-changing objective hazards—and also provides some free rope for rescue in the event of a crevasse fall. When you're hanging in a crevasse after a fall, a Kiwi coil adds an impressive amount of back support too. Each member (except at the end of the team) can also rope up using a cow's tail, which allows individual team members some freedom of movement as they travel.

If you're touring up a glacier that's very flat and predictable, on the other hand, it might be worthwhile to stow the excess rope in your pack instead of using a Kiwi coil. This gets the excess rope out of the way and you'll be more comfortable. Changes to rope length—and especially the subsequent changes back again—are a bit more complicated, so be sure to account for this.

Fig. 6.30 Using a probe to increase safety in crevassed terrain while relying on the security of the rope

If you're roping up because of crevasse-fall hazard, don't stop short in your safety precautions. Prerig for what would turn into your load-transfer system or self-rescue system. That said, try to avoid complicated-looking prerig systems that are constantly in your way while you're moving. *Try to find a balance of clean preparedness* (see "Prerigging for Glacier Travel" earlier in this chapter).

It is common practice to simply distribute the length of rope in equal amounts among team members. This often works out quite well, but in certain situations you might be better off with a larger distance between the first and second person. This way the team has more reaction time. Poor visibility can contribute to crevasse-fall hazard, and this technique can improve safety.

For example, say your rope team consists of three people and you have a 140-foot rope. One person can carry a few coils for a small Kiwi coil. Then take about 60 feet between the first and second person and about 30 feet between the second and third person. The knots for all three tie-ins will consume another 10 to 15 feet of rope. With more rope, members at each end of the team can carry coils.

ROPED UPHILL TRAVEL WITHOUT SKIS

In certain situations it is advantageous to travel without skis. This may seem a bit counterintuitive, but there are good reasons for it.

The most compelling reason for skiless travel in crevassed terrain is if the terrain is steep or frozen. Let's face it: boot crampons have more purchase than a ski edge will ever have. If you assess the objective hazard to be a potential slip that might land you in a crevasse, taking your skis off and putting your crampons on might be a simple and effective way to decrease the chances of a fall. It's important to distinguish this from leaving your skis *on* if you think you're at risk of falling into a crevasse because of a collapsing snowbridge, as mentioned earlier. It's crucial to find and analyze the objective hazard and then act accordingly.

Don't we all wish it were as simple as that? In the mountains, the reality is a bit more hazy. Sometimes you'll encounter situations that seem to encompass just about every possible hazard. No proscriptive formula will substitute for good judgment. Just keep this in mind: weigh the likelihood and the consequences of each hazard, and take steps to mitigate them. Stay flexible and be aware that you may need to change your mode of travel as the relative importance of each hazard changes with the terrain.

This approach will also determine your rope distance. Being roped up properly creates surprisingly high safety margins, and being roped up the wrong way can create a greater hazard than not being roped up at all.

Generally speaking, a direct crevasse-fall hazard demands a bigger rope distance between team members, while an indirect crevasse-fall hazard demands a shorter rope distance. This is an appropriate technique as long as proper rope length and disciplined travel techniques can mitigate the hazard. Make sure to determine whether a bigger or smaller distance will influence your reaction time positively or negatively. Keep this in mind and think about whether you need the next-most aggressive technique in order to keep the hazard level down.

UPHILL TRAVEL ON ROCK: SKI BOOTS

Since this is a ski touring book, we assume you'll be wearing alpine touring or telemark boots. Movement on rock in these boots can be awkward because of their high cuffs and lack of ankle mobility—especially compared to rock shoes or climbing boots.

A good ski boot is supposed to provide good lateral stability, meaning the ankle is immobilized side to side. You also have reduced articulation to the front and very little articulation toward the back. We're not making ski boots sound like very attractive climbing boots...that's because they're not! To make matters worse, the duck lip of a tele boot eliminates all toe sensitivity.

A good mountaineering boot, on the other hand, provides a sophisticated balance between ankle mobility, foot support, and sensitivity. Due to the basic nature of a ski boot, a great deal of this sensitivity is lost and this needs to be taken into account when climbing.

That said, steep terrain can actually be surprisingly manageable in ski boots, especially when it is stepped in nature. But traversing or downclimbing slabby rock—or any movement that requires rolling your ankles—can be challenging, since the ski boot does not allow for enough mobility.

If you anticipate using your boots a lot for true ski mountaineering, meaning you might be climbing without skis on your feet, consider a boot that has a bit shorter cuff. It might affect your skiing ability negatively, but the touring and walking/climbing performance will be better. When traveling in AT or tele boots, be aware of their limitations and adjust your expectations of performance accordingly.

UPHILL TRAVEL ON ROCK: SKI BOOTS AND CRAMPONS

Climbing rock in ski boots with crampons can be a mixed bag. On one hand, there is the lack of ankle mobility, severely limiting the climber in technical terrain. On the other hand, often the mountaineering element of a ski tour involves some sort of scrambling in mixed terrain or easy ridge climbing. In this terrain, movement with ski boots and crampons demands good balance and coordination, and developing these skills takes practice.

Not all crampons fit well with all AT and telemark boots, in the latter case primarily because of the duck bill at the toe. If you have telemark boots, get a crampon that has a metal toe bail so that the duck bill can fit neatly underneath it.

Caution: With either AT or tele boots, make sure you have crampons that fit correctly (see "Boot Crampons" in chapter 1).

Climbing and scrambling around with crampons in mixed and rocky terrain puts a lot of strain and torque on the boot-crampon connection. It is essential that this connection is absolutely solid. If you are moving on rock for long durations, periodically check your crampons to make sure they are still solid.

Fig. 6.31 Climbing in steep and frozen terrain near the Fieschersattel, Bernese Oberland, Switzerland

UPHILL TRAVEL ON ICE: SKI BOOTS AND CRAMPONS

If ice climbing is part of a ski mountaineering outing, the ice climbing section is usually of moderate difficulty. In the modern era of steep skiing and ski mountaineering, frozen 50-degree-plus slopes are being climbed often in order to ski them a few hours later (fig. 6.31). Whether this qualifies as proper ice climbing in the traditional sense could be discussed, but the techniques of rope handling and general movement skills certainly apply.

For this basic form of snow and ice climbing, AT and telemark boots are actually surprisingly useful. They seem powerful and comfortable. Your calves might even fatigue less in a ski boot than in a good mountaineering boot. The supportive feeling you get when you lean forward in the ski boot really saves some energy.

The feeling of AT and tele boots is not very sensitive, but the required motion repertoire is also not sophisticated. Even steep ice climbing can be a satisfactory experience in AT or telemark boots as long as the climbing does not involve any aggressive ankle articulation. The traditional techniques in moderate terrain that involve a lot of ankle articulation, such as the French technique, are hard to master in a ski boot. You will have to resort to front pointing earlier in order to compensate for the lack of ankle mobility.

Make sure that your crampons fit well to your boots. As mentioned above, a poor fit between boot and crampon is sometimes hard to detect in the store.

ADVANCED ROPE TECHNIQUES
Short Roping

Short roping: the oldest, purest, fastest, and hardest to learn form of roped mountain travel. It can provide safe freedom of movement when done right and a drastic increase in hazard when done wrong. Please learn this skill from someone you trust and who can teach it the right way. All else will lead to bad habits and potentially disastrous results.

The problem and allure with short roping, in general, is that it's very free flowing.

There are only a few principles you need to understand. But real-world terrain presents numerous variables to which these basic principles must be applied. A full understanding of the short-roping technique can only be obtained by roaming around in the proper terrain, and the safest way is with an experienced person.

Short roping without terrain features. Short roping can be divided into a couple of categories. We generally differentiate between terrain that offers natural features that can be used to augment security, and terrain that does not offer any form of natural protection. The latter is a scary form of short roping and you must be fully aware of its limitations.

In terrain without natural protection, short roping is based on the idea that the rope leader will not fall and is essentially a moving anchor (fig. 6.32). The technique further assumes that the rope leader can arrest a slip before it becomes a dynamic fall, and that the likelihood of a fall is rather small in the first place. There is obviously a lot of room for judgment here. The stronger rope team member will almost always be above the other team member, in both uphill and downhill travel.

Short roping in such circumstances is popular in the guiding world, because by nature of the arrangement there should be a difference in comfort level between guide and client. This technique finds plenty of application in ski mountaineering: much of the time, the same terrain could potentially have been skied and skinned if conditions had been more favorable.

Fig. 6.32 One of the authors short roping in the Ortler Mountains in Italy (Photo by Dan Patituci)

Caution: As the rope leader, you are the moving anchor and your biggest safety margin comes from your, and your partner's, basic movement skills in the given terrain. It does not come from rope-handling technique or the hope that you will be able to arrest your own or your rope partner's fall. Accident avoidance is of the utmost importance. If you think the chances of you or your partner falling for whatever reason are increasing, and/or the potential consequences are increasing at the same time, it is time to change the game.

Short roping with terrain features. Certain terrain—ridges, stepped blocky terrain, and the like—can offer a surprising amount of natural protection that allows for continuous movement and good use of short roping (fig. 6.33). Perpetual motion can be achieved without placing a lot of gear and, if done right, the technique can create a high level of security between the rope-team members.

When employing this technique, it is important to consider a few basic elements:

- Where is the danger coming from? Exposure? Difficult climbing?
- If there is a fall, in which direction would you or your rope-team member fall?
- Are you in the right spot to provide security when your rope-team member comes to the dangerous spot?
- Is the rope between your rope partner and yourself positioned in a way that decreases the danger?
- Is the rope length correct? Is there too much or too little slack to adequately protect you?

- And most of all: Recognize any looming hazard and ensure that, while you are moving, your rope partner's or your rope's position efficiently minimizes this danger.

When short roping in terrain with natural protection, you are slinging the rope around terrain features so that if one person falls, the other acts as a counterweight and holds the fall. These features might include the following:

- Rock horns (which must point in the right direction and must be solid).
- A small tower on a ridge that you simply walk around while your rope partner is still on the other side of the ridge.
- The ridge itself, with rope-team members walking or climbing on opposite sides of the ridge.
- A small moat that you are moving into while your rope partner is still exposed to the hazard.

Very often you will run into blank spots, meaning terrain that is not too difficult but is also not protectable. This is where many accidents occur; the trick is to realize when likelihood and consequence are going up at the same time. In the real world, terrain changes often between places where you don't need a rope and places where you do, going from easy to hard, then moderate but hard to protect, hard but easy to protect, and every possible combination in between. It's up to you to smooth out the transitions, which often turns into short pitching.

Fig. 6.33 On the way to the Mittaghorn in the Bernese Alps of Switzerland

Short Pitching

Short pitching is used in the mountains as a technique to isolate the crux of a short section of terrain. You move as close as possible to the crux in short-roping mode, then you create a suitable anchor below the crux, fix your partner to this anchor, and climb the short section with or without a belay. Once above this moderate crux, you create another anchor or use a terrain feature to belay your rope partner up.

If you fall without a belay (which should be low on the likelihood scale), the anchor below the crux would catch you and keep your partner from getting torn off the mountain. **Important:** the rope should go from you to the anchor below and then to your rope partner. When you set up, make sure that any potential pull will be on the anchor and not on your rope partner.

If you think the crux presents a higher likelihood of a fall, you create the same anchor, your partner clips into the anchor, then you ask for a belay and off you go. As you go up, you place some protection, maybe a cam, nut, piton, snow picket, or an ice screw. You place the amount of protection that seems needed and adequate, climb to the next suitable anchor spot, create an anchor, and bring your partner up. The consequence or the likelihood of a fall (or both) have gone up, and you need to deal with it. Don't count on the hope that you won't fall!

What happens if there is not a suitable anchor spot and the terrain does not let up? Keep climbing. At some point you may hear your partner yell that you are out of rope.

Careful here! Most likely you could have anticipated this. **Caution: Do not open**

your Kiwi coil from a desperate stance in order to lengthen your rope. You must be safe. This means being in a secure stance or clipping in to some form of solid protection, then getting the rope, opening up a few coils, and then retying the rope. Your partner takes up the slack and signals clearly that you are good to go again before you proceed.

Tip: When short roping, anticipate, adjust rope length and be fast at it, and read the terrain.

If you end up climbing a substantial distance from your original anchor to the next anchor with several pieces of protection in between, you have moved from short pitching to "pitching it out" in fully belayed climbing.

Belayed Climbing

The transition from short roping and short pitching to fully belayed climbing on a full pitch can be quite fluid. Once in the traditional climbing mode, climbing in full pitches can seem very tempting. Sometimes this is the best idea, and other times it is smarter to keep the pitches shorter so that you can see and communicate with your partner.

The best solution will depend on the situation, but we advise against going out of sight and especially out of earshot. As in so many other situations, good and easy communication is key. If you can't see and or hear your partner, the chances for a disastrous communication error go up substantially.

Rappelling with Skis

One of the most frequently used rope techniques in ski mountaineering is rappelling. We rappel into couloirs, off steep cols, and any place we are not comfortable skiing or downclimbing (fig. 6.34).

The following description of the rappelling sequence assumes knowledge of knots and climbing basics. See "Climbing and Mountaineering" in the appendix for additional resources.

Caution: Rappelling accidents are one of the most common accidents in mountaineering—often we rappel when we are tired, and mistakes happen easily. When in doubt, recheck it out.

1. First, determine if you or anyone in your group needs to rappel. This evaluation should be carefully considered. Assessing your group's abilities can be difficult. In easy terrain with low consequences, carefully downclimbing may be the quickest and ultimately the safest solution. But, when the terrain becomes too steep or technical and consequences increase, rappelling is often the easiest, fastest, and safest method.

2. Evaluate the length of the rappel. With the available rope, can it be done in one rappel? If not, can you see the next anchor location?

3. Determine a solid anchor. This may be an established anchor made from a tree, a large boulder, or a manmade anchor (bolts or pitons). If

Fig. 6.34 Rappelling with skis on

there is no anchor available, you may need to construct one (see earlier this chapter for details on anchors). Remember, the anchor must be unquestionably strong!

4. Make sure that the position of the anchor allows easy retrieval of your rope. If the anchor is too far back, once you have rappelled the rope may not pull easily and could even become jammed. One solution is to extend the anchor downhill with a sling or cord (this cord will be left behind).

5. If using a single strand of rope, thread one end through the anchor point and pull it through until you have both ends and the middle of the rope is around the anchor. If using two ropes, push one end through the anchor point and join it with the other using a knot. We recommend a flat overhand or a double fisherman's knot.

6. Before tossing the rope, coil each end independently using the butterfly coiling technique.

7. Determine if a knot in each end of the rope is appropriate to your situation. Knots prevent a person from coming off of the ends of the rope—an especially good feature if both ends were not carefully equaled in their length. In a multiple-rappel situation, this is usually a great idea. Use a bulky knot like a double overhand or stopper knot (one side of a fisherman's) for this. Putting knots in the rope ends is not an absolute: sometimes the rappel is short, straightforward, and both ends can be seen on safe ground.

8. Toss each rope end independently. Check to see that they *both* reach

their destination. Double-check that the midpoint or knot in the ropes is still located at the anchor point.

9. Attach yourself to *both* strands of the rope(s) using a rappel device or a Munter hitch. Double-check your connection.

10. Determine if a backup is needed. Backups are useful in complex terrain where the rope may become stuck and you'll need both hands to free it. They are also important in unknown terrain or rappels where snow, rock-, or icefall may strike the person rappelling. Use the autoblock or the prusik as the backup knot.

11. Before beginning the rappel, check and double-check everything. Is the anchor solid? Is the rope (or ropes) correctly attached to the anchor? Do both ends equally reach the ground or destination? Are you wearing your harness correctly? Is the rope (or ropes) correctly threaded through your rappel device?

12. Rappel. Pay close attention and do not remove your brake hand from the rope.

Tip: Rappelling without a harness. Often in ski touring we throw a rope in the pack, but choose not to include all the other technical items, such as a harness. We can still manage a rappel. Bring both ends coming from the anchor through your legs, around your back, across your chest, and then around the back of your neck and out your arm, grasping the rope with your hand. Using this technique should only be done in low-consequence and relatively low-angle terrain—you are *not* attached to the rope in a way that closes the system.

TIPS FOR RAPPELLING WITH SKIS

- Often we use a rappel to get us through the top steep section of a couloir. It may be possible to rappel on skis using the sideslip or sidestep technique. This allows a quicker and safer transition at the end of the rope.
- When rappelling with skis on, pay extra attention to your 5-foot-long-rope-cutting edges, particularly at the top station when you are getting yourself rigged.
- Sometimes the terrain will dictate that you put your skis on your pack for a rappel. If this is the case, the first person down can remain on rappel (preferably with a backup) and use his shovel to create a transition platform in the snow near the end of the rappel. The subsequent skiers will then have an easier time getting their skis on. For added security, skiers can remain on rappel as they put their skis on. **Note:** The skiers will have to have a backup or tie-off the rappel knot to do this.
- When snow stability is in question, you may consider setting up a rappel to check out the slope. This is best done with knots in the end of the ropes and using a backup.
- Rappelling can be a great way to manage moats found in couloirs and steep slopes.

PUTTING IT ALL TOGETHER ON A SKI TOUR

Last season you were touring with your three friends in classic low-angle glaciated terrain on Bagotricks Mountain. At first, snow conditions seemed great; all was nicely filled in. Then the snowpack seemed to become thinner (maybe due to wind exposure), and there seemed to be more crevasses. No problem, you roped up. The actual topography had not changed, so the rope distances between you were fairly big, you were all prerigged, and you all continued cautiously and without slack in the rope.

Excellent—you recognized and managed the objective hazard.

After a while the terrain became steeper and you had to weave through crevassed terrain, exposing yourself to a sliding fall into crevasses immediately below you. Snow conditions felt a bit firmer as well. So you put your ski crampons on, and since you had to travel parallel to many of the crevasses in this steeper terrain, you shortened the rope distances.

"All right, not bad," you thought. "It's almost like I know what I'm doing." But you had some nagging doubts about the reality of arresting a slipping rope partner in this situation.

Suddenly the terrain turned even icier, and now your nagging doubts turned to certainty. There would be no way to hold a slipping person here on skis. The good news was that the hardening terrain had decreased the direct crevasse-fall hazard and had only increased the indirect (sliding fall) crevasse hazard.

It was time to put your skis on your pack and pull out some more tools, namely your boot crampons and ice axes. Everybody in your team seemed confident on crampons and suddenly the chances of a slip seemed a lot more remote.

You were good and you knew it . . .

The terrain did not steepen any more, and there seemed to be fewer crevasses. Regrettably, the upper portion of the glacier was divided from the easy summit ridge by a short 50-degree headwall. The headwall featured a not terribly serious bergschrund at the bottom, and it had suffered horribly in the strong winter winds. It was scoured down to the ice.

"Let's face it," you thought, "there is just no way that anybody can hold anyone up there in case of a fall."

Well, instead of getting frustrated with the ice, you took advantage of it, built a quick but safe ice-screw anchor, and started cruising up the headwall. You were the strongest climber of the group, and you were confident that a slip was a remote possibility on this moderate angle. Your buddies were nicely anchored in down there, and you had been one step ahead of the hazard once again.

Suddenly, just a few meters before the ridge crest you felt that the ice was absolutely bone hard under the blow of your ice ax. Still, your feet felt secure in the old névé, and you were quite confident that you would be able to top out the last few meters without any additional protection. You were just about to carry on when the little smart voice in your head started piping up again.

"Are you pretty confident, or are you absolutely sure? What are the consequences of a fall?"

It didn't take you long to decide that you wanted a belay and that you were going to use your nice new ice screw for protection. You cranked in the screw while one of your buddies put you on belay. Just about when you were done cranking in the screw, you heard the reassuring call from below: "Dude, you're on belay."

Suddenly, it was like somebody had taken all the stress off you, stress you hadn't noticed consciously. You climbed the last 5 meters to the ridge crest and built an anchor for your friends to belay them from the top. The two tied in close to each other but with enough space that the first climber would not be kicking the second climber in the head if he fell, and they climbed up the headwall. Of course right as the first climber crested the ridge and his knot came to your nifty Munter belay hitch, the second climber was right in the iciest spot.

You were so glad you knew how to tie off that Munter belay with a mule hitch, and you were also glad you knew the Munter hitch in the first place. So you muled it off and prepared a second locking carabiner in your bomber anchor.

And right then it happened. The second climber fell. But your system was ready for it and he ended up falling 1 whole foot. He had fallen into your locked-off belay. Instead of getting scared, you were excited and proud that you had recognized the inherent dangers of the headwall.

The second climber stepped up a bit, which gave you enough slack in the rope to put him on belay behind the first climber's knot. You unclipped the first Munter hitch and then, a few seconds later, you all stood together on the summit ridge. A flat and simple ridge led to the nearby summit.

The snow seemed soft, unconsolidated, and an elevated level of crevasse-fall hazard was apparent. Again you recognized the changing hazard, roped up long for glacier-travel mode, made sure that you were properly prerigged, and continued to the summit without any trouble.

What a great ski tour! Hazards did exist. That's just the way it is in the mountains. But with good judgment and some skill you were able to mitigate them.

CHAPTER 7

Martin Volken enjoying early summer skiing on the Coleman Glacier, Mount Baker, Washington

Downhill Skiing Techniques

People often get into backcountry skiing because they want to get away from the lifts. Ironically, it is very difficult to become a good backcountry skier without spending a lot of time in the ski area.

You have to be a solid skier if you want to truly enjoy backcountry skiing. Becoming a solid skier involves making lots and lots of turns and skiing millions of feet of vertical. Accomplishing this in the backcountry is virtually impossible. If you're an aggressive and fit backcountry skier, you might be able to log about 30,000 feet of vertical in a week in the backcountry. You can accomplish this in a modern ski area in one day.

Tip: If you want to become a proficient backcountry skier, become a solid skier first. This will increase your enjoyment in the backcountry, your efficiency, and your safety.

You can practice what you'll need for the backcountry in the area: go skiing with your backcountry gear, including your pack. Subject yourself to varied surface conditions and bad snow. Maybe consider hiring a ski instructor. One day with a professional instructor could save you from ingraining bad habits or could help you unravel the ones you have. It could help you reach that next level that you've been trying to get to for so long.

BACKCOUNTRY VS. ALPINE GEAR

The lines are getting blurry between gear used for backcountry ski touring and gear used in the ski area, but there are undeniable differences. As discussed in chapter 1, Gear and Equipment, alpine touring (AT) and telemark gear was designed to be lighter, since ski touring means that you earn your turns, skinning up to get to them. A refined ski touring setup tries to optimize the contradictory demands of uphill and downhill travel.

When you ski in the backcountry, you most likely will have climbed up the hill for a while. You might be tired, the ski touring boots don't offer that same level of support you get in an alpine boot, and the ski touring bindings don't transfer power as well as an alpine binding. Your skis are lighter, get deflected easier, and your pack might throw you off balance. And when you start skiing at higher elevations and/or with an overnight pack, the demands on your skiing skill rise to a whole new level. It's pretty safe to assume that your skiing ability will not be as good as you remember it being in the area.

Tip: Choose your equipment wisely and for the application you intend.

Of course, these days there are ski touring boots that boost forward flex to equal high-end alpine boots, ski touring bindings with DIN settings up to 16, and lightweight skis that have astonishing skiing performance.

THE FRONT-SIDE SKIER

The industry seems to have recognized that the greatest growth of backcountry skiing will come from area skiers and not hikers and climbers. In order to accommodate the needs of these customers, the gear needs to come close to alpine gear performance. This new customer wants to access the backcountry, but she wants to access it ideally with a little help from the lift system. A new category has been born.

Front-side skiing is lift-assisted "backcountry" skiing that occurs within ski-area boundaries. The typical front-side skier has been skiing for a long time and has grown tired of skiing in the area. But purely earned turns sure do seem like a lot of work (not to mention a new gear setup), so the ever-increasing ski-area infrastructure and opening of backcountry gates makes the relatively low commitment of front-side skiing attractive.

The uphill touring portion of a typical front-side day can still amount to a decent amount of vertical gained, but this is generally only a fraction of the downhill portion skied. In many of the European resorts like Zermatt, Verbier, La Grave, and Chamonix it's not unusual to ski a couple of runs that amount to maybe 3000 feet of touring and 15,000 feet of downhill skiing.

The issue for the front-side skier is probably not skiing skill, but a lack of mountain knowledge. When you're an area skier, all you're trying to become is a better skier, which results ultimately in more dynamic turns.

If you're a front-side skier and you're just getting into it, take an avalanche course and a ski touring course. Even if you don't intend to do a lot of ski touring, such courses will help you start looking at terrain in a realistic way.

It can be hard to tone it down in high-avalanche-hazard conditions or high-consequence terrain when the powder is good. After all, that's why you got the touring gear in the first place. You want to access the goods. But keep in mind that you're out of the area and therefore further from help if you get hurt. You may want to ski less aggressively as a result.

SURVIVAL SKIING TECHNIQUES FOR THE BACKCOUNTRY

There are significant differences in equipment and snow conditions between the ski area and the backcountry. Both of these categories change the rules of the downhill skiing game. By understanding them and having the tools to deal with them, your backcountry experience can be much more fun and free of injury.

HOW GEAR AFFECTS TECHNIQUE

Depending on the backcountry tool you are using, you may need to deal with different gear configurations in the backcountry. Below are some general considerations that can apply.

Skiing with a pack. The added weight on your back—even with a day pack—shifts you back from the center of gravity you're accustomed to. As a result, you can end up driving from the back seat.

Boots. Your AT or telemark boots may be lighter, have softer flex, have fewer buckles, be lower on your calf, and have less aft support than what you're used to in an alpine boot. As a result, your stance and center of gravity can end up too far back.

Bindings. Some AT bindings have less forward angle to them. This can give you a much more upright stance than in alpine skiing, making it difficult to get forward on your skis as you turn.

DEALING WITH CHALLENGING SNOW CONDITIONS

Having techniques for skiing the highly varied snow conditions in the backcountry plays a huge role in your enjoyment of a tour. When the snow is less than powder—wind crust, sun crust, rain crust, frozen conditions, variable conditions, ACL-destroying glop—survival skiing techniques can help keep you safe from injury. Below are techniques to use when snow conditions are at their most horrendous, followed by techniques for better and better conditions.

Sidestep and sideslip. These are the basics, but they often get overlooked. In both sidestepping and sideslipping, your goal is to keep your tails and tips level with each other, so that your skis slide neither forward or backward. In sidestepping downhill, you must be well balanced enough (and have a wide/stable enough stance) to lift either your uphill or downhill ski (fig. 7.1). To sideslip straight down, ease the angle of your edges so that your skis will slip on the snow.

Traverse with downhill-facing kick turn. This technique is invaluable in breakable crust or heavy snow conditions, as it frees you from the struggle to initiate a

Fig. 7.1 Sidestepping stance with skis perpendicular to the fall line

turn. Traverse at as steep an angle as you can without gaining too much speed. In frozen conditions you might be able to combine sideslipping with traversing in order to maximize elevation loss without having to make a turn. When you reach a good spot, stop and execute a downhill-facing kick turn (see chapter 4 for instructions). Traverse again, do another kick turn, and so on. This is also an excellent way to safely navigate tight trees, variable conditions, or any terrain not uniform enough for a full turn.

Wedge turn. Don't be too proud to plow! If you can snowplow well, you can navigate any slope crowded with trees, crevasses, or other obstacles. The wedge turn allows you to control your speed through the apex of the turn, which is normally where you accelerate most. A good snowplow stance is a wide one, with your knees bent, quad muscles engaged, and body upright (fig. 7.2).

Stem turn. The snow conditions are almost good enough to link powder turns, but

Fig. 7.2 Wedge turn used in the backcountry

not quite. What can you do? Meet the snow halfway with a stem turn, also called a stem christy (figs. 7.3a–e). Stem turns are easier to initiate than a regular parallel turn in heavy or deep snow, and they allow you to control your speed similar to a wedge turn. This technique is indispensable in difficult conditions, especially in heavy, wet snow.

Fig. 7.3a Stem turn: Set up for the turn with a wide stance, moving across the fall line.

Fig. 7.3b Stem turn: Step the uphill ski out to form a wedge, keeping knees bent.

Fig. 7.3c Stem turn: Steer into the turn and shift your weight to the outside leg, beginning to lift the inside foot.

Fig. 7.3d Stem turn: Complete the step and bring the inside ski near parallel.

Fig. 7.3e Stem turn: Finish the turn by traversing across the fall line to control your speed.

TRANSITIONING FROM ALPINE SKIING TO TOURING

Transitioning from alpine skiing to ski touring is easier if you have solid alpine technical skills, as they are the basis of touring, but it can be difficult for several reasons related to gear: the skis are lighter and not so performance driven, so they don't hold as well on hardpack, nor do they carve as well. The boots are softer, and you have to stand more upright and hold yourself in a more balanced position. The biggest change from alpine skiing to touring might be the change of mass, as your backpack adds weight and moves your center of gravity up. To get used to touring gear, I recommend using it at a resort on familiar terrain before skiing in difficult backcountry conditions.

In addition to gear considerations, you can practice on machine-groomed runs those skiing techniques used in the backcountry, such as dynamic medium-radius parallel turns and short turns. The better you ski in the resort, the easier it will be in the backcountry. It's almost impossible to improve your skiing technique in the backcountry. You must learn to flip the kayak before you go in the rapids, as it were.

The first time you use backcountry equipment (in a resort), it feels like your knees are going to touch your ski tips and suddenly, conversely, that you're about to fall on your arse! But as you practice, you'll find your center over your feet and be more balanced. Try short turns, wide radius turns, and the most important turn: the stem christy (*the* backcountry turn).

Another big challenge is skiing a breakable crust, which is never easy. Most important in backcountry skiing is looking ahead and looking for changes in the surface snow so you can correct and prepare for a possible crust or wind slab ahead. In other words, *tactical decisions are as important as experience*. If you have ever skied full speed into a crust without recognizing it, you know what I'm talking about! Not a pretty sight.

In crust conditions, you jump to unweight your skis and turn them to the fall line. Once you turn your skis, steer them to complete the turn to control your speed. Short turns are useful as well, because you jump from turn to turn and this helps with the up and down motion. No matter how you slice it, this technique is exhausting, and you might have to stop quite often to give your legs a rest or resort to more conservative techniques. I once guided a tour where the crust was so bad we had to do kick turns down for at least 2000 vertical feet before we could actually ski a turn.

In powder, keep your stance a little narrow so the skis have a floating effect and a wider platform. Stay balanced over your feet and don't move laterally too much, as you won't to be able to adapt quickly to any changes in the conditions. You don't need a lot of edging skills in powder, as the snow builds under the base of your ski for a carving effect. Retract your feet as you start the turn and extend your legs away during the steering. This gives you a great sensation of floating and riding the snow. There is nothing greater then floating down an untouched slope.

If you get tired or conditions turn bad, use the stem christy to control the turns down to the end of the tour or to better snow. Simply put your uphill ski out to a stem and start cutting the snow into the fall line. Once comfortable, shift and transfer all of your weight to the outside ski and steer a completed turn.

Freddy Grossniklaus is a UIAGM-certified Swiss mountain guide, ski instructor, and ex Demo-team member.

ADVANCED SKIING TECHNIQUES: SKIING ON BELAY

Skiing on belay is a technique that can be used when the consequences of an uncontrolled fall and slide are unacceptable. It also lets you ski into a steep slope or couloir, and check snow stability in the heart of the hazard without endangering yourself. It might be the beginning of a steep ski descent and you might want to get a feel for the first few turns. Before skiing on belay, it is paramount for you to accurately evaluate your abilities in the given terrain and snow conditions. Ski on belay when the probability of a fall is low (because of good skiing technique), but the consequences of a fall are high. If you expect to fall every turn, you should consider another method of dealing with the slope.

Skiing on belay is an advanced technique for both the belayer and the skier. On the part of the belayer, it requires specific technique to allow the skier to move freely. On the part of the skier, it requires a fairly high level of skiing ability, as it can be difficult to turn with a rope on.

CONSIDERATIONS FOR THE BELAYER

Setting up a belay for a skier is different than most belays, primarily because the belayer's goal will be to feed rope out in a series of dynamic movements each time the skier makes a turn. The type of anchor used depends entirely on the terrain. However, the placement of the anchor and the belayer should take the following into consideration.

Security. Skiing on belay has the potential to dynamically load the belayer and the anchor. The belayer must evaluate the terrain; if the stance is not strong enough, he should add security by tying in to an anchor. Further, once attached to an anchor, the belayer must be prepared to hold a dynamic fall on a hip belay—belaying from a Munter hitch or belay device doesn't allow the rope to feed freely enough and either way will lock up and jerk the skier off her feet. If the terrain, anchor, or belayer is not suitably strong, another technique should be considered.

Visibility. In order to feed rope out at the right time and in the correct amount, the belayer must be able to see the skier. This can be accomplished by extending the anchor if necessary so that the belayer can see the skier.

Communication. Skier and belayer must work together.

Movement. The action of feeding rope out during each turn is dynamic, and it is very important that the belayer feed enough rope so as not to jerk the skier off her feet. To accomplish this, the belayer must have a stance in which he can move his arms and legs freely (fig. 7.4).

Belay techniques. To give a skier a good belay during each turn, the belayer must feed out slack in rapid periods during each turn, and then adjust to make sure there isn't too much slack in the system between turns. This must all be accomplished while still maintaining good control of the rope and the ability to stop a potential fall (fig. 7.5). See "Seated Belays" in chapter 6 for a discussion of these hip-belay techniques.

Fig. 7.4 Stance for belaying a skier using a hip belay backed up with an H-anchor

Fig. 7.5 Belayer feeding out slack to the skier during a turn

Fig. 7.6 Back tie-in for skiing on belay

CONSIDERATIONS FOR THE SKIER

If you decide to ski on belay, it is important to have the correct tie-in and to use highly controlled technique for each turn.

Tie-in for belayed skiing. The normal tie-in point on the front of the harness is awkward to ski with because the skier must constantly flip the rope over her head with each turn. More importantly, if the rope comes tight too soon from the belayer, the skier is instantly rotated into the hill and off her feet. To solve this problem, the skier must modify the tie-in as follows:

1. Tie in to the front of the harness, through waist and leg loops, just as you would in any mountaineering situation.
2. Clip a locking carabiner to the back loop of the harness (fig. 7.6). If the harness doesn't have a back loop, simply clip the biner through the whole

waist strap of the harness. Tie a figure eight on a bight or a clove hitch, and clip that to the carabiner. Leave enough slack between front and back tie-in points so that loading the back point won't affect the front point.

Ski technique while on belay. The key word for the belayed skier is *control*. Each turn must have a finite start and finish to allow the belayer to give enough rope through the turn and then adjust slack and prepare for the next turn. Good communication between skier and belayer is crucial. Regardless, the skier sets the pace for the turns and the length of pauses between turns. It is important to keep turns as methodical and regular (in radius and cadence) as possible.

CHAPTER 8

A fresh cup of brew in the Alaska backcountry

Taking Care of Yourself and the Mountains

The better you are at taking care of yourself and your surroundings, the more enjoyable your experience will be. This includes keeping yourself warm and dry, carrying or constructing effective shelter, and eating and drinking properly. As you care for yourself, remember to take equal care of the environment you are enjoying and always seek to have minimal impact on your surroundings. If you get into ski touring, odds are you'll want to do more than day trips. That means winter camping, which sounds like heaven to some and a frozen hell to others. Yes, you can actually stay comfortable in most conditions, sometimes even perfectly dry and toasty. And staying out overnight can get you to some of the best the backcountry has to offer. You did want to get away from the areas, didn't you?

STAYING DRY

Staying dry in a winter environment can be relatively easy in cold temperatures or next to impossible if the temperature hovers around the freezing point.

In terms of staying dry in moderately cold temperatures, you might as well confront the fact that there will be some discomfort involved. We (the authors) live in the Pacific Northwest and guide in the North Cascades of Washington a lot, where the mountains sometimes seem to be drowning in a 15- to 20-foot snowpack of $0°C/32°F$ snow. If a body of $37°C/98.6°F$ is put into this environment, some melting will occur. And with warm temperatures, the relative humidity can be high; in fact it's above 90 percent most of the time. This extremely maritime snowpack brings its own advantages, but ease of temperature regulation is certainly not one of them.

If this high relative humidity is coupled with actual snowfall, staying dry can be very difficult. You have to wear some form of weather protection, which tends to trap the warm and moist air inside your garment. So you try to ventilate and you end up mixing the warm moisture-laden air with cold air, which brings down the saturation point. If you don't wear any weather protection, you have snow melting on your steaming body.

You will get wet. What to do?

Clothing has come a long way in the recent past, but the industry can't change simple laws of physics. If the winter environment is relatively warm, you will be struggling with moisture, ventilation, staying dry, and drying time (see "Clothing" in chapter 1 for a detailed discussion).

Once you understand and accept these facts, you most likely will not only dress appropriately, you will also start moving appropriately. This takes some experimenting. Not all people weigh the same and work with the same level of efficiency. You will have to find out for yourself what it takes to overwhelm the moisture-transport capabilities of your garments.

STAYING WARM

Since we are warm-blooded animals, our bodies attempt to keep our internal temperature constant. We continually generate heat and our bodies must take active steps to lose that heat. The other side of this coin is in cold weather, in which your body must work to stay warm. The mechanisms for heat loss and retention that your body uses or that affect its function are conduction, convection, evaporation, respiration, and radiation, as discussed in chapter 1 (see the "Warmth is Personal" sidebar in chapter 1).

It's a lot easier to stay warm than to get warm, and one of the best ways to stay warm is not to get too hot. For example, you get out of your nicely heated car at the roadhead, where the temperature hovers around 25°F. Your body perceives this as very cold, so you put on more layers.

As you get ready to start touring, the thought of shedding layers is highly uninviting. So you keep the layers on, thinking you'll take a layer break when you get hot. By the time your body signals that it's hot, however, you've actually been hot for awhile. And when you shed layers you end up shocking your body. Your body was struggling to keep from overheating and was in full cooling mode, trying to lose heat through evaporation: your sweat glands working hard, the pores of your skin wide open. When you take your jacket off, you effectively achieve supercooling.

This feels okay for a while, but your body continues with its heat-loss program through evaporation and pretty soon you've gone from sweating to shivering. You have overcompensated. So you stop again and put a layer on, or you deal with the discomfort until exertion brings your body back into its comfort zone. Overall, you're making your body work very hard to stay in its thermal comfort equilibrium.

A better approach is to try to stay warm

without overheating. Come to a break nicely warm from exercise, put a layer on during the break in order to avoid heat loss, and take the layer off before you leave again.

PLANNED SHELTERS

After a long, hard day of ski touring, you have arrived at your camp. All went well and ideally you should still have some energy to build a nice camp. You carried your shelter with you, but which option did you choose? Shelters vary in efficiency and comfort, so choose one that meets your requirements for both.

Bivy Bags
Pros. Bivy bags are light and compact. They have a small footprint and take up very little space in your pack. They are good in alpine applications where there might not be enough room to pitch a tent. In good weather they can be the lightest option and make for great star gazing.

Cons. A good bivy bag weighs nearly half as much as a modern two-person tent and does not deliver the same amount of protective space. Tents are also more breathable. We recommend a modern two-person tent, unless you're on your own or need to camp somewhere with small camp platforms.

Lightweight Floorless Shelters
Pros. Floorless shelters (like Black Diamond's Mega Mid) are superlight, considering that they can accommodate three

Fig. 8.1 A floorless shelter—surprising comfort for very little weight

to four people in reasonable comfort (fig. 8.1). In conjunction with other group gear, this can mean a very light per person load. These shelters provide good headroom and can be dug out into small snow palaces. They're also cheaper than a fancy, light single-wall tent.

Cons. You saved energy carrying the light load, you arrived in camp, and... you have to keep working for a while. If the group is strong and the weather is decent, this is not that big of a deal, but if you have to set up camp in a storm, this extra exertion can be unpleasant. Floorless shelters can be quite strong and roomy, but all this takes some work.

Tents
Pros. Modern two- and three-person tents offer a broad spectrum of benefits, from lightweight with moderate protection to heavy with excellent protection (fig. 8.2). A decent single-wall two-person tent can weigh barely 3 pounds, while some expedition-type tents can weigh well over 7 pounds. Vestibules are a key feature if the weather is raging.

Fig. 8.2 Expedition camp setting on Mount Logan, Canada (Photograph by Greg Allen)

Cons. Pick your battle—if you take a superlight tent, it will most likely not be as weather worthy, but if the tent is absolutely stormproof, it will be heavier. There are some good single-wall tents out there, but they tend to be less breathable. Consider the duration of your trip and the weather forecast.

SNOW SHELTERS
Building a snow shelter is an option for winter camping. If you are venturing out into the more remote backcountry you should be able to build an emergency snow shelter (see chapter 10 for a discussion of emergency shelters). What follows are two nonemergency versions, should you have the time and inclination.

Side of a Snowbank:
The Snow Cave
If the snowpack is sufficiently high, you could use the side of a snowbank to create a

nice cave in order to get out of the elements (fig. 8.3). If there is enough snow, make sure to use a cold trap in your entrance, meaning the top of the entrance is lower than the platform you are sleeping on.

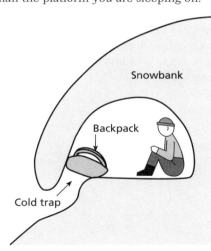

Fig. 8.3 Basic snow shelter on the side of a snowbank or hillside

It is impressive how much warmth you can create (relative to the outside) in a cave like this. Make sure you create a vent hole to keep the cave from dripping and to ensure proper ventilation.

Proper terrain selection is crucial. Please make sure that you are not building your snow cave below a cornice lip or in general avalanche terrain.

Building time for two- to three-person shelter: 1 hour.

The Digloo

The digloo, as the name implies, is a combination between the well-known but seldom-built igloo and a snow cave that is formed out of a mound of snow.

A digloo takes some time to build and is most suitable if there are multiple people involved. Digloos also have great base-camp applications if a storm might last for days. Staying in a tent that is constantly rattled by the wind for days on end, or having to cook in stormy conditions, can be rather demoralizing.

1. Simply start by mounding up snow (this works for shelters built to accommodate up to four people). The resulting cone should be about 8 feet in diameter at the base and about 5–6 feet tall at its highest point (fig. 8.4).
2. Then start hollowing out the inside of the cone from below. Make sure to incorporate a cold trap into the entrance—the top of the entrance should be lower than the platform you'll be sleeping on.
3. In the meantime, have someone stomp out an area of about 25 square

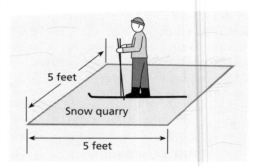

Fig. 8.5a Step 3: Digloo construction

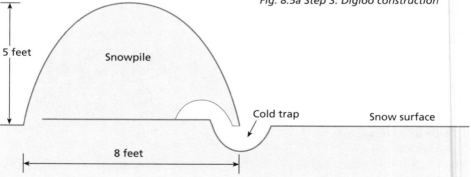

Fig. 8.4 Step 1: Digloo construction

feet with skis on. Let the snow of the stomped area settle a bit. This will be your block material (the snow quarry; see fig. 8.5a).

4. One person climbs to the top of the cone and starts digging down from the top. You want to dig down about 3 feet or so and have the top hole be about 2 feet in diameter (fig. 8.5b).

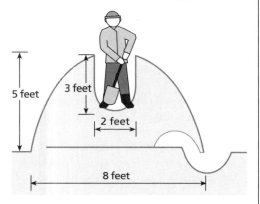

Fig. 8.5b Step 4: Digloo construction

5. The person who was digging below comes out and starts handing cut snow blocks from the snow quarry to the person standing on top of the cone. These snow blocks can be cut with a snow saw, a shovel, or, in a pinch, with a ski.

6. The person on top of the cone builds a small igloo around herself with these snow blocks (fig. 8.6). This is accomplished by cutting the bottom and one side of each snow block at a bit of an angle so that the blocks lean slightly forward and each successive block fits neatly next to the previous one. Make sure you offset the blocks of the next round so that the block seams of the various rounds don't overlap. The snow blocks will start supporting themselves. After a couple of rounds, the remaining hole should be small enough that one more block placed on top should complete the

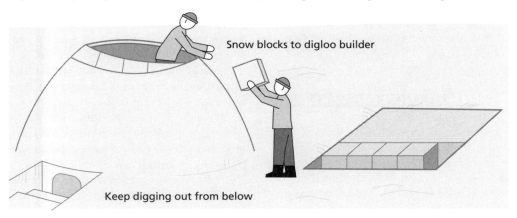

Snow blocks to digloo builder

Keep digging out from below

Fig. 8.6 Step 6: Digloo construction

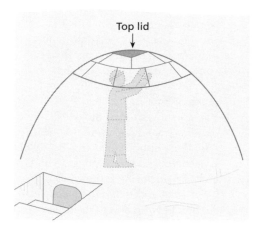

Top lid

Fig. 8.7 Step 6: Digloo construction

simple roof structure. If timed properly, the person digging from below will be close enough to the middle of the cone so that the person on top will end up popping through the ceiling of the lower hole (fig. 8.7). The digloo can then be improved, refined, and enlarged as much as you want. Building time for three-person shelter: 1.5–2 hours.

NUTRITION ON A SKI TOUR

In an endurance sport like backcountry skiing, where you carry your own food, planning for good nutrition is important not only for staying fueled and hydrated, but for managing the weight you carry in your pack. Much has been written about exercise nutrition, and we recommend *Conditioning for Outdoor Fitness* by David Musnick and Mark Pierce as a good place to start. Always keep in mind any of your own health problems that might trump particular recommendations.

Getting the fuel you need on a tour starts with your overall at-home diet. Shoot for 60 percent calories from carbohydrates, 15 percent from protein, and 25 percent from fat. Choose unprocessed carbs (legumes, whole grains, a variety of fruits and vegetables), eat foods low to midrange on the glycemic index, and choose healthy fats (avocados, seeds, nuts). The glycemic index measures the rate at which carbs increase blood-glucose levels—higher-glycemic carbs (honey, fruit juices, fruit) spike blood-sugar levels, while lower-rated carbs (like brown rice) cause a more gentle change in blood sugar.

Your muscles need glycogen to fire, and glycogen is generally replenished with glucose from your bloodstream. Glycogen reserves vary person to person, but you can expect anywhere from 1.5 to 6 hours of fuel before you work through your reserves and you need to replenish. If you don't replenish muscle glycogen, your body seeks fuel by burning fat or protein. Energy from burning fat is hard to access, resulting in significantly decreased performance (the all-too-familiar "bonk"). For longer-duration or higher-intensity activities, like backcountry skiing, you need to start off with high glycogen reserves, replenish them throughout a tour, and completely replenish them after you're done.

ON A DAY TOUR

Before. In the morning before your tour, avoid simple carbs like honey, fruit juices, and fruit (including bananas) that will spike your blood sugar and then make it drop. If you do eat these, also eat some fat and protein to lower the glycemic response. Make sure you get enough protein in the morning—a protein shake or protein bars work great. Drink 12–16 ounces of fluid 1.5–2 hours prior to your tour. Caffeine will squeeze some of the water out of your cells, so keep hydrating after your morning coffee.

During. Don't wait until you're hungry or thirsty to eat or drink. Eat a snack every 1–2 hours, depending on your exertion level. Trail mixes of nuts and dried fruit, cheese, and some meat (or fish, like sardines) all travel well and will help you achieve your recommended 60-15-25 ratio of carbs-protein-fat. A fast way to replenish depleted muscle glycogen is with simple carbs (like energy drinks, Gu, gummies, honey), but you will burn through them more quickly—combine them with fats, protein, and fiber to keep your blood sugar up after the immediate sugar burn. Aim for 6–8 ounces of fluid every 15–20 minutes, or 16–32 ounces per hour.

After. Replenish the fuel your exercise has burned, restore your body's hydration, and make sure enough protein is available for muscle repair and growth. High-glycemic carbs are a good way to replace depleted glycogen, especially in the first four hours post-tour. Hydrate to replace lost fluids (drink until your urine becomes clear). Drink energy drinks with electrolytes (salts), and don't be afraid to eat salted foods (like nuts). Your body can't rehydrate without salt.

ON A MULTIDAY TOUR

Before. You may be able to increase your glycogen reserves by carbohydrate loading, consuming higher than usual levels of carbs (70 percent of your calories) for the week prior to your tour. **Important:** Only do this if you are in excellent condition and free from health problems like diabetes. Continue to get adequate protein. Taper your exercise one week prior, and take a rest day the day before.

During. Carry calorie-dense foods to keep your pack weight down. This means including foods with fats. Plan on enough snacks to eat once every 1–2 hours, with a mix of carbs, protein, and fat. Look for high-calorie, high-protein energy bars (but make sure they're palatable!). Bars with extra vitamins are good too. Bring lots of drink powder, with at least 6–8 percent carb content.

After each day of the tour. Evening meals should replenish glycogen levels—dehydrated potatoes are always a good idea because they're light and high on the glycemic index. Bring enough protein (dried sausage is light; sardines have protein and good fats in them), especially if you plan on strenuous days. Some evidence suggests that protein needs rise with repeated high-intensity exercise. When choosing dehydrated meals, read the labels—some pack a better carb-protein-fat punch than others. Rehydrate after every day, with hot drinks as well as cold ones.

AT ALTITUDE

Above 8000 feet, your body becomes significantly affected by the decrease in available oxygen. One major issue becomes dehydration; your oxygen requirements increase at high altitude. Bring drink mixes to make the needed volume of water more palatable; drink noncaffeinated hot drinks whenever possible; make your water easy to reach while moving. Monitor your urine for output and color, and drink more than you think you need to.

Growing evidence suggests an increased reliance on carbohydrates—and slightly decreased reliance on fats—as altitude increases. Fat requires more oxygen to metabolize at altitude than carbs do. Maintain a high level of carbs at altitude, but consume enough protein to protect against muscle loss. One of the biggest problems with eating at higher altitudes can be loss of appetite. If you're out for a long trip, bring a variety of food and drink, and be aware that bland foods are often more appetizing at high altitudes.

MOUNTAIN ETHICS

The Leave No Trace (LNT) Principles of outdoor ethics form the framework of Leave No Trace's message. Not all the principles have obvious applications in ski touring and ski mountaineering, so we have included them here with some elaboration on what they can mean for backcountry skiing. For more detailed information about the basic principles, refer to the LNT website at *www.LNT.org.*

Leave No Trace principles:
Text in *italics* is particularly relevant for backcountry skiing

1. **Plan Ahead and Prepare**
   - *Know the regulations and special concerns for the areas you'll visit.*
   - *Prepare for extreme weather, hazards, and emergencies.*
   - *Schedule your trip to avoid times of high use.*
   - *Visit in small groups when possible. Consider splitting larger groups into smaller groups.*
   - *Repackage food to minimize waste.*
   - *Use a map and compass to eliminate the use of marking paint, rock cairns, or flagging.*

2. **Travel and Camp on Durable Surfaces**
   - *Durable surfaces include established campsites, rock, gravel, dry grasses, or snow.*
   - *Protect riparian areas by camping at least 200 feet from lakes and streams.*
   - Good campsites are found, not made. Altering a site is not necessary.
   - In popular areas:
     - Concentrate use on existing trails and campsites.
     - Walk single file in the middle of the trail, even when wet or muddy.

- Keep campsites small. Focus activities in areas where vegetation is absent.
- In pristine areas:
  - Disperse use to prevent the creation of campsites and trails.
  - Avoid places where impacts are just beginning.

3. Dispose of Waste Properly

- *Pack it in, pack it out. Inspect your campsite and rest areas for trash or spilled foods. Pack out all trash, leftover food, and litter.*
- *Deposit solid human waste in catholes dug 6 to 8 inches deep at least 200 feet from water, camp, and trails. Cover and disguise the cathole when finished.*
- *Pack out toilet paper and hygiene products.*
- *To wash yourself or your dishes, carry water 200 feet away from streams or lakes and use small amounts of biodegradable soap. Scatter strained dishwater.*

4. Leave What You Find

- Preserve the past: examine, but do not touch, cultural or historic structures and artifacts.
- Leave rocks, plants and other natural objects as you find them.
- Avoid introducing or transporting non-native species.
- Do not build structures, furniture, or dig trenches.

5. Minimize Campfire Impacts

- *Campfires can cause lasting impacts to the backcountry. Use a lightweight stove for cooking and enjoy a candle lantern for light.*
- Where fires are permitted, use established fire rings, fire pans, or mound fires.
- Keep fires small. Only use sticks from the ground that can be broken by hand.
- Burn all wood and coals to ash, put out campfires completely, then scatter cool ashes.

6. Respect Wildlife

- *Observe wildlife from a distance. Do not follow or approach them.*
- *Never feed animals. Feeding wildlife damages their health, alters natural behaviors, and exposes them to predators and other dangers.*
- *Protect wildlife and your food by storing rations and trash securely.*
- *Control pets at all times, or leave them at home.*
- *Avoid wildlife during sensitive times: mating, nesting, raising young, or winter.*

7. Be Considerate of Other Visitors

- *Respect other visitors and protect the quality of their experience.*
- *Be courteous. Yield to other users on the trail.*
- Step to the downhill side of the trail when encountering pack stock.
- *Take breaks and camp away from trails and other visitors.*
- *Let nature's sounds prevail. Avoid loud voices and noises.*

BEYOND LEAVE NO TRACE: A PERSONAL APPROACH

The Leave No Trace principles are firmly established and have been incorporated into the general practices of guide services, land-management agencies, and the visiting public. There is growing consensus that these principles are a good step in environmental awareness, but though they focus on protecting a particular resource it is sometimes hard to link this directly to our everyday world.

To protect our precious natural resources, permit systems had to be established in many parks and wilderness areas. We believe this management style turns many people away from enjoying wildlands, thus denying them a connection to the natural world. Developing this connection could ultimately help to protect this resource. Our population is becoming more and more urban and as a result is more detached from the natural world than ever. It's hard to connect with the natural world if you have never seen it. It's also a big turnoff for potential outdoor users that they can't just up and go. Access restrictions make it feel like you're not going to a free place, which is a principal reason people flock to the mountains in the first place.

So we pose these questions:

- Is it worth straining an ecologically intact resource a bit in order to foster a more environmentally aware attitude in the general population?
- Conversely, what if there was *carte blanche* access and our LNT practices were so widespread due to basic education in schools that virtually no impact occurred on protected land?
- How do we get to the mountains, and how much environmental damage do we cause by driving and flying to these places?
- How much damage do we cause outfitting ourselves with high-quality gear that was shipped halfway around the world?

We believe the long-term solution to environmental awareness lies in more education on a large scale and maybe less restriction. We're not saying we're right, but we're convinced that these questions should be on your mind both when you're in the backcountry and the civilized world.

Perfect weather, perfect place, perfect sport. Camp in the Forbidden Peak area, North Cascades, Washington

CHAPTER 9

The Mountain Environment

Just about everybody who has spent significant time in the mountains has a good weather story. Of course, weather stories can resemble fishing stories: as time goes on, temperatures tend to get colder, snow dumps deeper, and wind speeds get higher. Nonetheless, mountain weather can be extreme and changes can come about abruptly.

Weather happens all the time all around us, but not until we leave our sheltered 21°C/70°F homes do we really start to pay attention to it. Once we enter the relative wildness of the mountains, talking about the weather becomes more than water-cooler chitchat—it's one of the most important topics of the day. The weather affects just about everything on a ski tour: whether or not we go in the first place, what route we take, what we wear, and, in the end, how much fun we have.

MOUNTAIN WEATHER BASICS

So how does the weather happen, and more particularly, how does mountain weather happen? What follows is a brief overview of complex processes. For more detail, *Mountain Weather* by Jeff Renner is an excellent resource.

The earth's axis and rotation relative to the sun cause strong heating and cooling of the earth's surface and atmosphere as different regions are exposed to more or less solar radiation. This differential heating of air drives our weather. The heating and cooling of air occurs with the following general patterns. Warm air can absorb more moisture than cold air (i.e., is more humid), and warm air is also less dense than cold air. Pressure, temperature, and humidity differentials in the atmosphere drive movement of air masses. Higher-density air flows toward lower-density air, and warm air rises above colder air and the air starts circulating.

Mountains form great barriers against the natural flow of these air masses. Mountains stall air masses over an area or cause them to rise in elevation. This causes changes in air density, temperature, and humidity, and mountain weather occurs.

ATMOSPHERIC PRESSURE

Atmospheric pressure is a measure of the weight of the air. It is expressed in millibars (1013 millibars at sea level) or in inches of mercury (29.92 inches of mercury at sea level). The atmosphere is thicker at the equator; thus atmospheric pressure is higher there than at sea level somewhere in the Arctic.

As you go up in altitude, atmospheric pressure decreases. At first, the decrease is about 100 millibars per 1000 meters of altitude gain (or 1 inch of mercury per 1000 feet). But, unlike the altitude increase, the atmospheric pressure decrease is not linear (fig. 9.1).

Atmospheric pressure drops to one half its sea-level value at about 18,000 feet. The implication is that one half of all the mass of the atmosphere lies below this altitude. Further, almost (but not quite) a third of the total lies below 10,000 feet. On the other hand, more than one-fifth of the total lies above 35,000 feet.

What does this mean for the backcountry skier?

The atmosphere contains about 21 percent oxygen. Commonly people say there is less oxygen the higher up you go. This is slightly misleading because the percentage of oxygen does not change at all throughout the atmosphere. It is just the air density

ALTITUDE (FT/M)	PRESSURE (IN HG/MB)	ALTITUDE (FT/M)	PRESSURE (IN HG/MB)
0	29.92 / 1013	20,000 / 6097	13.75 / 464
1000 / 305	28.86 / 977	22,000 / 6707	12.64 / 428
2000 / 610	27.82 / 941	24,000 / 7317	11.56 / 392
3000 / 914	26.82 / 908	26,000 / 7926	10.62 / 360
4000 / 1220	25.84 / 875	28,000 / 8536	9.70 / 329
5000 / 1524	24.89 / 842	30,000 / 9146	8.87 / 301
10,000 / 3048	20.58 / 697		
15,000 / 4573	16.88 / 571		
18,000 / 5487*	14.94 / 508		

This is almost exactly one half the sea-level value.

Fig. 9.1 Altitude/Barometric pressure conversion chart

that decreases as you climb higher. In other words, at 18,000 feet, you inhale about half the amount of oxygen as at sea level, even though your respiratory volume remains the same. You would have to inhale twice in order to obtain the same amount of oxygen compared to sea level.

This matters to backcountry skiers because we're gaining altitude to get our turns in, and we're exerting ourselves, using oxygen, to do it. That means we have to adapt to lesser oxygen availability at altitude. Physical adaptation to higher altitude happens in two basic stages: short-term adaptation is the initial phase in which your body reacts to the shortage of oxygen concentration by increasing your respiratory and pulse rates. Long-term adaptation begins after a few days at higher altitude, when your body starts producing more red blood cells, which are effectively the oxygen delivery system in your body.

There is a wealth of information about physical exertion and adaptation at altitude, for example in James Wilkerson's *Medicine for Mountaineering*, and we encourage you to delve deeper.

FRONTS

Fronts are the boundaries between different air masses. Meteorologists differentiate between four different types of fronts:

Warm front. This is a front where a warm air mass is replacing a colder air mass (fig. 9.2). In the mountains this could mean:
- The temperature could rise.
- The snow quality could decrease.
- The avalanche hazard could increase, if higher density snow falls on lower density snow.
- Since warm air is not as dense as cold air, temperature inversions could occur.
- If this warm front is associated with precipitation, it could bring freezing rain.

Cold front. This is a front where a cold air mass is replacing a warmer air mass (fig. 9.3). In the mountains this could mean:

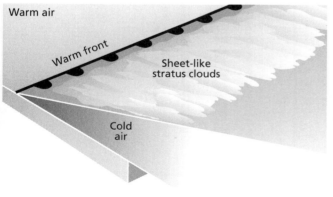

Fig. 9.2 Warm front

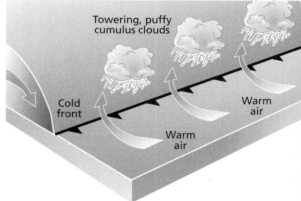

Fig. 9.3 Cold front

- The temperature could decrease.
- The snow quality could increase.
- The avalanche hazard could increase, if the front is associated with a lot of fresh snow.
- The avalanche hazard could also increase if the warm front is replaced by cold weather without precipitation and then the new, low-density snow falls on this potentially frozen old layer.

Generally speaking, cold fronts bring lower precipitation amounts than warm fronts, since the saturation point of the air is lower in cold air.

Occluded front. This is a front where a cold air mass is mixing with warmer air masses (fig. 9.4). The result could be just about anything, and in the mountains this could mean:

- Prolonged precipitation with strong bursts and maybe even lightning
- Rather quick passage of the front

Stationary front. As their name implies, stationary fronts do not really move and not much happens. In the mountains this could mean:

- Prolonged precipitation
- Widespread cloud cover

TEMPERATURE

Finally, something not so fuzzy. Air temperature is an absolute measurement. Of course different people perceive it differently and changing humidity saturation can change the perceived temperature like not much else. Wind also changes the

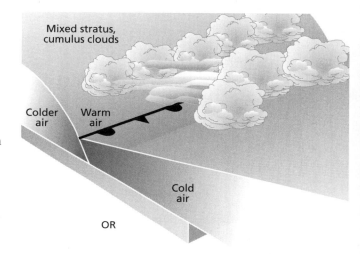

OR

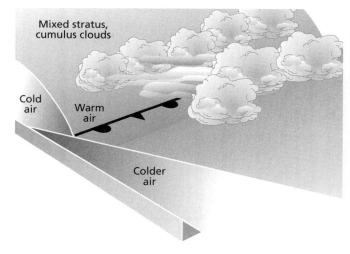

Fig. 9.4 Occluded front

perceived temperature, though new wind-chill calculations make the numbers seem less frightening (fig. 9.5).

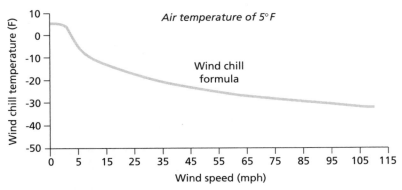

Fig. 9.5 Wind chill temperature chart

Temperature and elevation. As you gain elevation, temperature drops about 0.6°C per 100 meters (or about 3°F per 1000 feet, roughly 10°F per 10,000 feet).

Temperature inversion. A temperature inversion is when colder, denser air sinks to a low-lying area and is capped by warmer air sitting on top. This occurs quite often in the winter, and cold air pockets that form in shady valley bottoms can persist for a long time. An inversion can also result from two fronts of radically different temperatures meeting, with the cold air forcing the lighter warm air to rise.

ANATOMY OF A GLACIER

Glaciers are relatively simple in their makeup, but very complex in how they behave. Explaining and understanding fully how glaciers work exceeds the scope of this book, but a basic understanding of glaciology will increase your safety and enjoyment in the mountains.

Most of the glaciers in the world are receding at an alarming rate, and the reasons for it are well documented. It is also equally well documented that glaciers have surged and receded for as long as they have been around. If all is well, a glacier exists in a delicate state of equilibrium between precipitation in the form of snow, melting, mean temperature, and surface area.

HOW GLACIERS FORM

All glaciers are born from snow. The snow that settles onto the mountain landscape builds a snowpack and consolidates over time (figs. 9.6–9.9 show glaciers and their components). Some of this snow melts in the summer and some of it survives. Snow that survives a full summer cycle turns into névé, or firn.

At this point the snow has reached a density of around 60 percent. If all goes well, the firn gets covered by a new blanket of snow in the fall, and further compaction increases its density to about 75 percent. If the new blanket of snow can keep the first

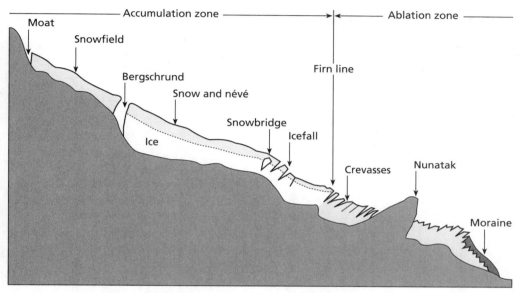

Fig. 9.6 Anatomy of a glacier—side view

firn layer covered over the next summer, this firn layer will start to progress in the direction of young glacial ice. Its density is now around 85 percent, and to the climber or ski mountaineer it feels like ice.

When is it snow and when does it turn into ice? At around 85-percent density, the spaces between the isolated ice grains are reduced enough to call it a solid mass of ice. Right around this time the glacier also starts flowing as a solid unit.

HOW GLACIERS FLUCTUATE

Just about any alpine glacier can be divided into two sections:

Accumulation zone: In the accumulation zone, the total amount of annual precipitation in the form of snow exceeds the total amount of melt-off.

Ablation zone: In the ablation zone, the total amount of melt-off exceeds the total amount of accumulation.

Naturally, then, there is a zone where accumulation and ablation are in balance. This zone travels up the glacier through the summer season. Where it ends up in the fall before the new snow season starts is called the firn line, or the zone of equilibrium.

If a glacier's size is stable, the total volume of water gained in the accumulation area is very close to the same volume of water that was lost due to melting below the zone of equilibrium. Annual

267

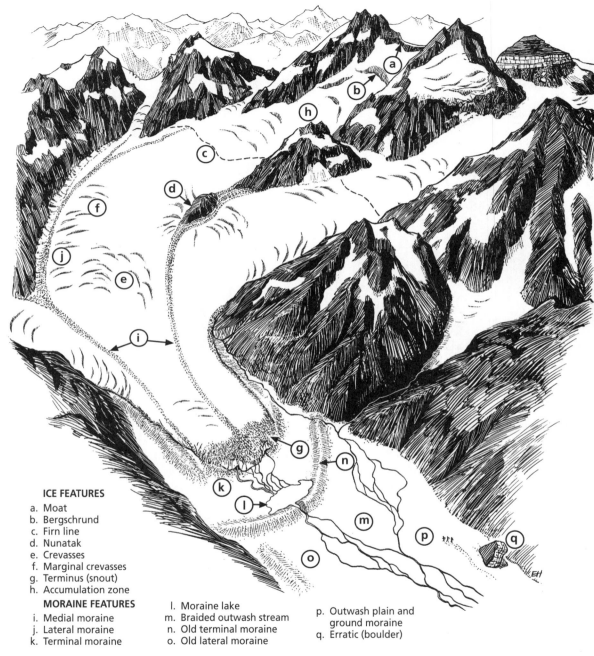

ICE FEATURES

a. Moat
b. Bergschrund
c. Firn line
d. Nunatak
e. Crevasses
f. Marginal crevasses
g. Terminus (snout)
h. Accumulation zone

MORAINE FEATURES

i. Medial moraine
j. Lateral moraine
k. Terminal moraine

l. Moraine lake
m. Braided outwash stream
n. Old terminal moraine
o. Old lateral moraine

p. Outwash plain and
  ground moraine
q. Erratic (boulder)

Fig. 9.7 Anatomy of a glacier—top view

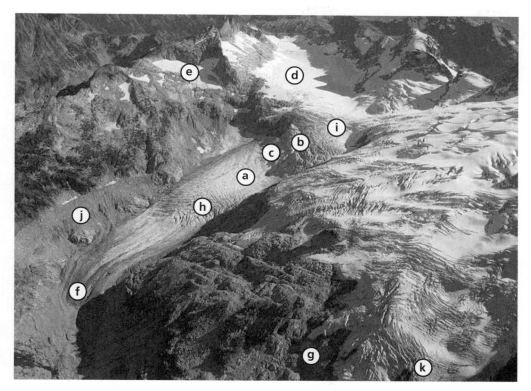

a. Ogives
b. Icefall
c. Compression zone
d. Accumulation basin
e. Pocket glacier
f. Snout of retreating glacier
g. Glacier polished bedrock
h. Crevasse zone
i. Approximate firn line
j. 19th century lateral moraine
k. Extreme crevasse zone due to glacial thinning

Fig. 9.8 Chickamin Glacier in the North Cascades, Washington (Photograph by John Scurlock)

fluctuations are normal, but observed over a few years the firn line should end up roughly in the same spot at the end of each summer.

Though glaciers worldwide are retreating at a rapid rate, this doesn't necessarily mean they are all dying. They are adjusting, downsizing so to speak. They will retreat until the total melt-off volume equals the accumulation volume again and, as long as that equation stays even, a glacier is technically still "alive." Current studies suggest that many glaciers won't survive, however. If a glacier receives tremendous

a. Accumulation zone
b. Firn line
c. Ablation zone
d. Pocket glacier without current accumulation zone
e. Icefall
f. Small valley glacier
g. Glacial plateau
h. Nunatak
i. Bergschrund

Fig. 9.9 Eldorado/Klawatti area in the North Cascades in early fall of 2005 after the "non-winter" of 2004–2005 (Photograph by John Scurlock)

amounts of snowfall, if temperatures remain cold enough, and if all the factors are just right so that accumulation exceeds ablation, some glaciers will start increasing in length and volume until things are in balance again.

HOW CREVASSES FORM

Crevasses! They are probably the principal reason why ski mountaineers are interested in glaciers. Crevasses form on just about all glaciers of any size, and crevasse falls have resulted in many fatalities. Crevasses are frightening enough that their size and hazard have been exaggerated, but they nonetheless present a primary mountain hazard for the ski mountaineer. A bit of knowledge on how crevasses form and how a glacier flows in general can increase your ability to make safe decisions when in crevassed terrain.

Just about all temperate glaciers (as opposed to arctic glaciers) "flow" down the mountain. This is a simple function of gravity coupled with bedrock lubrication. Bedrock lubrication occurs because meltwater from the glacier's surface flows to the bedrock and also because the lower layers of any "warm" glacier are in a near liquid state. For a discussion of the complex physics of glacial flow, *Living Ice* by Robert Sharp is a good resource (see "Avalanche and Weather Publications" in the appendix).

Crevasses form because the outer brittle crust of the glacier flows over topographical features at a different speed than the more plastic interior layers. This causes the ice to shear and break in multiple dimensions. The flow rate is faster near the surface of a glacier and also in the middle than near its outer edges. Most of the shifting and fracturing that occurs on the surface are considered crevasses.

There are different types of crevasses, and their exact locations are difficult to anticipate when they are snowed-in. There are, however, certain types of crevasses that tend to form in a certain way in certain areas of a glacier.

Bergschrunds

A bergschrund is a crevasse that occurs where a glacier detaches itself at its highest margin from a rock face, a couloir, or a mountainside where it is too steep for a glacier to form.

What you should know. A bergschrund wall normally forms perpendicular to the slope. This means that if the upside slope of a bergschrund has an angle of 40 degrees, the upper wall of the bergschrund will most likely be quite overhung.

Keep this in mind if you are approaching a bergschrund from the top. Conversely if you are approaching the same bergschrund from below and the angle is still quite steep, you might be surprised to see that the lower bergschrund wall seems at a friendlier angle.

Be very careful with these crevasses. Quite often they bend into a more plumb direction farther down. This curved appearance can make crevasse rescues very tricky.

Crevasses in Stress Zones

These so-called V-shaped crevasses are generally the most visible ones. The stress zones are areas where a differential in gravitational pull occurs. This could be a rapid change in topography. The classic feature is a mellow slope changing into a steeper slope. Gravitational pull accelerates the flow and the brittle crust fractures, forming the crevasse.

What you should know. Be aware

that these stress zones can also produce crevasses uphill from the actual zone. The increased flowage starts pulling the ice apart a bit above the stress zone. Also watch for crevasses once you are below the visible stress zone, since crevasses that were created above are moving down with the glacier and are only closing gradually over time.

Icefalls

If the change in gravitational pull is quite severe and the topography goes through an abrupt change (maybe a cliff in the bedrock), the resulting crevasses can be so chaotic and severe that they can make up a very unstable and generally dangerous section of the glacier.

What you should know. Try to avoid spending time in and below icefalls. The calving that occurs in icefalls is unpredictable and correlates only to a certain extent to the seasonal and daily warming cycles.

Crevasses in Compression Zones

These so-called A-shaped crevasses are tricky because they are less visible than other crevasse types. They occur in transition zones where the glacial flow slows down rapidly (for example, the transition from steep to flat terrain). The glacier is compressed more at the surface and the crevasse is thus bigger toward the depths of the crevasse.

What you should know. These crevasses are very dangerous. They are not only hard to spot, they can also be severely overhung. This means that you might spot the hole in time, but you'll already be standing on a crevasse lip.

Crevasses Around the Lateral Margins

A glacier flows faster in the middle than toward its edge, where it is being slowed down by the friction against the lateral moraines. This causes crevasses that are diagonally downward facing. Over time, the flow of the glacier turns these crevasses more perpendicular to the glacier's flow direction.

What you should know. Anticipate that there might be crevasses if you are leaving the lateral margins of a glacier.

Seracs and Serac Zones

If a glacier flows over a topographical feature that causes gravitational pull in multiple directions (like a knob of some sort), the ice will fracture in multiple directions and create this very unstable feature.

What you should know: Try to avoid close contact with serac zones. If you have to pass under one, it's time to hurry.

What You Should Really Know About Crevasses

Crevasses seem to form in the strangest places. It would be foolish to simply look at basic topographic features, potential stress and compression zones, and then think you can make solid judgments about where crevasses are. Glaciology is a very complex topic and just about any glaciologist will confirm that predicting the location of crevasses with 100 percent accuracy is just about impossible. You can, however, be prepared with an awake mind, the right equipment, and the proper training to use it.

CHAPTER 10

Skier in the hole! North Cascades, Washington

Rescue Techniques and Emergency Preparedness

The two most important kinds of technical rescue skills you need for ski touring and ski mountaineering are companion rescue and crevasse rescue. Companion rescue occurs in the event of an avalanche and involves using avalanche beacons, shovels, and probes to find and dig out a buried ski partner. We discussed the basics of beacon function and use in chapter 1; here, in chapter 10, we focus on the vital skills necessary to carry out a beacon rescue.

Crevasse rescue is necessary if someone falls into a crevasse while traveling roped on a glacier. Crevasse rescue can occur as self-rescue—where the fallen skier ascends the rope to get out of the crevasse—or can involve a hauling system, where other members of the rope team pull the fallen skier out of the crevasse. In both cases, your ultimate goals are prevention and practice: learn the systems and techniques well, and then use your terrain skills and travel techniques to avoid having to use them in the mountains.

AVALANCHE COMPANION RESCUE

Your best protection against dying in an avalanche is prevention. Use terrain selection and travel techniques (as discussed in chapter 2) with a healthy dose of caution to avoid getting caught in the first place.

Trauma is what kills 25 percent of people buried in an avalanche. That's one in four—not very good odds. The remaining fatalities are mainly from asphyxiation. Figure 10.1 shows the time needed to keep survival odds reasonable for victims not killed by trauma.

If you are caught in an avalanche and not killed by trauma, the best chance you have for survival is to be rescued by your companions. In the event of a burial, you

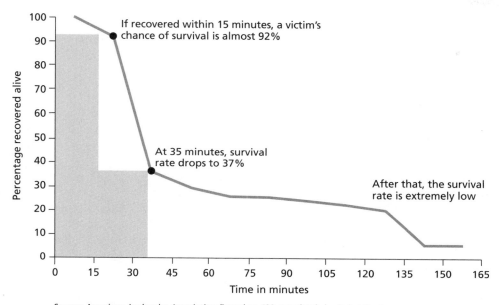

Source: American Avalanche Association (based on 422 completely buried victims)

Fig. 10.1 Survival chances of avalanche victims not killed by trauma

and your fellow skiers can provide each other with the fastest means of rescue. Organized rescue involving search and rescue, ski patrol, or any rescuers outside the immediate party may take many hours or days to reach an accident site. This timeline is not realistic for finding avalanche victims alive.

To travel in avalanche terrain, each person *must* have a beacon, dedicated probe, shovel, and the knowledge to use them. Remember, your knowledge of rescue doesn't benefit you, only your partners, so insist on competent, well-equipped ski partners.

Take note: Companion rescue has one key limitation. There must be companions not buried by the avalanche in order to effect a rescue.

Take note: Your only real chance of surviving an avalanche will come from your partners, not outside help. They must have the skills, knowledge, and equipment to be able to help you.

WHAT IF YOU ARE CAUGHT IN AN AVALANCHE?

If you are caught in an avalanche, your survival is mostly a matter of luck. However, there are some things you can do to help yourself:

- **Yell.** Get the attention of your partners to get their eyes on you.
- **Try to ski off the slab or moving snow.** This may involve skiing downward or to the side.
- **Jettison all your equipment** if you are unable to ski off the slab. Items such as poles, skis, and large backpacks only weigh you down. Getting rid of gear sounds easier than it actually is. It may be unrealistic to shed these items, and you may need to rely on the releasability of your bindings.

  There has been some debate about whether to leave your pack on or let it go. If you're carrying a large pack, such as an overnight pack, it may be best to remove it because the extra weight may make you sink. To prepare for this, loosen or unbuckle the straps prior to heading onto a suspect avalanche slope. Small day packs are best left on: if you do get buried they may provide some back protection, and if you don't you might need your rescue gear to help your friend.

- **Look for items to grab onto.** Maybe it's possible to grab a tree and let the slab go by. If nothing else, pay attention to the objects on the slope and try to be prepared to hit them.
- **Fight to stay on the surface.** Once again, easier said than done, but do your best to stay afloat—it's human nature. People who have been in an avalanche describe using a violent swimming motion.

As you slow down:

- **Try to make it to the surface of the snow.**
- **Try to make an airspace around your face.**
- **Try to get a hand or leg up and visible.** This can greatly improve your odds of survival.

Note that the three techniques listed above are last-ditch efforts; each one is potentially life-saving but each also has a potential cost. (For instance, thrusting your hand upwards means you can't give yourself much of an air pocket.)

After the snow stops moving:

- **Try digging yourself out.** Maybe you're close to the surface and you can rescue yourself.
- **Yell out for help.** This might give the rescuers a jump on your location.
- **If all else fails, remain as calm as possible.** Hopefully you've chosen competent ski partners and rescue is only minutes away. It's crucial to conserve as much oxygen as possible, and staying calm helps with this.

OUTLINE OF THE RESCUE

Rescue does not come easy. Imagine you need to rescue your partner from under the snow. Knowing the odds of survival only increases the stress. The best way to ensure a competent rescue is to adopt the tactic the fire department uses: rescue repetition. The more practice the better. Be sure to practice all aspects of various types of rescue scenarios (see the "Tips for Rescue Training" sidebar).

You must move quickly in a rescue, but you must also be methodical. You must organize the search and then carry it out rather than just rushing around in a panic.

Organization

1. **Determine the last seen point.** This is the location to begin the search. Hopefully, you were using appropriate travel techniques, were skiing the suspect slope one at a time, and had eyes on each skier.
2. **Determine a leader.** Sometimes this just happens, and the natural-born leader in the group takes charge. It's not a bad idea to figure out who a leader might be prior to embarking on your trip, but sometimes you need to decide on the leader in the field. Either way, don't waste time—figure it out quickly.
3. **Determine the safety of the slope** before rushing out onto it. A buried rescuer is not a very effective rescuer. Look around: could another avalanche occur? Two big things to look out for are the presence of hang

fire (snow above the crown) and multiple slide paths that lead into the deposition area. You may need to assign someone to stand watch if you think danger still exists and you have decided to proceed with the rescue anyway. Establish an escape route for the rescuers.

4. **Do a head count.** It's important to know how many people you're looking for.
5. **Assign tasks.** Who will perform the transceiver search? Who should have shovels and probes ready? Who should get the first aid ready? Maybe you're the only searcher, then it's obvious—it's all up to you.

The Search

1. **Do a visual search.** Don't get so focused on your beacon that you don't see a hand sticking above the snow. If you see any visual clues, go pull on them and see if they're attached to the person you're looking for.
2. **Turn all nonsearching transceivers to off.** Perform a visual check of everyone's beacons. Searching with a transceiver is hard enough, try not to make it any harder with a false signal.
3. **Mark the last seen point if possible.** Marking this point helps define the search pattern, especially if the scene becomes confusing.
4. **Begin the transceiver search.** See "Transceiver Search," below, for detailed information about the three phases of the beacon search: Primary,

Secondary, and Pinpoint.

5. **Once the signal is pinpointed, probe.** See "Probing," below.

6. **Dig.** See "Shoveling Technique," below.

7. **Tend to the victims.** Remember, 25 percent of victims caught are killed by trauma. This means that many of the remaining 75 percent may be injured and may need first aid.

THE THREE COMPONENTS OF COMPANION RESCUE

Companion rescue involves three main components to get to the buried person: the transceiver search, probing, and shoveling. After the person is uncovered and has an established airway, another set of rescue and first-aid skills need to be employed (see "Wilderness First Aid" in the appendix).

Transceiver Search

Practicing beacon searches can be a confusing and frustrating experience. We've observed this on many occasions while teaching avalanche courses with new and experienced users alike. There is no question that using a beacon to search for a buried partner is currently the fastest way to recover a buried person. So why is it so confusing?

From our observations, one reason is that people become affected by *beeper tunnel vision*. In other words, you become so overwhelmed by the technology in your hands that the world around you gets overlooked.

One of the keys to a fast beacon search is being good at spatial recognition. This requires you as a searcher to look up from the beacon and recognize where to go and where you've been. A system to methodically cover ground, and to keep track of this, results in fast search times.

In order to do this as quickly as possible, you should use these three phases of a beacon search: primary search, secondary search, and pinpoint search—think: run, walk, crawl (fig. 10.2). Beacons vary in their

TIPS FOR RESCUE TRAINING

- Take a modern avalanche course that has a beacon training and rescue scenario component.
- Take some time after your tour with your ski buddies to practice. Put beacons in backpacks and bury them in open terrain (away from avalanche risks).
- Practice beacon searches on the beach in the sand (this works great, just make sure you seal the beacons in plastic before training).
- Visit a beacon training park. These are free training sites around North America and Europe sponsored by Backcountry Access (BCA) and are often hosted by others, including ski areas.
- Take an instructional course or clinic to learn multiple beacon search techniques.

distance and directional indicators, but the methods below will work for any beacon. It's up to you to understand the specific functions of your beacon.

What follows are the basic steps for a *single-beacon* search. Then we address techniques for a *multiple-beacon* search. There is some overlap between the two kinds of searches.

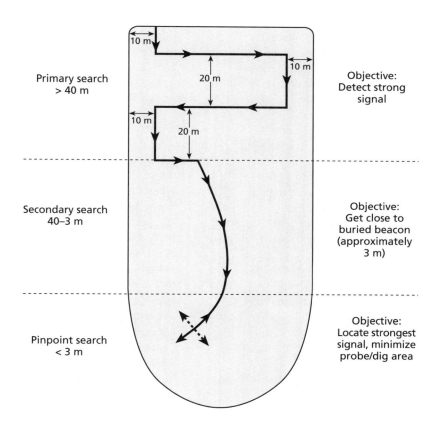

Primary search
> 40 m

Objective:
Detect strong
signal

10 m
20 m
10 m
10 m
20 m

Secondary search
40–3 m

Objective:
Get close to
buried beacon
(approximately
3 m)

Pinpoint search
< 3 m

Objective:
Locate strongest
signal, minimize
probe/dig area

Fig. 10.2 Three phases of a beacon search

Primary Search: Run

Here the main objective is to obtain a signal with the searching beacon.

1. Begin at the last seen point. If there is no last seen point, begin at the start of the avalanche path. If a signal is immediately found, move on to "Secondary Search: Walk," below (but only if you're searching for a single burial).

2. Zigzag horizontally across the path in the pattern shown in figure 10.2. Follow the path, making switchbacks 20 meters apart and within 10 meters of the edge (flank) of the path. Do this as quickly as possible.

3. Keep moving. The key here is to cover the ground in a methodical way, leaving no part of the slope unchecked.

4. Move the beacon back and forth in front of you in a slow sweeping motion to aid in signal detection.

5. Once a useable signal is found, move on to the secondary search.

Tip: If you find yourself standing in place, rotating your beacon around, confused—*move*. Walk forward and your beacon will give you more information.

Secondary Search: Walk

Begin the secondary search once a useable signal is found.

1. At a fast walk, follow the directional indication given by the searching beacon. Decreasing numbers and directional arrows found on most beacons will guide you along the flux line (see "Avalanche Safety Equipment" in chapter 1). Often a curving path leads to the pinpoint search. If using an analog beacon, remember to reduce the antenna's sensitivity control as you get closer. Don't forget to look around for your location and other clues in the slide path.

2. As you get closer, slow down and watch your indicators carefully so that you don't walk past the buried beacon.

Pinpoint Search: Crawl

The pinpoint search begins when you are within 3 meters of the buried victim. The primary goal here is to find the strongest signal on the snow surface so you can pinpoint the probing location.

1. When the beacon indicates 3 meters, lower the beacon to the snow surface and proceed low to the ground (fig. 10.3). This removes the 1 meter or so of unnecessary distance between the searching and transmitting beacons that exists when you're standing up. Slow down here. Thirty extra seconds of caution can save several minutes later on.

2. Continue on the same path you were following in the secondary search, moving the beacon slowly forward until the distance numbers begin to increase. Mark that point with a line in the snow. Keep the beacon in the same orientation (do not rotate), and

Fig. 10.3 A correctly performed pinpoint search with the beacon at the snow surface

move the beacon backward along the same path to find the lowest reading along the path. Move the beacon (in the same direction) *past* this point, and mark the first place where the distance numbers increase. You now have the upper and lower bounds marked.

3. Move the beacon back to the lowest distance reading. Now move it to one side, in a direction perpendicular to your path in step 2. Mark the point where the numbers increase. Repeat this process to the other side. Now you have the left and right bounds marked. Remember to keep your beacon oriented in the same direction in steps 2 and 3.

You have created a square marked in the snow, and the pinpoint location will be inside of it, usually about in the center.

Multiple-Beacon Search

An avalanche with a buried skier is the backcountry traveler's worst nightmare. Multiple buried skiers are even worse. Multiple-beacon searches are exponentially more difficult than a single search for several reasons. Multiple buried beacons simultaneously sending out signals confuses even the most experienced beacon user. To complicate matters, once you've located the buried person you still need to extricate him and then move on to the next person(s)—this takes a tremendous amount of time. *Remember, good terrain selection is the key to not getting caught in an avalanche, and correctly implementing travel techniques is the key to not having multiple people caught.*

A focus of beacon technology is in reducing the complexity of the multiple signals that the user must decipher. At present, many beacons function similarly to each other in a single search. How to search for multiple victims differs between manufacturers, as each company uses the technology it thinks will best expedite a search. Each beacon functions slightly differently in its multiple search mode, and familiarity with this mode is fundamental to completing a search. The key to improving your chances in the event of a multiple burial is practice. Due to the array of differing technology, having a standardized search technique for practicing has been difficult—until recently.

The Three Circle Method (TCM) is a multiple beacon search technique that builds on the single beacon search pattern described in "Transceiver Search," above. There are other search techniques unique to each beacon, and some of these may prove faster when carried out by an experienced user. The benefit of the TCM is that it is easily adaptable to any beacon—a huge plus for anyone looking to gain training experience in searching for multiple beacons.

The TCM focuses on a systematic and methodical technique to define the search area. As you move you are always checking off your search area and noting where you need to go next. The TCM is a good technique we recommend for getting started in your training and practice for locating mul-tiple beacons. "Beacon Searches with the Three Circle Method" by Chris Semmel and Dieter Stopper describes the technique in detail (see "Avalanche and Weather Publications" in the appendix).

Probing

Probing prior to digging can save you precious time in the recovery of your partner. In the shoveling section, below, you'll find out how much snow you need to excavate for a typical burial—it's a ton (literally). Without an exact pinpoint using a probe, the search time will go up dramatically and the results are often not good. The best way to target which snow to remove and exactly where your partner lies is through effective probing.

By the time you are into your pinpoint search, you and your searching partners should have a probe out. If there are multiple rescuers, someone can start probing around.

1. Begin probing at the pinpoint location,

PROBING TIPS

- Keep both hands spaced apart on the probe with one hand low and near the surface of the snow; this will minimize probe breakage.
- Use a fair amount of force when probing to penetrate all the layers of the snow; some layers can be surprisingly dense.
- If your probe has incremental marks, note the depth of the buried person—this depth will come into play for shoveling.
- To feel the difference between a dense layer and a buried person, push your probe against your partner while out practicing with your beacons.
- The general rule is to probe down to a depth of 2 meters (6 feet). If the area was pinpointed using a beacon, probe as deep as necessary to find the skier.
- Wear gloves while probing to prevent snow from freezing to the probe.

with the probe held perpendicular to the snow surface.

2. Probe in an expanding spiral pattern, with each spiral 10 inches (25 centimeters) apart. Do this as quickly as possible.

3. Once you have a confirmed probe strike, *leave the probe in place.* This ensures you don't dig in the wrong area, a mistake common given the frantic nature of a rescue.

Spot Probing

If you cover all the deposition area with your beacon and you are unable to pick up a signal, you can still look for the buried skier. If you need to search for someone without a beacon signal, you can use the spot-probing technique. Spot probing differs from probe lines common to search and rescue protocol, which require a fair amount of manpower and rarely have live results.

Hopefully, you have a last seen point. This will provide a good starting point to begin your spot probing.

1. Start at the last seen point.

2. Determine the likely burial areas below the last seen point. These include:
   - The uphill side of trees, rocks, and other obstacles
   - Depressions, holes, and creek beds
   - In the fall line directly below the last seen point. Flowing snow has characteristics similar to flowing water—imagine the direction that water flows from the last seen point.

   - Around gear on the surface—don't forget to pull on the gear; someone may be attached to it.

3. Probe in these areas to a depth of 2 meters (6 feet). Probing deeper wastes too much time.

Shoveling Technique

You're telling yourself, "I already know how to dig—what techniques do I need?" Avalanche debris can weigh up to 400 kilograms per cubic meter. In a typical burial (1 meter deep) around 3 cubic meters of snow must be moved. If you do the math, that's 1200 kilograms (a little more than 1 ton) of snow that needs to be moved by your power. You'll need to dig like hell.

Many of us focus on the beacon search when we train for rescue (that is, if we train at all). But new research on avalanche burials suggests that taking a methodical approach to shoveling can reduce burial time. Analysis of avalanche rescues indicates that most of the total burial time is taken up by the shoveling part of the rescue, so techniques that expedite shoveling are worth discussing and practicing. Bruce Edgerly and Dale Atkins's "Strategic Shoveling" paper is an excellent resource for more information (see "Avalanche and Weather Publications" in the appendix).

These are the recommended steps for a single rescuer in a companion rescue scenario.

1. Leave the probe in place (as discussed in "Probing," above), and note the burial depth using the probe markings.

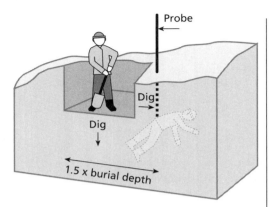

Source: Backcountry Access and "Strategic Shoveling" by Bruce Edgerly and Dale Atkins (see appendix)

Fig. 10.4 Strategic shoveling—a properly located starter hole

2. Map out the starter hole (fig. 10.4).
   - Move downhill 1.5 times the burial depth. (If the area is flat, step away 1.5 times the burial depth in any direction where the snow can most easily be removed.)
   - The hole should be 1.5–2 meters, one wingspan wide (spread your arms and measure fingertip to fingertip).

3. Begin the shoveling on your knees. This is a more efficient method than standing. Toss snow to the sides to prevent having to move it again. Due to the hardness of avalanche debris, you will most likely be *chopping*, then *excavating*. *Shoveling* is a bit of a misnomer; the debris is far too hard and dense.

4. Dig on the downhill side, removing two shovel depths before moving uphill toward the probe.

5. The starter hole is complete once it is waist deep.

6. Remove the snow between the starter hole and the probe, tossing the snow downhill.

7. As you remove the snow in between the starter hole and the buried person, keep the downhill side of the probe exposed. If the probe is perpendicular to the snow surface and you dig a wall plumb from the top of the probe, you risk removing more snow than necessary.

8. As soon as some part of the victim is reached, establish the location of his head and focus digging toward his airway.

If you have multiple rescuers, here are tips to add to the above steps:
- With two shovelers: work side by side, tossing the debris sideways out of the starter hole.
- With more than two shovelers: two people begin the starter hole in the normal location. The remaining shovelers can begin digging at the probe.

Once the starter hole is finished (waist deep), begin to rotate shovelers. One minute of digging followed by one minute of rest is the most effective use of manpower.

By using these techniques you can avoid many possible problems: these include moving more snow than necessary, collapsing the air pocket of the victim, and being unable to move or roll the victim because the hole is too small.

Keep in mind that you now have your partner uncovered and likely injured—the hardest part of the rescue may still be ahead of you. You must administer first aid as best you can, figure out how to transport yourself and the victim(s), and deal with backcountry terrain and conditions. These challenges are also relevant to actions you may need to take after a crevasse rescue. We discuss them in greater detail later in this chapter.

CREVASSE FALL: SELF-RESCUE

In the event that you fall into a crevasse, one of the faster ways back up to the surface is to ascend the rope that you're hanging on. To safely and successfully self-rescue, you must focus on three tasks: how to communicate with your rope team, how to create backup protection against another fall, and how to ascend the rope.

COMMUNICATION

Communication between you and those holding your weight can be very difficult because snow is such a good sound insulator. At the same time, communication is vital to prevent further hazard after the fall has been arrested. The skier up on the snow surface is responsible for managing communication. You must be sure that your partners are expecting you to self-rescue before you begin to ascend the rope, and they must be able to tell you when they've transferred the load to the anchor and are ready for you to ascend.

If you're lucky, you'll be able to shout back and forth; if not, you may have to wait until your partners are able to transfer the load to an anchor and come to the lip of the crevasse (see "Crevasse Rescue" later this chapter).

BACKUP

If you can reach a crevasse wall, you should create a backup as soon as possible after your fall. Until you communicate with your partners, you have no idea if they are holding you in a good arrest stance in solid snow a good distance from the edge, or if they are clawing for purchase on frozen snow or ice. If you can attach yourself to the crevasse wall, you provide increased safety for yourself in the event that they slip or lose hold.

The fastest way to build a backup is to place an ice screw near shoulder height in the crevasse wall and clip in to it. Remember that slings are static, so it is very important that the connection between your harness and the ice screw has minimal slack in it to prevent injury in case of dynamic loading. Use a sling and clip in to your harness directly; and tie an overhand knot to adjust the length and keep slack out of the sling.

The ice screw provides a backup as long as you remain below it; once you begin ascending out of the crevasse (or are hauled out), then you must remove it. Until then, however, it is best to keep yourself clipped in until you and your partners have communicated.

In the worst case, where you are unable

to communicate before you begin ascending, it is possible to place ice screws in the crevasse wall above you as you ascend. Doing so requires having two or more ice screws so that you can always be clipped in to one.

PREPARATION

Once you have communicated with your partners, decided to self-rescue, and backed yourself up, it's time to rig to climb the rope.

The first thing you need to do is get your skis off your feet and connect them to your body. Hopefully, you have ski straps on because you're traveling on a glacier; this means that getting your feet free is just a matter of releasing your bindings.

If you don't have ski straps, or if you want to hang your skis from your harness, make sure you clip your skis in to something before taking them off. The last thing you want to do is drop a ski in the crevasse! Hanging them on the back of your harness is a good way to keep them out of the way while you ascend.

If you have a heavy pack on you may want to consider removing it before you ascend. If you decide to remove your pack, you will attach it to the rope with a friction hitch and haul it up behind you.

Make sure to rig your hanging system and clip the pack in before you take it off your back. To put the weight of the pack on the rope, tie a long cordelette to the rope with a friction hitch. Clip a load bearing strap of the pack (not just a small strap that could rip) to the long loop of the cordelette, and lower the pack until it's hanging below you.

ASCENDING

There are many options in deciding how to ascend the rope. Your goal is to choose the quickest and safest method, and your choice of technique will be largely dictated by the gear you have on your harness. This means you should consider your self-rescue plan when deciding what gear to put on your harness for glacier travel.

Tip: Develop and practice your self-rescue system before you go into the mountains, and plan the gear on your harness accordingly.

An ascension system has three requirements: the waist loop, the leg loop (or loops), and the backup. (These loops are also called waist and leg prusiks, after the commonly used friction hitch.) You can ascend using these loops and friction hitches, or you can use a combination of the leg loop and some type of autolocking device in place of the waist loop. We will focus on a system that is simple to rig and that requires no special gear. "Climbing and Mountaineering" in the appendix lists resources for more information on various systems.

Ascending with Friction Hitches

The basic concept here is to attach two cordelettes or slings to the rope using friction hitches, resulting in a waist loop above a single leg loop.

1. For the waist loop, rig one friction hitch with a shorter cordelette or sling, and clip it through your harness with a locking carabiner (at the same

Waist loop

Leg loop

Overhand knot in leg loop, and locker clipped in to it for backup

Fig. 10.5 Waist loop and leg loop setup for self rescue

Fig. 10.6 Leg loop length and setup for self rescue

place as your rope tie-in point; fig. 10.5). If you are prerigged for glacier travel, the cordelette/hitch will already be on the rope.

2. For the leg loop, rig another friction hitch below the first with a long cordelette or sling (fig. 10.5). The sling should allow you to get one foot in it with your knee bent, but should be as short as possible (fig. 10.6). Often a double-length sling is a good length. If you need to shorten the loop, tie an overhand knot in the cordelette or sling.

Tip: Your legs are below your waist—use this as a way to remember the order in which to rig your hitches, leg loop below waist loop.

3. To rig a backup, tie an overhand knot in the upper part of your leg loop (fig. 10.5). Clip a locking carabiner through your harness and into the leg loop above the knot. (There are many other ways to rig a backup; see "Climbing and Mountaineering" in the appendix.)

Tip: Use a klemheist knot for ascending a rope. It provides plenty of friction on wet or frozen ropes and can be undone easily after it has been weighted by pushing the loop around the rope (fig. 10.7).

Fig. 10.7 Releasing a klemheist

How to Ascend

Once you are rigged and backed up, you will be inch-worming your way up the rope as follows:

1. Stand in the leg loop, letting it hold your weight, and slide the waist loop as high as you can up the rope (fig. 10.8). Hold on to the rope for balance, and brace your foot against the crevasse wall if you can reach it.
2. Sit down in the waist loop. This takes your weight off of the leg loop and allows you to slide the leg loop up the rope to meet the waist loop (fig. 10.9).

Fig. 10.8 Stand in leg loop and slide waist loop up the rope

Fig. 10.9 Sit in waist loop and slide leg loop up the rope.

CREVASSE RESCUE

We describe crevasse rescue in five components: arresting the fall, building the anchor, transferring the load to the anchor, checking on the person in the crevasse, and building a haul system. This progression assumes the rescuer is wearing rope in a Kiwi coil (or that it's in her pack) and is in glacier-travel mode, prerigged with a cordelette/friction hitch on the rope. What follows assumes the worst-case scenario: that you are solely responsible for rescuing your friend in the crevasse. Where applicable, we refer to other methods you can use if you have more people available. For more information about crevasse rescue, see "Climbing and Mountaineering" in the appendix.

ARRESTING THE FALL

Arresting a fall on skis gives you the advantage of extra surface area for holding power. On the other hand, if you get pulled head-first toward the load, it can be harder to bring your skis around beneath you to hold the fall. You must position your skis and your body to hold the weight of a person while you dig an anchor.

The strongest position to hold a fall is with your edges perpendicular to the direction of pull. You should be positioned such that the pulling force and the rope are oriented in the same direction as your body (fig. 10.10).

Fig. 10.10 Good arrest position on skis

Arresting a fall on skis is also different from self-arrest on foot because you may or may not have an ice ax in your hand. As such, your ski edges replace the ice ax pick for holding the fall. Once you have caught the fall, stamp a solid hold with your skis (similar to kicking good steps for your feet after arresting a fall without skis). This platform and your leg strength will hold the weight of your fellow skier while you dig an anchor.

Fig. 10.11 After the uphill ski is removed it can be stuck in the snow while you dig your anchor.

Tip: Once you have a good platform, take your uphill ski off and kick a solid foothold for your skiless boot (fig. 10.11). You can use your ski for a T-slot anchor or to brace your body.

At best, holding the full weight of a person on your harness is hard work; at worst, it is exhausting. As mentioned in "Rope Handling and Roping Up" in chapter 6, tying knots in the rope can take the load off your body if the knots can dig into the crevasse edge. With or without knots in the rope, you must build an anchor to take the weight of the fallen skier.

Tip: Before you start digging an anchor, remove your pack and slip the coils of rope off your neck (but make sure to keep them tied!). Doing so will free your upper body to create the anchor and will allow the load to pull from your harness instead of from your neck.

BUILDING THE ANCHOR

When building an anchor, there are several important things to keep in mind. You must make an anchor that is above all very strong, and you want to make an anchor that can be dug from your arrest position. For a full discussion of anchors and anchor selection, refer to Chapter 6, Ski Mountaineering Techniques.

Here, we describe using a T-anchor. In winter or spring snow conditions you will most likely be digging a T-anchor. In the right conditions these anchors are very strong, and they are relatively simple to create.

What to bury? Use whatever piece of gear is best suited for the snow conditions and the situation. Pulling force and snow/ice density will determine the size of the buried object. Think ahead: What will you use to pad the lip of the crevasse? Will you need your ice ax to get in and out of the crevasse (which you'll need to do if the person who fell is injured and needs assistance)?

Anchor placement. Dig the trench for the T in the vicinity of your shoulders (fig. 10.12). This puts the anchor as high as possible while still allowing you some leverage to chop at the snow and a clear view into the trench to check its depth and uniformity.

Direction. Make sure the trench of your T-anchor is perpendicular to the direction of pull, and that the slot for the attachment sling is perpendicular to the trench.

Attachment. Use a sling or cordelette girth- or clove-hitched around the object you slot into the trench (usually one of your skis). Make sure the master point of the sling is low enough (i.e., close to or below your harness) for you to transfer the load to it. Tie an overhand knot in the attachment sling to give yourself a "shelf" to clip in to (fig. 10.13). Make sure you pad the sling if it wraps around your ski edges.

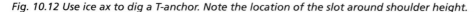

Tip: Dig a trench a few inches deep to clear your work space at the anchor. This will keep your ratchet out of the snow and the whole system will run more smoothly.

TRANSFERRING THE LOAD

In order to transfer the load from your harness, you need to clip your prerigged load-transfer cordelette to the anchor sling. In doing so, it is important to keep your body in the system until the anchor is

Fig. 10.12 Use ice ax to dig a T-anchor. Note the location of the slot around shoulder height.

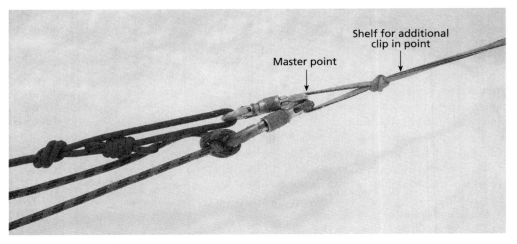

Master point

Shelf for additional clip in point

Fig. 10.13 Master point with a knot creating a 'shelf'

holding the full load, making the transition from you to the anchor slowly so there will be no dynamic load on the anchor.

1. Use a locking carabiner to attach the load-transfer cordelette to the anchor sling (fig. 10.14). Check your system (load perpendicular, biner is locked) before you allow the anchor to take the weight.

2. Once you have transferred the load to the anchor, it's vitally important that you create a backup for the system *before* you undo your Kiwi coils. Until you build a backup, the entire weight (and fate) of one person is hanging on the single friction hitch of your load-transfer cordelette, and by unloading your coils you introduce all that rope as slack into the system. A quick way to create a backup is to add another cordelette to the rope (the load line)

using a second friction hitch below the first one; then clip this second cordelette to the anchor with minimal slack. Now you are free to remove your Kiwi coils and move about.

Tip: When taking off your Kiwi coil, don't just dump the whole stack of coils on the ground! Doing so will create a mighty tangle of rope. Take the time to remove the coils one by one and stack them off to the side.

3. After you have taken your coils off and stacked them, you can use the rope to tie a clove hitch or a figure-eight on a bight to a locking carabiner in the master point of the anchor sling (fig. 10.14). This is a backup, and you can remove the second cordelette from the rope and have it available for your haul system.

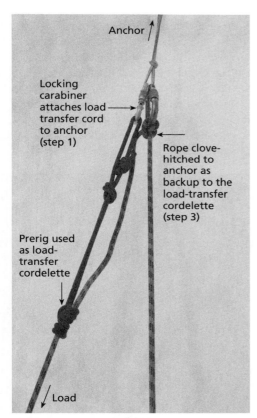

Locking carabiner attaches load transfer cord to anchor (step 1)

Anchor ↑

Rope clove-hitched to anchor as backup to the load-transfer cordelette (step 3)

Prerig used as load-transfer cordelette

↙ Load

Fig. 10.14 Load transfer complete with clove hitch in the rope for backup

Important: If you are concerned with the strength of your anchor for hauling purposes, build another anchor and create a new master point using both anchors.

Take a deep breath. You have just accomplished the most critical steps of crevasse rescue: you stopped the fall, you built an anchor and transferred the load, and you escaped the system—you have arrived at base line. From this point, self-rescue is preferred over hauling, but you may have to haul if the fallen skier is injured or is not experienced in self-rescue.

CHECK ON THE PERSON IN THE CREVASSE

Once you have dropped your coils and can move about, the most important thing to do is to communicate with and check on the person in the crevasse.

Protecting yourself. Whether you only go to the crevasse lip or rappel down into the hole, it is very important that you protect yourself from falling into the crevasse or into one nearby. It is good practice to attach yourself to the anchor. Remember that you clipped the rope into the anchor with a clove hitch (or figure eight on a bight) already. Put yourself on rappel on the free end of this rope to go to the lip of the crevasse, and use an autoblock or similar hitch to back up your rappel (fig. 10.15). Now you can move around safely, adjusting the rappel to keep minimal slack in the system. If you are uncertain about additional crevasses or a large, overhanging lip, you may want to probe the area around you.

Preparing the lip. The rope holding the weight of the person in the crevasse will have already dug deeply into the snow with the force of the fall. You may need to haul the person out on that stand (see "Building a Hauling System" later this chapter), in which case it is crucial to minimize the friction at the lip of the crevasse. Regardless

Fig. 10.15 Rappel with a backup

of which haul system you use, you must prevent the haul line from digging farther into the snow. You may just need to keep the rope from digging farther into the snow so that the person can more easily move past the lip as she climbs out herself (as described in "Crevasse Fall: Self-Rescue" earlier this chapter). In either case, you must remove the rope from contact with the snow at the point where it bends to go into the crevasse.

Note: If you have knots in your rope, you will need to pad the lip for the haul line, *not* for the rope with knots in it (see "Direct Haul vs. Drop-Loop Haul" later this chapter).

You can use a backpack, ice ax handle, ski poles—anything that will keep the rope out of the snow at the bend point (fig. 10.16). Go to the very edge of the lip (with your

Fig. 10.16 Using ski poles to prepare the lip of the crevasse to minimize friction for hauling

rappel and backup) and take the time to dig out the rope and shove your pack or ice ax underneath it, and make sure the rope runs over the padding correctly. As you pad the lip, communicate with the person below, being careful not to shower her with heavy snow chunks or ice as you clear the rope.

Rappelling to the person in the crevasse. If the person in the hole is unconscious or needs immediate first aid, it may be necessary to continue rappelling past the lip to reach her. If the person is okay, she may be able to self-rescue. Bring slings or cord to rig a chest harness, an extra puffy jacket to keep your partner warm, and any first-aid gear you expect to need.

Ascending out of the crevasse. Once you have reached and tended to your partner, ascend the rope just as you would in self-rescue (see "Crevasse Fall: Self-Rescue," above). Leave your rappel and backup rigged while you transition.

1. Attach a short cord to the rope using a klemheist or prusik and clip it to your harness with a locking carabiner. This is your waist loop.
2. Attach another cord or double-length sling below the first, again using a friction hitch. This is your leg loop.
3. Back yourself up: tie an overhand knot in your leg loop near the friction hitch. Girth-hitch a short sling or cord through your harness and clip it to your leg loop between the overhand knot and the hitch using a locking carabiner.
4. Check your ascension system before undoing your rappel system.

BUILDING A HAUL SYSTEM

Once a person is in a crevasse, it will take a certain amount of pulling force to get him back to the surface. The weight of the person in the hole and the resistance (friction) resulting from the rope digging into the snow dictate the magnitude of force needed.

Pulling power can be created in many ways: multiple rescuers can pull together, or you can build a hauling system that creates enough mechanical advantage for one person to do the hauling alone. To understand hauling and crevasse-rescue systems, you must first understand the following terms:

Load line. The load line is the rope connected to the fallen skier, the strand of rope that holds the skier's weight in the fall.

Haul line. The haul line is the strand of rope you will be pulling on to rescue the skier in the crevasse. In a direct-haul system, described a few paragraphs below, the haul line is the same section of rope as the load line.

Ratchet. The ratchet is a hitch or device that allows rope to slide through it in one direction only. The ratchet slides on the rope as you pull it in, but holds the rope and keeps it from sliding backward when you release it (fig. 10.17).

Mechanical advantage. Mechanical advantage is expressed as a ratio, like 3:1 or 5:1. What does this mean? The science-geek dictionary definition is "the ratio of output force to input force in a mechanism." In our case, the mechanism is a hauling system made of cordelettes and carabiners; the output force is the force needed to pull the

Load line →

Rope moves this way only; garda locks when the load line is weighted

Fig. 10.17 Garda hitch is one option for a ratchet.

skier up out of the crevasse; and the input force is the amount of pull the rescuer applies to the haul line.

Let's try rewriting the definition in crevasse-rescue terms: mechanical advantage is the ratio of *the force needed to pull the skier upward* to *the amount of pull applied by the rescuer* using a hauling system. Think of it in terms of human power: a mechanical advantage of 5:1 means that when one person pulls on the haul line, the force of five people pulls on the load line.

Direct Haul vs. Drop-Loop Haul

In general, you can pull someone out of crevasse in one of two ways: with a direct haul or with a drop-loop haul. In a direct haul, you are pulling on the rope that leads to the person in the crevasse, and any mechanical advantage you add is built off that same line. In a drop-loop haul, you are pulling on one end of a loop that begins fixed at the anchor, runs through a pulley (read: carabiner) clipped to the fallen skier, and then runs back up to you on the surface.

How will you know which system to use, direct haul or drop-loop haul? Think once again of applying the right tool at the right time. Each system has advantages and limitations that you must understand in order to decide which tool is right for a given application. These are the factors to consider:

- Rope length available. Direct haul systems use less rope than drop-loop haul systems. How much rope do you plan to have with you?

- Number of rescuers. Are there two people on the rope, or four? Are there other parties in the same area? It can be very fast to use a drop-loop haul if you have five people available to pull and mind the system.

- Knots in the rope. If you are traveling in poor conditions, or have just two people on the rope, you may be tying knots in the rope to help hold a potential fall. Doing so commits you to using a drop-loop system.

- Snow conditions. If the rope digs very deep into the snow during the fall, it may be more efficient to use a drop-loop system because you can prepare the lip of the crevasse more easily. In a direct haul, you must dig the load line out of the snow and find a way to minimize friction as you haul. In a drop-loop haul, preparing the lip is as simple as making sure the loop runs over your padding.

Tip: If you are learning about crevasse rescue for the first time, the best plan is to learn one system well and practice it, and adjust your gear selection and travel techniques to match that system.

Drop-Loop: Team Haul 2:1

With multiple rescuers present, this is often the fastest way to get someone out of a crevasse (fig. 10.18). After arresting the fall, transferring the load, and checking on the person in the crevasse, the setup is as follows:

1. Drop the loop. Send a loop of rope down to the fallen skier and have him clip it through a locking carabiner through the tie-in point of his harness (if he is unconscious, you will have to rappel into the crevasse and do this for him). To fix your rappel line, tie a hard knot (figure eight on a bight) in the rope and clip it to the anchor with a locking carabiner. Now you can use the long end of this "fixed" line to loop into the hole and back up to the surface.

2. Create a backup. As the team hauls your fallen skier upward, they will create slack in the load line that was holding the fallen skier's weight. If the haulers let the haul line go slack, the skier will fall back down onto the load line, creating a dynamic load on the anchor and losing height gained in the haul. To protect against this you must create a backup for your haul using either the load line or the haul line. To back up the system using the load line, a rescuer must pull slack through the load-transfer cordelette as the team creates slack in the load line.

   - Tie a figure eight on a bight with a cow's tail in the middle of a long cordelette.
   - Create a friction hitch using a stitch prusik on the haul line of the rope. Make sure the distance from the figure eight to the stitch prusik is the length of one arm's reach.
   - Create the same friction hitch again on the other side of the C line (fig. 10.18).

   In addition to creating a ratchet to back up the haul, this system provides a backup for the rescuer when moving around near the crevasse edge. It allows the rescuer to pull from a stance close to the edge, creating a better hauling angle and reducing friction.

What Is A Stitch Prusik?

A stitch prusik, or rolling hitch, is a prusik hitch tied with an untied length of cord. See "Climbing and Mountaineering" in the appendix.

Backup for haul

Clipped to harness
with cow's tail

The **C** loop dropped
down to the skier

Load line
(fallen skier)

Fig. 10.18 Team haul with a drop loop 2:1

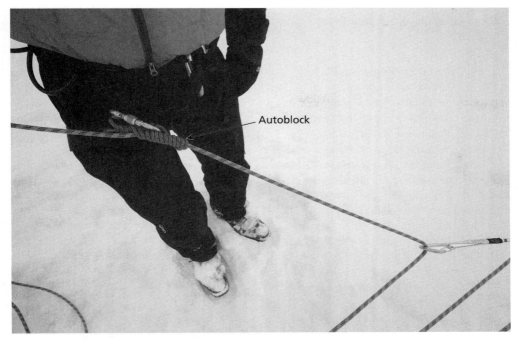

Fig. 10.19 Autoblock clipped to harness to aid in hauling

3. Haul! Clip your hauling team in at various points along the haul line using friction hitches on the rope clipped in to team members' tie-in points (fig. 10.19). This not only provides backup to the single friction-hitch ratchet, it also allows for rapid adjustment of the team's place on the rope as you haul. Connecting to the rope at the tie-in point also allows everyone to use the strongest work muscles in their bodies—their legs—to pull.

Tips and warnings:

- In this and any system, be aware of creating slack in the system as you haul and of how you protect against it. Avoid hanging the whole show on one friction hitch—once your haulers have clipped in to the rope, monitor the slack in the haul line and guard against everyone unclipping at once.

- Monitor the ratchet so that it functions correctly.

- Two nonlocking carabiners reversed and opposed are equivalent to one locking carabiner. Use lockers for rappel back-ups, clipping the rope in to the master point, or for any situation where you can't afford the rope to come out of the carabiners. Nonlockers can be used when building hauling systems.

- The long haul: if conditions permit, begin hauling below the anchor and walk/crawl until you are up above it.

Drop Loop: Single Haul 6:1

In the absence of a team to haul someone, you need to create more mechanical advantage. The following system adds to the 2:1 drop-loop system described above by adding mechanical advantage to the haul line, which creates a 6:1 advantage (see the "Counting Mechanical Advantage" sidebar later in this chapter).

1. Drop a loop to the fallen skier as described in the 2:1 system above ("A" indicates this C-shaped loop in fig. 10.20)

2. Create a ratchet by building a garda hitch using the haul line ("B" in fig. 10.20). Attach the garda hitch to the anchor using an overhand knot in the drop-loop line ("C" in fig. 10.20).

3. Add a friction hitch to the haul line with a short cord or sling ("D" in fig. 10.20). Make this cord as short as possible by using a small prusik loop. Clip a nonlocking carabiner into the short loop.

4. Take the free end of the haul line

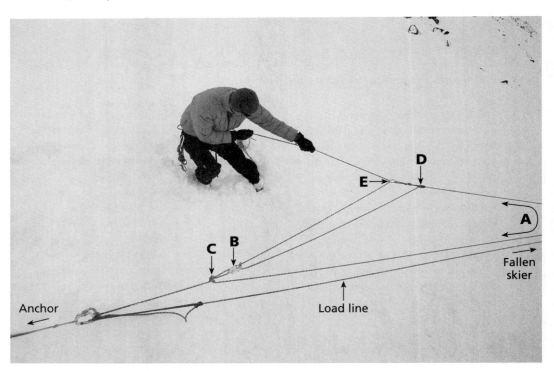

Fig. 10.20 Drop Loop 6:1 haul system

and clip it through the nonlocker of the short loop you just created ("E" in fig. 10.20)

You have built a drop-loop haul with a Z-drag, creating a 6:1 mechanical advantage. Clip the haul line to your tie-in point using a friction hitch (fig. 10.19), and start hauling.

Direct Haul 3:1

There are several variations of mechanical advantage in a direct haul. We discuss building a 3:1 system and then expanding it to a 6:1 system. For additional resources, see "Climbing and Mountaineering" in the appendix.

The 3:1 direct haul is built on the load line (instead of on the haul line). After arresting the fall, transferring the load, and checking on the person in the crevasse, this is the setup. (**Note:** Your load-transfer cordelette will become your ratchet in this system.)

1. Attach a cordelette via friction hitch on the load line. Make the clip-in for this cordelette as short as possible, then clip a nonlocking carabiner to the cordelette ("A" in fig. 10.21).
2. Clip the load line to the anchor with a locker ("B" in fig. 10.21). If you

Fig. 10.21 Direct haul 3:1 system

have used the rope to back up your load-transfer cordelette, it will already be clipped in hard (i.e., with a knot or clove hitch) to the anchor (see step 3 of "Transferring the Load" earlier in the chapter). Leave it that way until you have built and backed up your hauling system.

Caution: A prusik ratchet is not self-minding. If you don't monitor the ratchet as you haul, it can get pulled through the locking carabiner at the anchor which effectively ends the functioning of your hauling system. In order to get out of this predicament, you would need to build another system to unload the weight on your hauling system. See "Climbing and Mountaineering" in the appendix for more information.

3. Take the end of the rope coming from the anchor (now the haul line—the load line becomes the haul line in this system), and clip the rope through the nonlocker on the short cordelette from step 1 ("C" in fig. 10.21).
4. Your 3:1 is complete! You can see where it gets the name Z-drag. As with the drop-loop 2:1 direct haul, you can back the system up by using a friction hitch on the haul line clipped to the tie-in point of your harness (fig. 10.19).

Tip: If your load/haul line is still clipped in with a locking carabiner to the master point of the anchor, you will need to undo the clove

hitch so the rope can move through that locker as you haul. You can avoid suddenly introducing slack into the system by leaving one loop of the rope in the locker at all times, even as you undo the clove hitch.

Direct Haul 6:1

To increase your mechanical advantage from 3:1 to 6:1, you add a 2:1 system onto the haul line of a 3:1 (fig. 10.22).

1. Add a short cordelette via friction hitch to the haul line of the 3:1. Tie this off as short as possible, and clip a nonlocking carabiner to the cordelette.
2. Take an extra long cordelette and clip one end of it to the anchor using a hard knot (and a locker). You can do this using two nonlockers reversed and opposed and a figure eight on a bight.
3. Clip the free end of the long cordelette into the single nonlocker attached to the haul line of the 3:1. You have just added a C to your Z. Your new haul line will be the end of the long cordelette.

While we have described the basics of a few crevasse rescue systems—a drop loop haul 2:1 and 6:1, and direct haul 3:1 and 6:1—getting the fallen skier out of the crevasse may be only part of the battle. As in the case of an avalanche accident, once you have an injured person on the surface, you may still need to deal with first aid, broken or lost gear, emergency communication, and transport back to safety.

C of the added 2:1

B

C

A

A,B,C are the 3:1

Fig. 10.22 Direct haul 6:1 system

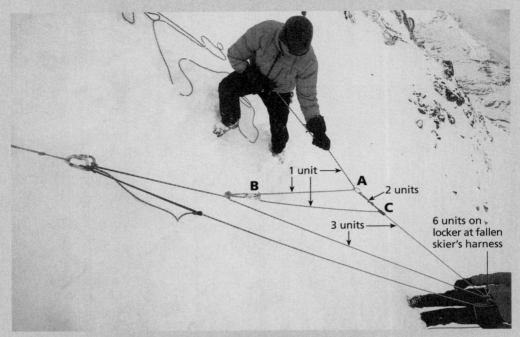

Fig. 10.23 Counting mechanical advantage for drop loop 6:1 haul system

COUNTING MECHANICAL ADVANTAGE

Until you have practiced several times, hauling systems can easily create much confusion and head scratching. How can you keep it all straight? One good tool is to understand how to count up your mechanical advantage. This can help you figure out if you built what you meant to build (we've seen folks build a 9:1 system when they were shooting for a 3:1!).

Let's use the drop-loop 6:1 system as a practice example (fig. 10.23):

1. Begin counting at the hauling end, with the rope in your hands. You are equal to the pulling power of one person, so assign the haul end of the rope a unit of 1.
2. Follow the rope as it goes through the nonlocking carabiner at "A." You can easily picture that the force on the rope on one side of the carabiner is equal to the force coming out the other side—1 unit going in, 1 unit coming out.
3. Now add the forces on the carabiner at "A" (and the cordelette clipped to it)—there is 1 unit in each strand of rope on either side of the carabiner, so the carabiner has 2 units of force acting on it.
4. Keep following the rope through the garda hitch (at "B"). The rope still has 1 unit of force—1 unit going in, 1 going out (the garda adds friction, but does not change units of force).
5. Keep following the rope through the system. The next thing you encounter is the short-loop friction hitch (at "C"). Add forces again: 1 unit from the rope, 2 units for

the cordelette/carabiner ("A" from step 3). That brings the units of force applied to the rope below the hitch to 3.

6. Now follow the rope down into the crevasse until it goes through the locking carabiner on the skier's harness. The rope has 3 units going down to the biner, and 3 coming up toward the anchor. That means that the skier clipped in to the locker is experiencing 6 units of force. Voilà—a 6:1 system.

Note: This method of counting mechanical advantage gives us the hauling ratio as it would be in a frictionless world. In the real world of carabiners, dynamic ropes, and other hauling efficiency losses, you can expect a lower ratio to be applied to the load.

EMERGENCY SHELTERS

The decision to use an emergency shelter can be boiled down to one question: in order to deal with your situation, is it better to move toward safety or to stay put? The factors you have to consider in this decision can include the following:

- What is the nature of the emergency? This can range from a time/location problem (it's getting dark and/or you're lost) to a serious injury or accident.
- How far from help and safety are you?
- What are the conditions you are experiencing? This includes weather, terrain, snowpack, and time of day.
- What emergency equipment do you have with you?
- What hazards will be created by moving? What hazards will be created by staying where you are?
- What other special considerations do you have in the situation?

As in any decision-making in the backcountry, there are no hard and fast rules about when to build a shelter. Instead, always have shelter as an option for dealing with an emergency. Overall, the benefits of building an emergency shelter must outweigh the hazards or disadvantages.

HOW TO BUILD AN EMERGENCY SHELTER

There are countless ways to create shelter in the winter backcountry environment—build an igloo (or digloo), pitch a tent, create a snow cave (all discussed in chapter 8). However, creating an *emergency* shelter is different than creating a backcountry shelter, and there are a different set of criteria to guide you.

Time matters. Your goal is to create effective shelter as quickly as possible.

Equipment available. Your shelter must keep its inhabitants as warm as possible, and often you will need to do this without the luxury of overnight gear (tent, sleeping pad, sleeping bag).

Goal of the shelter. Are you digging a shelter to get an injured skier out of a storm for part of a day, or are you digging shelter for three people to spend the night without sleeping bags?

Consequences of building the shelter. Can you build a shelter without getting soaked to the bone? Can you get warm again if you do get wet and cold creating the shelter?

An ideal shelter will be fast to create (about half an hour is a good goal), will make maximum use of your available equipment, and will keep you warm enough and dry enough to be safe in the situation.

THE TRENCH/EMERGENCY BIVY SHELTER

There are many ways you can meet the above criteria in any given situation. Here we describe one way of creating a snow shelter that is fast and effective. Snow is an easily sculptable material and it has amazing insulative qualities. A good snow shelter will shield you from cold temperatures, wind, and generally tough winter conditions that might make it hard to survive an unplanned night out. A snow cave can also be used as an emergency shelter—it can take longer to create than a trench shelter, but requires no gear other than a shovel (see "Snow Shelters" in chapter 8).

For the following trench shelter we assume you have the basic gear for a day tour: skis, poles, and shovel. This shelter is a trench dug in the snow, with the bottom of the trench wider than the top. The roof of the shelter is then created by laying skis and poles across the top of the trench and creating a roof of snow on the skis and poles (figs. 10.24–10.27).

1. Begin by digging a narrow trench in the snow, about as wide as your body. Dig until the trench is at least up to your ribs—you can go deeper for a more comfortable shelter. The length of the trench will be determined by the length of your skis.

2. Excavate the snow on the bottom few feet of both sides of the trench. Dig the sides out for as much space as you want. Again, the depth and extent of this side excavation will determine the size and comfort of your shelter.

3. Once your shelter is large enough, place your poles side to side and then your skis lengthwise across the poles (fig. 10.25). Cover these with snow (fig. 10.26).

4. You will need an entrance for your shelter once it has a roof. Dig a slide or steps leading down into the trench. Keep this as small as possible—this is where heat can escape from your shelter (fig. 10.27).

Tip: Before you begin digging, probe the spot to make sure it's clear of trees or rocks. Keep the top of your trench as narrow as possible, and be careful of making it too long. Excavate the sides of the trench fully before you put the roof on. Once the shelter is built, use blocks of snow or a pack to block the entrance.

Tip: If you have only one pair of skis or if you need to make a larger (longer) shelter, you can use your emergency tarp as part of the shelter. Rest the tarp across your skis and cover it with snow. You may need to anchor the tarp corners with ski poles or snow anchors (fig. 10.26).

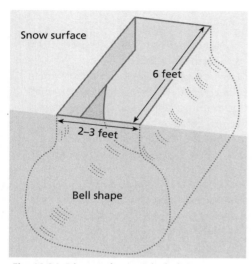

Snow surface

6 feet

2–3 feet

Bell shape

Fig. 10.24 Dig out the trench shelter.

Fig. 10.25 Lay skis on top of the poles to frame the roof of your trench shelter.

Snow or tarp and snow

Fig. 10.26 With a tarp your trench shelter will be even toastier!

Fig. 10.27 Finished trench shelter. Place a pack over the entrance to keep heat in.

IT'S ALL GOOD UNTIL IT ISN'T

The sky was clear, temperature in the mid 20's. Winds were moderate. We were skiing low-angled terrain approaching the flats a few thousand feet above the parking lot. The snow was hard packed, icy. Wind had scoured the surface for several days, leaving a frozen sastrugi pattern on the slope. Not an ideal ski descent, but we were having fun. The uphill exercise had been good, the scenery spectacular. Plenty of daylight was left, and we were all looking forward to a hot cup of coffee on the way home.

My ski tip caught the front of a frozen wind lip. I fell head first onto the hard pack. I heard a crunching sound in my neck and back as I hit the surface. My left arm went numb. This was definitely Not Good.

My friends were right there. They knew a casual day on easy terrain had just turned into a rescue operation. They improvised a neck splint. Someone had a bivy sack. Someone else had a thermal pad. They dug a trench to keep me out of the wind. Everyone pulled extra clothes from their packs to keep me warm. A call was made for help; self rescue would be risky with an unstable spine injury.

A helicopter arrived just before sunset and I was safely evacuated back to town. I spent the next three months in a body brace, followed by six months of rehabilitation. My recovery is complete, but the questions remain.

How much equipment is enough? Super light is all good until something goes wrong. Carrying enough equipment for the worst case scenario will sap energy, increasing the chance for injury. This is an age old debate of wilderness travel.

Keep a few things in mind as you pack:

- Longer, more remote trips require more safety equipment than short tours near the road. We were only carrying the basics on the tour where I was injured.
- Safety equipment can be shared among the party. Check that your group has adequate shared equipment before departure. There was enough equipment for my situation primarily because my group was a large group.
- Be prepared for cold. Traumatic injury increases susceptibility to hypothermia. I was shivering within minutes of my injury even though I was plenty warm while skiing. An injured person will require more warmth than an uninjured person.
- Ask yourself what type of self rescue you are prepared to carry out. A rope can take the place of several hands if you have to lower someone to a safe location.

Finally, cultivate the decision-making process. Determining the right gear for the tour is part of the art of ski mountaineering. Learn from your mistakes, and revel in your successes.

Benjamin Haskell is an AMGA certified ski mountaineering guide, an EMT, and a lieutenant with the Seattle Fire Department.

EMERGENCY SLEDS

At its most basic, the decision to build a sled is a decision to move toward safety rather than to stay put and wait for rescue, daylight, or a break in the weather. Moving someone in a rescue sled is difficult, exhausting, and slow work. Building a rescue sled in any terrain—steep or benign—is something of a last resort, when rescue by mechanized means is not possible and the injured skier can't move himself to safety.

Deciding to build an emergency sled includes the same considerations used in deciding to build an emergency shelter, but with added concerns. In addition to the considerations of time, equipment available, goals of creating a sled, and consequences of building a sled, you will have another very important consideration: terrain. On skis, the location of an injured skier may well be in steep and technical terrain, or you may be deep in the wilderness with long distances to safety. In deciding to build a sled to execute a rescue you will be asking yourself these general questions:

- What is the distance you must travel?
- Are there periods of sidehill traversing, or can you get to safety moving down the fall line or over flat ground?
- What are the snow conditions—deep powder or hardpack?
- Are you in steep or technical terrain that will require anchoring and lowering the sled once it is built?

HOW TO BUILD AN EMERGENCY SLED

The form and nature of your emergency sled will be dictated by the following considerations:

Materials. What do you have available to you? Do you have a manufactured rescue sled? Do you have skis with holes in their tips (and/or tails)? Do you have the equipment to build an improvised sled? As we describe below, you can build a decent sled using skis (with holes), rubber ski straps, adjustable poles, several cordelettes and carabiners, and a bivy tarp.

Durability. The forces trying to pull your sled apart will be powerful and acting in many directions. Your sled must be durable enough to stay together as the system is loaded, wrenched, and shoved down steep inclines and through deep snow—all with a full-sized human strapped to it. Your sled must have reinforcement built into it in tensile, compressive, and torsional axes. You won't know if your rescue sled will stand up to these forces until you have practiced building and using it.

Nature of injury. It's one thing to strap a healthy, sound individual into a rescue sled while practicing; it's another experience altogether trying to secure an injured person in a sled. You must take into consideration the most comfortable position for the injured person, and this may not always be lying on their back with hands folded. What if the injured person will only lie on his side? Can you interface splinting with the sled? If you are worried about severe bleeding, either internal or external, place the injured person in the sled so that the site of the bleeding is on the uphill end. Otherwise, strap the person to the more comfortable "head-uphill" position.

Padding and security for the injured. Once the sled is built, how will you attach the person to the sled and pad him? How will you keep him secure as the sled moves around? This can be done using backpacks and clothing, cordelettes, and a bivy sack—we discuss these techniques below.

Attachment. Will you be lowering the sled or pulling it across terrain? How will you control the motion of your loaded rescue sled? If you are lowering a sled on a rope, you must be careful that your attachment does not pull the sled apart with the weight of the injured person. At the same time, you must be sure that the injured person is tied in, but that her tie-in point is not holding all the weight (we describe this below). If you are dragging the sled, you will need to control it from the front and the back, and you will be using your attachment points to keep it from rolling on traverses or bogging down in deep snow.

Manufactured Sled

Manufactured sleds include those commercially available as well as the homemade versions. We define manufactured sleds as those that include pieces specifically created to make a rescue sled. In contrast, improvised sleds are created using gear that you carry for other uses.

Manufactured sleds are currently available from Brooks Range, or they can be made with a strong sewing machine and some patience (fig. 10.28).

Components. Manufactured sleds usually include crossbars for the ski tips and tails, plus a nylon sleeve that stretches between them with straps for adjustment and loops to strap a person in. You will need to pad the sled once it is built. This can be done using any soft material you have on hand: packs, clothes, tents, sleeping bags, and foam pads, for example.

Pros and cons. Manufactured sleds can be fast and easy to construct, and provide a built-in method for attaching the injured skier to the sled. Their main disadvantages are excess weight and single use—their components are designed for a sled and don't provide any other use.

Building a manufactured sled. Building these sleds according to manufacturer's directions is a simple matter, but making these sleds strong enough for use requires some reinforcement. Assemble the sled by sliding the crossbar pieces onto the ski tips and tails and then sliding the nylon sleeves or loops over the crossbars. Pull the adjustment straps tight and—voilà!—the sled is built (fig. 10.29).

Tip: If the skis you are using have brakes, use rubber ski straps to hold the brakes in the engaged position (fig. 10.30).

No matter how tight you pull the adjustment straps, the sled will most likely come apart when you strap someone into it. To prevent this, you can add torsional and longitudinal reinforcement as follows (fig. 10.31):

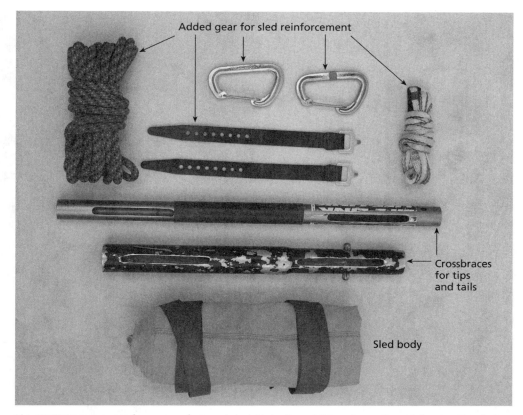

Added gear for sled reinforcement

Crossbraces for tips and tails

Sled body

Fig. 10.28 Components for a manufactured sled. Note the additional gear for reinforcing the sled.

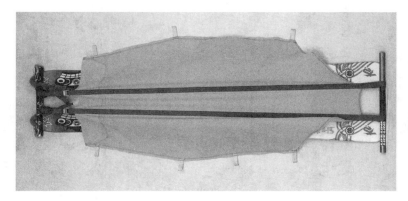

Fig. 10.29 Manufactured sled constructed without reinforcement

Fig. 10.30 Brake held with a ski strap

Fig. 10.31 Manufactured sled with cordelette reinforcement added

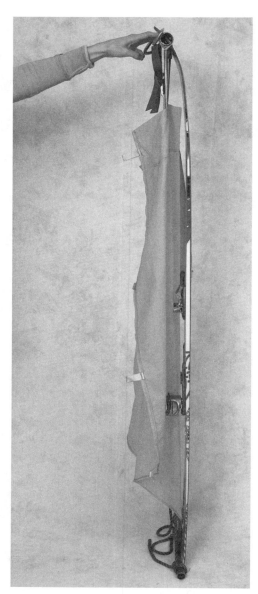

Fig. 10.32 Tighten cordelette so the skis have reverse camber.

■ Attach each end of a short piece of cordelette to opposite sides of one of the crossbars.

■ On the other crossbar, attach one end of a long cordelette to one side of the crossbar. Run the long cordelette through the loop created by the short cordelette at the other end and bring it back toward the end of sled. You have now formed two interlocked V's of cordelettes.

■ Build a trucker's hitch connecting the long end of the cordelette to the unte-thered end of crossbar. Crank the hitch tight—you'll know it's tight enough when the skis have some reverse camber to them (fig. 10.32).

Test your sled once you have built it—see if you can pull it apart or tweak it. And before you deem your sled strong enough, put someone in it and drag her around a parking lot or lower them a pitch or two (see "Lowering a Sled," below).

Improvised Sled

In creating an improvised sled, consider all of the factors listed above: materials available, durability, nature of the injury, padding and security for the injured person, and the attachment/hauling system.

Components. The components of an improvised sled can be broadly defined. You need some form of crossbars to connect and brace your skis. You need a method for attaching those crossbars to the skis and a method for holding the injured skier on the sled. You need attachment points to drag or lower the sled. Finally, you need to make sure that the whole assembly remains intact through use. You can choose from a host of materials: rubber ski straps, telescoping poles in two or three segments, shovel handles, carabiners, cordelettes, bivy tarp or sack, foam pads, plastic zip ties, and hose clamps. Don't forget to include padding for the injured person.

Pros and cons. Advantages are that you only have to carry minimal single use gear, and you can build a sled anywhere, anytime. But improvised sleds can be more complicated and more difficult to set up than manufactured ones, and they may require more practice.

Building an improvised sled. Here is one example of improvising a sled. There are a million ways to skin a cat, so use this as a jumping-off point.

1. Create the sled structure. Use the segments from telescoping poles, rubber ski straps, and cordelettes to create cross braces for the sled (fig. 10.33). This can be done in a wedge or parallel shape with skis—a wedge is often easier to build, but is more prone to tipping over when you are dragging the sled.

2. Create a system to secure the injured person. Attach cordelettes to the sled on both sides. Make sure that the attachment points are strong—be wary of bending pole pieces or of weak plastic binding parts.

3. Create a system for moving the sled. Use the holes in the ski tips to attach cord or rope to the ski tips.

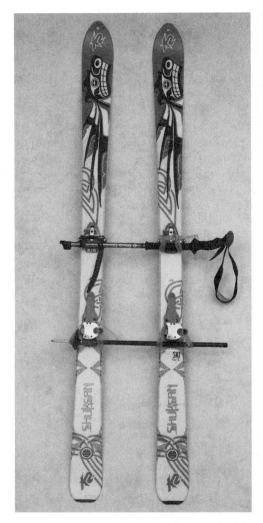

Fig. 10.33 Using poles as a cross brace to build an improvised sled. To significantly strengthen this sled further, cross-bracing is necessary. This can be done between the tips and the bindings.

Tip: You can easily drill holes in the tips—or tails—of your skis. Doing so does not adversely affect the performance of the ski, and can make it very simple to create a hauling system for your sled.

Lowering a Sled

In some situations the terrain might be steep or exposed enough that you must build an anchor and lower the injured skier in the rescue sled. We discuss building anchors in Chapter 6, Ski Mountaineering Techniques. Additional considerations in lowering a sled follow:

Secure your start platform. Make sure that you can safely build a sled and safely strap the injured skier into the sled. This can be as simple as staging the sled in flat ground or as complicated as digging or chopping out a platform to work on.

Avoid shock-loading the anchor. This is particularly important as you transition from flat ground to weighting the anchor. Set the anchor and master point high enough above the platform so that the rope is almost tight to the sled before you weight the anchor.

Tie in to the harness and the sled. This is crucial: the load-bearing tie-in point needs to be attached to the sled, but you also need to tie the person in through his harness. Figure 10.34 shows a good configuration for this dual tie-in system.

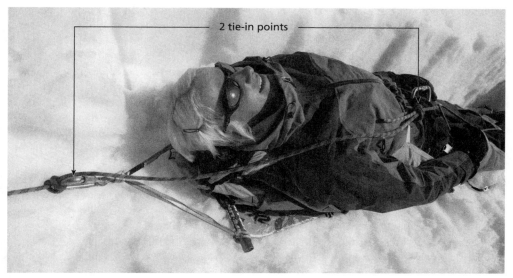

Fig. 10.34 Dual tie-in system for a sled lower

FIRST-AID KITS

A first-aid kit for ski tours will ideally contain everything you need for dealing with injury or emergency in the mountains. The difficulty arises in creating a kit that will be effective and appropriate, both in content and in size and weight. Before you build up your first-aid kit we highly recommend taking a first-aid course with a wilderness focus (see "Wilderness First Aid" in the appendix). This will give you a realistic feel for what can and can't be accomplished in wilderness first aid, and how wilderness emergencies are dealt with.

The following are some questions and their implications to guide you in building your first-aid kit.

What is the commitment level of your trip? What methods of emergency communication are available to you, and how far are you from mechanized rescue? How does the weather affect your access to mechanized rescue?

Implications. Consider the two ends of the spectrum. If the weather is perfect and you are in an area with highly developed rescue infrastructure, you will be mostly focused on stabilizing an injured person until help comes (for example, a sunny day in Switzerland, where response time for helicopter rescue is under a half hour). On the other hand, if you are two days into the wilderness in whiteout conditions with no cell phone coverage, you will need to treat the injured person with the expectation of having to wait hours or days for rescue, or you will have to move to safety using human power. As a potential first responder, you must bring the first-aid and safety gear appropriate to the commitment level of your ski trip.

What is the duration of your trip? Are you on a day trip in Colorado or a four-week ski traverse in Alaska?

Implications. If you are out for a long haul, the contents of your first-aid kit become much more geared toward dealing with injuries in the field and over a period of time. You may also carry more redundancy in your first-aid supplies.

What medical emergencies or injuries could occur on your trip? This list often includes trauma in various forms: cuts and lacerations, broken bones, blown knees, dislocated shoulders, spinal injury. Are you traveling at high altitude or in extreme cold or wet? Are you traveling with someone who is allergic to bees or to the nuts you put in the trail mix? Will you be cooking? Is there any potential for someone to get burned?

Implications. One of the most important things to understand is that wilderness medicine is quite limited in the depth of treatment you can provide. As a first responder, you must decide how to stabilize the injury, and the tools available to you in the wilderness are usually in the categories of trauma kit, splinting, and drugs. You will almost always be in a cold environment; if someone gets hurt, you will need to protect against cold and hypothermia.

What are the medical histories of the people with you? Do they have specific medications they take for allergies, heart problems, and so on? Do they have previous or recurring injuries?

Implications. Knowing what medications you may need beyond the normal scope of a first-aid kit is crucial to dealing with a backcountry emergency. Knowing about previous injuries can spark a dialog about preparedness and dealing with them.

FIRST-AID KIT MODULES

The answers to the above questions will help you choose from the following menu of possible first-aid components.

Personal safety kit. Designed to keep you, the rescuer, safe from blood and body fluids. *Includes:* Several pairs of latex gloves, compact mask, eye protection (light-lens sunglasses).

Trauma kit. Designed to effectively clean wounds in the field and keep them clean while controlling bleeding. *Includes:* Water syringe for cleaning wounds, alcohol pads, hydrogen peroxide, povidone iodine, gauze pads and rolls, nonstick trauma bandages, trauma shears, tweezers, medical tape, bandaids of various sizes.

Allergy kit. Designed to deal with allergic or anaphylactic reactions in the field. *Includes:* EpiPen or similar and Benadryl or similar and Prednisone.

Splint kit. Designed to split wounds to decrease further injury and provide mobility and/or comfort. *Includes:* Rigid splints (ski poles, SAM splints, foam pad, shovel handle...anything that works), straps (rubber ski straps, cordelette, tied clothing, etc.), padding, ace bandages, pain killers and/or muscle relaxants.

Altitude kit. Designed to mitigate the effects of altitude sickness. *Includes:* Aspirin, altitude drugs (acetazolamide, dexamethasone).

Blister kit. Designed to deal with and mitigate blisters. *Includes:* Duct tape, moleskin, athletic tape, blister pads, foam donuts.

Comfort kit. Designed to deal with nonserious ailments. *Includes:* Ibuprofen or other anti-inflammatory, antacid tablets.

Expedition kit. Designed to deal with medical emergencies deep in the wilderness, often for trips of longer duration. *Includes:* Pain killers, antibiotics (cephalexin), in-depth trauma kit.

SAMPLE DAY TRIP FIRST-AID KIT
- Personal safety kit
- Trauma kit
- Allergy kit
- Splint kit—minimal
- Blister kit
- Comfort kit

Figure 10.35 shows an example of a day trip first-aid kit (minus the blister kit). Note that all the items in the splint kit are pieces of equipment with multiple functions and that the volume of bandages is targeted for one day's worth of injury.

SAMPLE MULTIDAY FIRST-AID KIT
- Personal safety kit
- Trauma kit—multiday

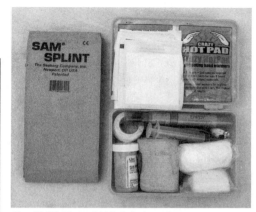

Fig. 10.35 First-aid kit for day trips

- Allergy kit
- Splint kit—extensive
- Expedition kit
- Comfort kit
- Blister kit

Your trauma kit should include enough equipment to deal with more than one injury, and your comfort and blister kits become more important on trips where you won't be returning to the comforts of home each night. Figure 10.36 shows an example

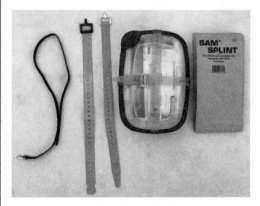

Fig. 10.36 First-aid kit for multiday trips

of a multiday first-aid kit. For trips with particular circumstances, such as extensive (multiweek) trips, trips at high altitudes, and trips in developing countries, consult other sources specifically devoted to the topic.

REPAIR KITS

Having a good repair kit can easily mean the difference between accomplishing the objectives of a trip and getting stuck going nowhere at all when you have gear failure. An ideal repair kit has many useful components, most of which have more than one use, but is still as compact and light as possible. That said, all repair kits are not created equal, and you should tailor your repair kit to your expectations for the trip's length, commitment level, and potential for wear and tear on your gear (figs. 10.37 and 10.38).

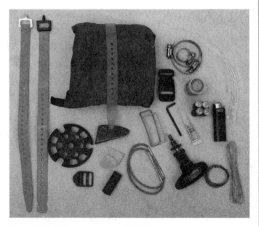

Fig. 10.37 Day trip repair kit

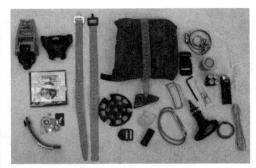

Fig. 10.38 Multiday repair kit

When deciding what items to take or leave on any given trip, think about your worst case scenarios: if anything breaks, how well can you fix it, and how far will you have to travel with broken gear? The most bare-minimum repair kit consists of duct tape, zip ties, and a few rubber ski straps; the deluxe model may start to look like the back room of a small ski shop. Build the kit that's right for your trip, and don't be afraid to adjust it constantly as trips vary.

General items. Duct tape, rubber ski straps, safety pins, extra batteries (AA and AAA), multipurpose tool (with pliers, screwdriver, scissors), dental floss, and needle(s).

Binding items. Zip ties, bailing wire, hose clamps, compact screwdriver for binding adjustments, spare cables for your telemark bindings, spare parts if on a longer tour. Telemark binding screws and plumber's putty allow you to remount a binding in ripped out or stripped binding holes.

Other fix-specific items. Extra skin bales, extra boot buckles, pack buckles, tent pole fix kit, patch kit for air mattress.

SAMPLE DAY TRIP REPAIR KIT

Binding fix. Large plastic zip ties allow you to permanently fix a broken ski/walk mechanism on many of the bar-style AT bindings. Telebinding screws and plumber's putty repair poles.

Boot fix. Extra buckles/bales can make it much easier to ski down. Ever tried skiing chop or powder with your boots unbuckled? The experience is the same if you have a buckle blowout.

Skin fix. Extra skin-tip bales if old ones break or wear through; skin wax and antiballing spray come to the rescue when snow builds up under your skis because of snow temperatures or old skins.

Pole fix. Extra baskets to replace a broken/lost one make a long skate out far easier (try doing without once and you won't do it again); a broken pole kit (hose clamps and short segment of tube) does the same.

SAMPLE MULTIDAY REPAIR KIT

All of the above, plus:

Binding fix. Extra toe- and heelpieces in case one breaks or shatters; telemark binding screws and plumber's putty; zip ties and pole segments can fix a broken binding bar on a Fritschi.

Boot fix. Extra parts as for the day trip kit, plus screw-in rivets in case the rivets in the boot hinge shear.

Tent fix. Dental floss for sewing, tent pole fix kit.

Air-mattress fix. A patch kit is a mandatory item in your kit, especially if your gear includes crampons. Patch kits are available in any good shop.

Pack fix. Dental floss and needle, pack buckles, large safety pins.

Stove repair kit. Most manufacturers provide these with their stoves. Go one step further: what if you lose a piece of the stove? Bring an extra fuel pump and materials to replace any lost pieces (fig. 10.38).

EMERGENCY COMMUNICATION EQUIPMENT

Communications are a crucial part of a rescue plan and are key to emergency procedures. There are a variety of ways to provide communications for emergency purposes, each suited to different parameters.

CELL PHONES

Cell phones are the most widely carried way to call for help from the backcountry. If you are considering your cell phone as a means of calling for rescue, you should know a few important things about cell phone technology.

All phones are not created equal. There is significant variation among the cell phones available in Europe, Canada, and the United States. Differences involve the networks the phones can access and the frequency band those networks use. When using your cell phone as emergency rescue equipment, you want it to be able to access as many networks as possible in the regions where you travel.

The language describing phone function can be confusing. Here is what you need to know in order to purchase a mountain-friendly phone:

Tri-mode designates a phone that can access three different combinations of frequency band and technology (mode). Tri-mode phones can access networks that are CDMA (digital) in two frequency bands, 850 and 1900, plus networks that are AMPS (analog) in the 850 frequency band.

Tri-band or quad band phones are compatible with a different network, GSM, which is used all over the world. A quad band GSM phone is necessary if you want to use a cell phone purchased in the United States in Europe, Africa, and Asia. These phones work on networks of four different bands (800/850, 1800, 1900), thereby allowing compatibility across continents.

Cell phone technology and infrastructure is constantly evolving, so the best thing to do in selecting a phone is to find out (via word of mouth) which carriers have the best coverage in your mountains, and then work with the carrier to get the right type of phone. In general, tri-mode phones are better for coverage in the United States because the analog network can give you better coverage in rural areas. If you are looking for a phone that works overseas, you should look into the quad mode GSM phones.

Pros. Cell phones are ubiquitous—everyone has one! They are easy to use and are cheaper than radios, satellite phones, or personal locator beacons.

Cons. Limited coverage—no cell towers, no cell coverage. Batteries die quickly. When cell phones are used in remote places, the signal must travel long distances, using more power. A cell phone will also often be in analog mode when used in the mountains, which uses more power than digital.

SATELLITE PHONES

Satellite phones work on similar principles as cell phones, but with network support via satellite instead of via cell phone tower. There are two basic types of satellite phones: geostationary and low earth orbit. Geostationary satellites are far away (about 22,000 miles), whereas low earth orbit satellites are much closer (400–700 miles). As communication for mountain rescue, satellite phones are most often used in cases where cell phone coverage and help from radio communications are both unavailable.

Pros. You can make calls from all over the world, and you can access the land-based and mobile phone systems in any country using a satellite phone.

Cons. Satellite phones are expensive to purchase and can be expensive to use. Coverage can vary depending on the type of network and location.

As with any technology, satellite phones are constantly evolving. If you are thinking of using one for your emergency communication device in the mountains, research the latest technologies and phones available before you make a purchase.

UHF/VHF RADIOS

This subject could fill an entire book. The types of radios available are described by the frequency bands on which they can transmit and receive. UHF/VHF (ultra high frequency and very high frequency) radios are those used for more long-distance communications, whereas the person-to-person (talkabout) radios work at shorter distances. The longer range of UHF/VHF radios makes them suited for rescue and emergency communications; the latter are more effective for basic communication over small areas.

Using UHF/VHF radios effectively for rescue requires a fair amount of knowledge and/or training on the part of the user. Two things must be in place: a radio infrastructure and access to that infrastructure. Radio infrastructure means that someone must be listening and that someone must be able to hear your signal. Access to that infrastructure means you must have the rescue frequencies for any organizations involved (like national parks) or an amateur license to talk to the network of amateur users.

Pros. If you have the right transmit and receive frequencies and an amateur license, you can almost always reach someone for help. With the right infrastructure, radios can transmit and receive long distances and can access mechanized services like helicopters, snowcats, and snowmobilers.

Cons. Radios are more expensive than cell phones and much more complicated.

This includes the difficulty of accessing the right frequencies, getting an amateur license, and learning to use the radio itself.

If you travel often in an area with poor cell phone coverage but good radio support, it might be worth investing the time and money in a radio. Getting an amateur license isn't that difficult, and in doing so you have access to people who can help you all over the world.

PERSONAL LOCATER BEACONS (PLB)

When activated, a PLB will send out an emergency signal. Organizations like NOAA monitor the frequencies of the beacon and use them to locate and rescue the people who set off the PLB. PLBs transmit two frequencies: one of the frequencies is used to locate you within a few miles, while the other allows a ground team to find you within closer range. Some PLBs now have GPS capabilities built into them.

Pros. PLBs work very well for organized rescue and require very little training to use.

Cons. PLBs are more expensive than cell phones, radios, and some satellite phones (you can rent them, however). You must be in a country with enough of a rescue infrastructure for them to be effective.

Resources Appendix

AVALANCHE CENTERS

US AND CANADA
Avalanche.org

ALASKA
Chugach National Forest Avalanche Information Center, *www.fs.fed.us/r10 /chugach/glacier/snow.html*
Southeast Alaska Avalanche Center, *www.avalanche.org/ ~ seaac*

CALIFORNIA
Eastern Sierra Avalanche Center (ESAC), *www.esavalanche.org*
Mount Shasta Avalanche Center and Wilderness Department (MSAC), *www.shastaavalanche.org*
Sierra Avalanche Center (SAC), *www.sierraavalanchecenter.org*

COLORADO
Colorado Avalanche Information Center (CAIC), *http://avalanche.state.co.us*

IDAHO
Panhandle National Forest Avalanche Center, *www.fs.fed.us/ipnf/visit /conditions/backcountry/index.html*
Payette Avalanche Center, *www.payetteavalanche.org*
Sawtooth National Forest Avalanche Center, *www.avalanche.org/ ~ svavctr*

MONTANA
Gallatin National Forest Avalanche Center, *www.mtavalanche.com*
Glacier Country Avalanche Center, *www.glacieravalanche.org*
West Central Montana Avalanche Foundation, *www.missoulaavalanche.org*

NEW HAMPSHIRE

Mount Washington Avalanche Center,
www.tuckerman.org

OREGON

Northwest Weather and Avalanche Center
(NWAC), *www.nwac.us*

UTAH

Utah Avalanche Center,
www.avalanche.org/ ~uac

WASHINGTON

Northwest Weather and Avalanche Center
(NWAC), *www.nwac.us*

WYOMING

Bridger-Teton National Forest Backcountry Avalanche Hazard and Weather
Forecast, *www.jhavalanche.org*

CANADA

Canadian Avalanche Association (CAA),
www.avalanche.ca

EUROPE

Chamonix Avalanche Information,
*www.ohm-chamonix.com
/fiche.php?id = 00&ling = En*
European Avalanche Services,
www.slf.ch/laworg/map.html
French Avalanche Service,
*www.meteo.fr/meteonet/temps/activite
/mont/france_bna.htm*
Swiss Federal Institute for Snow and
Avalanche Research,
www.slf.ch/welcome-en.html

AVALANCHE ORGANIZATIONS

American Avalanche Association (AAA),
www.americanavalancheassociation.org
American Institute for Avalanche
Research and Education (AIARE),
www.avtraining.org

AVALANCHE AND WEATHER PUBLICATIONS

The Avalanche Handbook, 3rd edition, by
David McClung and Peter Schaerer,
The Mountaineers Books, 2006.
The Avalanche Review, American
Avalanche Association,
*www.americanavalancheassociation
.org/publications.html.*
Avalanche Safety for Skiers and Climbers,
2nd edition, by Tony Daffern,
The Mountaineers Books, 2000.
"Beacon Searches with the Three Circle
Method," by Chris Semmel and Dieter
Stopper, *DAV Panorama* (January 2004).
"Field Experiments on the Effectiveness
of Some New Avalanche Equipment,"
by Martin Kern, Frank Tschirky, and
Jürg. Schweizer, *www.slf.ch/staff
/pers-home/kern/kern-de.html.*
"Heuristic Traps in Recreational Ava-
lanche Accidents: Evidence and Impli-
cations," by Ian McCammon, *The Ava-
lanche Review* 22, nos. 2 and 3 (2004).
*Living Ice: Understanding Glaciers and
Glaciation*, by Robert Sharp, Cambridge
University Press, 1991.

Mountain Weather: Backcountry Forecasting for Hikers, Campers, Climbers, Skiers, Snowboarders, by Jeff Renner, The Mountaineers Books, 2005.

Observation Guidelines and Recording Standards for Weather, Snowpack, and Avalanches (OGRES), Canadian Avalanche Center, 2002.

Powderguide: Managing Avalanche Risk, Tobias Kurzeder and Holger Feist, Mountain Sports Press, 2003.

"Snow, Weather, and Avalanches: Observational Guidelines for Avalanche Programs in the United States (SWAG)," American Avalanche Association, 2004, *www.avalanche.org/~research /guidelines.*

Staying Alive in Avalanche Terrain, second edition, by Bruce Tremper, The Mountaineers Books, 2008.

"Strategic Shoveling: The Next Frontier in Companion Rescue," by Bruce Edgerly and Dale Atkins, presented at the 2006 International Snow Science Workshop, *www.bcaccess.com/documents /EdgerlyAtkinsISSW06.pdf.*

CLIMBING AND MOUNTAINEERING

Alpine Climbing: Techniques to Take You Higher, by Mark Houston and Kathy Cosley, The Mountaineers Books, 2004.

Climbing Anchors, 2nd edition, by John Long, Falcon Press, 2006.

Climbing Self-Rescue: Improvising Solutions for Serious Situations, by Andy Tyson and Molly Loomis, The Mountaineers Books, 2006.

Ice and Mixed Climbing: Modern Technique, by Will Gadd, The Mountaineers Books, 2003.

Mountaineering: The Freedom of the Hills, 7th edition, edited by Steven M. Cox and Kris Fulsaas, The Mountaineers Books, 2003.

Climbing: From Gym to Crag, by S. Peter Lewis and Dan Cauthorn, The Mountaineers Books, 2000.

Rock Climbing: Mastering Basic Skills, by Craig Luebben, The Mountaineers Books, 2004.

Rock Climbing Anchors, by Craig Luebben, The Mountaineers Books, 2007.

TECHNICAL SPECIFICATIONS AND MECHANICS OF CLIMBING

International Testing Standards for Climbing Gear, *www.uiaa.ch*

Technical Explanations of the Mechanics of Climbing, *www.en.petzl.com*

NAVIGATION

GPS Made Easy, 4th edition,
by Lawrence Letham, The Mountaineers Books, 2003.
Wilderness Navigation, 2nd edition,
by Bob Burns and Mike Burns,
The Mountaineers Books, 2004.

TRAINING AND NUTRITION

Climbing: Training for Peak Performance,
2nd edition, by Clyde Soles, The Mountaineers Books, 2008.
Conditioning for Outdoor Fitness, 2nd edition, by David Musnick, M.D. and Mark
Pierce, The Mountaineers Books, 2004.

WILDERNESS FIRST AID

*Medicine for Mountaineering and Other
Wilderness Activities*, 6th edition, edited
by James A. Wilkerson, M.D., The
Mountaineers Books, 2009.
National Outdoor Leadership School
(NOLS) and Wilderness Medicine
Institute (WMI), *www.nols.edu/wmi*
Stonehearth Open Learning Opportuni-
ties (SOLO), *www.soloschools.com*
Wilderness Medical Associates,
www.wildmed.com

EMERGENCY PHONE NUMBERS

Emergency Call Numbers:

USA	911
Canada	911
Europe	112

Alpine Emergencies/Search and Rescue:

Germany	19222
Switzerland	1414
Austria	140
Italy	118

OTHER ORGANIZATIONS

Alpine Club (AC), *www.alpine-club.org.uk*
American Alpine Club (AAC),
www.americanalpineclub.org
American Mountain Guides Association
(AMGA), *www.amga.com*
Association of Canadian Mountain Guides
(ACMG), *www.acmg.ca*
International Federation of Mountain
Guides Association (IFMGA),
www.ivbv.info/

Glossary

457 kHZ International frequency for avalanche transceivers

Abalakov anchor *See* V-thread

Ablation zone Lower zone on a glacier where more annual melting than accumulating occurs

ABS Avalanche Airbag system: a backcountry ski pack with an integrated airbag, gas canister, and pull handle; it is designed to inflate when the wearer is caught in an avalanche and pulls the handle, thereby allowing him to remain on the surface of the slide

Accumulation zone Upper zone on a glacier where more annual accumulating than melting occurs

ACMG Association of Canadian Mountain Guides: a professional association of trained and certified guides and instructors

Active snow stability tests Non-standardized snow stability/bonding tests that require little time; can be done while moving through the snow

AIARE American Institute for Avalanche Research and Education: a not-for-profit organization providing a standardized approach to avalanche course curriculums for member providers

AMGA American Mountain Guides Association: a national organization devoted to the training and certification of mountain guides in the United States

Anchor Temporary or permanent method (using ice screw, cam, nut, ski, piton, bolt, natural features, etc.) of securing person or gear to the mountain

Angle piton Steel piton used in cracks too wide for a knife blade piton

Antiballing plate Plate that attaches to the bottom of a crampon, used to minimize snow balling up between the points

Arête ridge crest

A-shaped crevasse Crevasse created in a compression zone, where the glacial ice is more pulled apart near the bedrock than it is on the surface

Atmospheric pressure Air pressure at any point in the Earth's atmosphere, caused by the weight of the atmosphere above the measurement point

Autoblock Friction hitch that can be released under load commonly used as a rappel backup; also know as a French prusik

AVA turn Uphill turn on skis accomplished by alternating between converging and diverging steps

Avalanche probe Sectioned and collapsible pole used to pinpoint the location of a person buried in avalanche debris

Avalanche terrain Any terrain that can produce an avalanche or terrain that an avalanche can run through

Avalanche transceiver Device that can transmit and receive an electromagnetic signal on an internationally normed frequency of 457 kHz; used to locate and rescue buried avalanche victims

Avalung Device designed to facilitate breathing while buried in an avalanche produced by Black Diamond Equipment

Backcountry skiing Skiing outside a controlled ski area

Back-up system Any system, knot, or hitch offering another layer of protection if some or all of an existing system fails

Barometric pressure Atmospheric pressure as measured by a barometer

Bedrock lubrication Lubrication caused by meltwater that drains to the bedrock surface and promotes flow of the glacier by lubricating the surface

Bedrock surface Surface that the glacier is gliding on

Bergschrund Crevasse that forms at the location where the moving part of the glacier separates from the stagnant part of the glacier

Bight of rope Loop that is formed when a rope is doubled back on itself

Bollard Teardrop shape cut into the snow or ice to create an anchor

Cairn Pile of rocks used to mark a trail

Caloric efficiency Maximum amount of work performed with the minimum amount of calories consumed

Cam Active protection device for rock that uses a spring to hold itself in place

Cold front Leading edge of a cooler and drier mass of air

Companion rescue Rescue of a buried avalanche victim carried out by his backcountry partners using an avalanche transceiver, probe, and shovel

Compression zone Zone in a glacier where the ice is compressed due to a rapid deceleration; caused by change in topography from steep to flat

Conduction Transfer of thermal energy (i.e. heat) by direct physical contact

Continental snow climate Drier, colder winter climate that produces generally a lower snowpack

Contour lines Lines on a map indicating locations of constant elevation, used to represent a three-dimensional landscape on a two-dimensional surface

Contour-Tangent method Specific technique using a compass to determine slope aspect in the field

Convection Transfer of thermal energy (i.e. heat) by the movement of a fluid (e.g. air)

Cordelette A precut length of 5- to 7-mm cord used in climbing applications from crevasse rescue to anchor building

Cow's tail Loop created by tying a bight of rope with a knot

Crevasse Crack in the snow and ice of a glacier caused by decreasing and increasing rates of speed in the glacial ice

Cross loading In avalanche applications, wind causing the movement of snow horizontally across a slope and the buildup of wind slabs of vertical orientation. In technical systems, the loading of a carabiner across the axis of its gate (the weakest axis)

Declination Difference between true north, as drawn on maps, and magnetic north, indicated by the needle of a compass

Deposition zone Location of avalanche debris after it comes to rest

Depth hoar Angular, cup-shaped snow crystals formed within the snowpack due to the faceting process

Destructive potential chart Rating system used to determine the destructive potential of an avalanche; they range from D1 to D5, D5 being the largest

Digloo Snow shelter that combines the virtues of a hollowed out snowmound and an igloo cap on top of it

Direct haul In crevasse rescue, a simple method of pulling on the rope that leads to the fallen person

Direct weather effect Effect that weather has on or near the surface of the snowpack

Directional carabiner Carabiner that redirects the rope in a rescue or belay system

DMF (Decision-making Framework) Visual structure designed to indicate the presence and interplay of the factors involved in decision-making in avalanche terrain

Drop-loop haul Pulley system where a loop is lowered and attached to the fallen person

Dual Mode Pivot Telemark Bindings Type of telemark binding that has a ski mode and a separate mode for more efficient uphill travel

Dynamic rope Climbing rope designed to stretch upon loading to lessen the force to the climber, the points of protection, and the anchor

EARNEST Acronym used to remember the characteristics of a sound climbing anchor; Equalized, Angle less than 90, Redundant, No Extension, Strong, and Timely

Escaping the belay Process by which a belayer removes herself from a belay and ties the rope off so she can move about freely

Faceting Metamorphic process by which snow crystals form angular, layered structures

Flux line Visual representation of a magnetic field

Fracture line Distinct uppermost line of a slab avalanche; also referred to as the crown line

Friction hitches Any hitch that will lock onto the rope when loaded, but can be slid along the rope when not loaded; includes prusik, klemheist, and autoblock

Front-side skiing Lift-access skiing that takes place within some form of a controlled boundary

Garda hitch Ratchet using two identical carabiners in the same orientation

Glacial snout Frontal boundary of a glacier

Glycemic index Index of the glucose and insulin responses of the human body induced by carbohydrate foods

Glycogen Stored form of glucose found in your muscles and liver, used by your muscle cells for energy during exercise

GPS unit Global Positioning System: an electronic device that uses satellites to give the location of the user

Half rope Dynamic climbing rope designed to use in pairs but clipped in separately when climbing steep terrain; may be used singularly for glacier climbing

Handrailing Use of a prominent or easily recognizable terrain feature as a guide in whiteout navigation

Haul line Stand of rope pulled on to rescue a person in a crevasse

Heel lifter Elevator bar on a telemark or randonnée binding that reduces foot angle relative to slope angle

Heuristic Rule of thumb that guides decisions in everyday life

Heuristic traps Oversimplified decision-making based on existing simple rules of thumb that lead to poor results

Hip belay Belay technique in which the rope passes around the hips of the belayer; it is used frequently in moderate terrain

Human factor Role played by human nature and behavior patterns in the decision-making process

Icefall Rapid flow of glacial ice over a drastic change in topography which causes a chaotic zone of crevasses

Igloo Shelter constructed from blocks of snow generally in the form of a dome

Indirect weather effect Role weather plays on metamorphism inside the snowpack

Intermountain snow climate Snow climate with characteristics that fall in between maritime and continental; known as the Interior snow climate in Canada

Kick turn Technique to change direction 180 degrees

Kiwi coil Method for storing extra climbing rope by coiling it around your chest

Klemheist Type of friction hitch

Knifeblade piton Steel piton used in thin cracks

Lee side Mountainside opposite the windward side

LNT Leave No Trace: a list of guidelines designed to minimize human impact in backcountry travel

Load strand Strand of rope holding the weight of a person who has fallen in a crevasse; also called the load line

Load transfer In crevasse rescue, the process of shifting a load from one location (usually a person who has arrested a crevasse fall) to another (usually an anchor)

Loose snow avalanche Avalanche resulting from the lack of cohesion of surface snow, often resembling a teardrop; also known as a point release avalanche

Maritime snow climate Snow climate located near a large body of water that often experiences mild temperatures and high rates of snowfall

Master carabiner Large carabiner used as a master point in applications where a sling may be under so much tension that clipping carabiners in and out of it is difficult

Master point Central clip-in point of an anchor; the master point can be created with a sling, cord, rope, or carabiner, but is designed to be the central point of connection to the anchor

Mechanical advantage Ratio of the force needed to pull the skier upward to the amount of pull applied by the rescuer

Melt-freeze cycle Result of swings in daily temperatures which repeatedly melts and refreezes the upper layer of the snowpack

Moat Gap that forms between the steep part of the mountain and the snowpack that lies at the base of the steep slope, caused by creep of the snowpack

Moldable liners Closed cell foam liners that can be custom molded by a heating process

Mule knot Knot used to tie off hitches which enables them to be released under load; often used with a Munter hitch

Munter hitch Hitch used for belaying and rappelling

NTN New Telemark Norm: a telemark binding/boot system which eliminates the classic duckbill of the 75mm telemark standard while retaining the flex of the bellows of the boot

Nut Passive camming device used for protection in rock

Occluded front Cold front overtaking a warm front

Organized rescue Rescue requiring outside party help often in the form of ski patrol or search and rescue organizations

Panel loading pack Backpack that allows loading/access through the main compartment via a panel that opens

Personal Locator Beacon (PLB) Portable device that sends out an emergency signal once activated

Piton Metal spike that can be pounded into a rock crack for anchoring

"Primary, secondary and pinpoint search" Search progression during the three phases of transceiver search

Prusik hitch Friction hitch created by passing a loop of cord through itself several times

PTFE membrane Thin porous Polytetrafluoroethylene layer; when used in clothing, creates a layer that is both waterproof and breathable

Quad band Cell phone technology that accesses four frequency bands

Radiation Transfer of energy in the form of infrared waves

Radius In skis, describes the distance from the center of an arc that the ski would carve if fully decambered

Rappel backup Any method used to provide extra security on a rappel; can be created using a friction hitch above or below the rappel device, or via a fireman's belay

Ratchet Friction hitch or device that can be used to allow rope to move through it in one direction, but locks and holds the rope in place in the other direction

Recco System Rescue system utilizing radar to locate skiers wearing a Recco reflector when buried in an avalanche

Relative humidity Ratio of the current absolute humidity to the highest possible absolute humidity

Rescue repetition Technique of practicing rescue progressions repeatedly; designed to help rescuers use the correct steps during the stress of an actual emergency

Resection Method used in navigation to determine location using bearings from two or more visible known points

Risky shift effect Process of individuals finding security in groups; group members shift the risk that otherwise would be on them individually to the group as a whole

Ropeman Device designed to be used in ascending a rope, manufactured by Wild Country Inc.; it can be used as a ratchet in crevasse rescue applications provided it is not the load bearing redirect

Rounding Process the snowpack goes through when the temperatures are consistently warm and the snowpack is deep; sometimes referred to as sintering, this process usually creates a strong, dense layer

Run–walk–crawl Search progression during the phases of transceiver search; run during the primary search, walk in the secondary search, and crawl for the pinpoint search

Rutschblock test Quantifiable snow bonding test using a column of snow with a 2-meter x 1.5-meter surface area, with the skier's weight as the load

SAM splint A lightweight splint made of flexible aluminum alloy and closed-cell foam, manufactured by SAM Medical

Seated belay Any belay that uses some combination of body weight, body position and terrain to provide security for an individual on a rope

Serac Unstable, freestanding iceblock on a glacier, often in an icefall, created by multidirectional pull

Shelf Secondary clip-in location in anchor slings, usually created by a knot in the master sling or cordelette

Short pitching Rope-climbing technique used to isolate the crux of a short section of technical climbing

Short roping Rope team roped up in short distance which allows for optimal simultaneous movement

Shovel shear test Quantifiable, but very subjective, snow bonding test that works well on low-angle terrain

Side cut Geometry of a ski in terms of tip/waist/tail dimensions

Single rope Dynamic rope that is strong enough to be used as a single strand for all climbing activities

Ski crampon Metal device that clips to the binding to improve uphill traction in icy or firm snow conditions

Ski mountaineering Backcountry skiing in high alpine and glaciated terrain involving technical mountaineering elements

Ski mountaineering harness Lightweight and low bulk harness designed for ski mountaineering; usually features adjustable or releasable leg loops

Ski platform Surface area of the ski determined by width and sidecut

Ski touring Skiing without the aid of lifts outside a controlled ski area setting

Ski waist Dimension of the narrowest part of the ski, generally in the middle of the ski

Skin adhesive Glue that holds the climbing skin to the base of the ski

Skin plush Synthetic or natural fiber side of a skin that touches the snow allowing the ski to grip the snow, then glide

Skinning Act of walking uphill on skis using a climbing skin

Skins Nylon or mohair plush that attaches to the base of skis in order to facilitate uphill travel

Slab avalanche Avalanche that begins as a cohesive unit of snow

Slope configuration Shape of a slope; different slope shapes affect the amount of tension in the snowpack thereby changing avalanche potential

Slope support Compressive support the topography has upon the slab of snow above

Sluff Small, loose-snow avalanche

Spiral probing Method used in companion rescue to locate the buried person using a probe, based on a spiral pattern

Spot probing Method of probing for a buried person searching the most likely locations of burial; often performed in the absence of avalanche transceivers

Static rope Nylon climbing rope with minimal stretch; often used in rappelling and rescue scenarios.

Stauchwall Lower fracture line of a slab avalanche

Surface hoar Frost that forms feathery crystals on the surface of the snowpack during clear, cold and locally humid conditions

TCM (three circle method) Method of searching for multiple buried persons in an avalanche using a transceiver

Telescopic pole Skipole that can be lengthened or shortened

Temperature inversion Inverted temperature gradient in which air gets temporarily warmer with rising altitude

Temperature lapse rate Rate at which temperature decreases with height

Terrain features Variables in terrain, including slope configuration, slope angle, aspect, and elevation

Terrain traps Sections of terrain, such as gulleys, trees, cliffs, depressions, etc., that increase the consequence to a person should the person become caught in an avalanche

Texas kick System of two leg loops used to ascend a rope

THINX Acronym used for the different types of anchors that can be built using skis

Tibloc Lightweight device designed for ascending ropes, manufactured by Petzl

Top loading pack Backpack that can be loaded/accessed through the top of the pack

Triangulation Navigation method that uses geometry to calculate location and distance from a known point

Tri-band Cell phones that support three frequency bands

Trigger points Areas of terrain where the stress of the snowpack is more concentrated or the snowpack is weaker

Tri-mode Cell phone technology that can access both digital and analog frequency bands

Trucker's hitch Simple pulley system that is generally used to tie something down

Twin ropes Ropes designed to be used in pairs and clipped together as if they were one strand

UHF/VHF radio Ultra High Frequency/ Very High Frequency, radio frequency bands that work for long distances

UIAGM/IFMGA *Union International des Associations des Guides de Montagne,* an international umbrella organization of mountain guiding associations responsible for developing and setting guiding certification standards

UTM grid Universal Transverse Mercator coordinate grid system; method of specifying locations using the metric system

V-shape crevasse Crevasse created in a stress zone, where the glacier is pulled apart more near the surface due to a topographical feature

V-thread Ice anchor created by boring a V-shaped tunnel into a piece of ice; also known as an Abalakov anchor

V-thread tool long pointy hooking tool used to pull a cordelette or piece of rope from one end of the V-thread to the other

Warm front the leading edge of a mass of warm air

Waypoint Known point on a map used for navigation, usually with a GPS, expressed by two coordinates

Whumphing Sound the snowpack makes upon collapsing that indicates poor stability

Windward side Side of the mountain into which the wind blows

Index

About the Authors

Martin Volken received his IFMGA certification in his native Switzerland and is the owner of Pro Ski and Guiding Service in North Bend, Washington. He has been guiding all facets of mountaineering since 1992 in the United States and abroad. He has pioneered several first ascents, ski descents, and ski mountaineering traverses in the North Cascades. Martin has appeared on the cover of *Outside* magazine as well as in several other industry publications. He is involved in product development for K2 and Outdoor Research and is an examiner for the American Mountain Guides Association.

He resides in North Bend with his wife, Gina and his two daughters, Andrea and Christina. Martin has also published *Back-country Skiing Snoqualmie Pass,* a guidebook for the Snoqualmie Pass area in Washington State.

Scott Schell is a certified AMGA Ski Mountaineering Guide and has guided extensively throughout the United States, including Alaska, as well as in Canada and Europe. An avid ski mountaineer, Scott has been involved in avalanche and guiding education as an instructor and trainer for AIARE and a former AMGA ski discipline instructor. As the former manager of Pro Ski Service in Seattle, he saw the need for a ski mountaineering book that would provide a comprehensive source for the backcountry skier. While toting his cameras throughout North America and Europe, Scott has captured many memorable and compelling images through the trained eye of both a photographer and mountain guide. To learn more about Scott's work, please visit *www .schellphoto.com.*

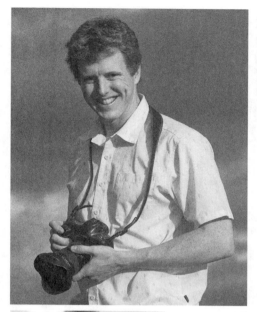

Margaret Wheeler is a ski, alpine, and rock climbing guide who has led trips throughout Europe and North America. An active member of the guiding community, she is an instructor of guide training for the American Mountain Guides Association (AMGA) and serves on its board of directors and as president of the organization. She is involved in avalanche education through her work as an AIARE (American Institute for Avalanche Research and Education) instructor and trainer. In the development of her ski mountaineering career, Margaret has been a member of several women's expeditions, pioneering first ski descents in India and the Altai mountains of Mongolia. In 2006, she became the second woman in the United States to complete her international IFMGA/UIAGM guide certification. She holds a bachelor's degree in history from Dartmouth College and a master's in mechanical engineering from the University of Washington.